Fitzroy Park allotments

Highgate

Close to the Veg

A book of allotment tales

MICHAEL RAND

Illustrations by the author

Marlin Press

To Pamela Winterton and Mick Smith

First published in Great Britain in 2005
by Marlin Press
PO Box 8076
Stansted CM24 8XQ

2 4 6 8 10 9 7 5 3 1

ISBN 0-9547988-1-3

A catalogue record for this book is available from the British Library

Printed and bound in Singapore

ACKNOWLEDGEMENTS

Many thanks to all those who appear in this book, whether anonymous, or named, and amongst the latter I am particularly grateful to the following: Theresa O'Neill, Sally and Mike Gallagher, Michael Grice, Dave Mundy, Fiona MacKie, Alan Blakeman and Matt Young. Profound apologies to Mike Taylor.

For support, translations and other expert advice, many thanks also to Norman Russell, Laura Eagles, Susan R Eilenberg, Hilary Burden, Tim Cole, Corin Purcell, Sarah Soulsby, Anne Elton, Melody Brown, Alex Dwight, Christa Langheiter, Rory Moore, Glyn Thomas, Stephen Wade and Roslyn McKendry.

"Know your own small patch and the rest of the world becomes readable."

Iain Sinclair,
London Orbital

Contents

CHAPTER ONE

Off the Plot

I am an Englishman, born in what must have been the twilight years of the travelling midwife, at Totternhoe in South Bedfordshire. The year was 1960, a time when "home delivery" meant something quite different from scooting around the houses on a moped, with a stack of pizzas lashed over the back wheel. Back then, few people in this country had even *heard* of pizza, hard to believe as it may be. But that's how long ago it was.

Totternhoe – that sombre village – is plonked along a mile or so of minor road between the towns of Dunstable and Leighton Buzzard, on the lower slopes of a headland of the Downs, which pokes its chalky nose out from the easterly hills into the broad Vale of Aylesbury stretching to the west.

With an ancient church stranded at its eastern end, it seems as if the village has crept towards the low land over the centuries, though whether to escape from the dawn shadows cast by the hills or from God, or from both, is a question best left to a landscape historian, should one ever drop by to work out the vagaries of the local past. Such an effort might well be worth something, because the environs of Totternhoe are thick with ancient banks, mounds and ditches, traces of a more exciting antiquity than its quiet modern ambience might at first glance suggest. For many thousands of years it was indeed *somewhere*. Stone Age farmers convened upon the hilltop above the modern village. Thousands of years later, their scratched enclosure was converted into a fort by an Iron Age tribe, and a couple of thousand years after that, the Normans constructed a motte and bailey castle close by.

My own arrival at this (pre)historical site was preceded by that of my parents by only a couple of years. They were people on the move, part of the massive post-second world war internal migration – millions in search of a new living – that in terms of sudden change to the country's social geography has probably dwarfed anything since the Black Death, and maybe that as well. So I can't claim to have ancient roots in South Beds., or anywhere else for that matter. By the time I came along the Times Were very much A-Changin'. No less so in Totternhoe, as in pretty much everywhere else in south-east England. Half the Iron Age fort had recently been eaten by a gigantic chalk quarry, without the benefit of an archaeological investigation. For reasons nobody we knew could fathom, the wild primrose plants were disappearing from the hillside. And new suburban cul-de-sacs, or culs-de-sac, I'll never know which, raced upslope at right angles off the through-road, in complete defiance of the ancient topography. It was at the end of one such cul-de-sac that I was born.

My father tells me that my early years were characterised by my running away as often as possible. There was only one way out. As soon as I could crawl, I was off down the slope in the direction of The Cross Keys, the local pub. The descending angle of travel and goal seem nowadays more sensible to me than ever, though whether I would have made it any further than "the local" we never found out, because although my mother was iconoclast enough to wonder out loud how much easier her life might be, if one fine day she refused to take up the chase, her motherly instincts would always win out, and prompt her to drag me time and again, yelling and struggling, back indoors.

So much for my early days in Totternhoe. Before my third birthday the family had migrated even further to the south, as my father pursued his career in the civil service, and the truth is I scarcely remember the place. Whilst we did revisit a number of times during my childhood, many of the physical details given above aren't taken from memory, mine or anyone else's, but were gleaned from twenty minutes with a 1:50,000 Ordnance Survey map and archaeological gazetteer. Including them at the start is meant as a gesture somewhat less towards my own biography, or to the actual landscape of my birth, as towards the cultural landscape in which I was brought up, of post-war boom. This was an increasingly well-fed, well-oiled world, just setting out on that motorway of white-heat style consumerism which has done nothing but gain in strength and intensity over my four-and-a-half decades, as very many people besides myself have, of course, observed.

This is the briefest effort at an introductory counterpoint, because this book isn't strictly about that mainstream world, although I'm not nearly hippy enough to attempt to deny that it exists. We all profit tremendously from our technologies, even as we serve them, or even if we're lucky enough to do no more than measure the distance we've managed to put between them and our immediate and daily lives. Without Christianity – no Atheism... Which has often been pointed out. Nor is this book an out-and-out autobiography, which is a thing only a some-way remarkable person should attempt. But whilst not either entirely political, or entirely personal, it contains elements of both.

The general subject is my interest in allotment gardening. To be more honest, *obsession* with allotment gardening. Specifically, Plot 3, Fitzroy Park Allotments, Highgate, London N6, England, to give the full address. Not – as I should point out – that the Post Office actually delivers to the site.

What follows is "political" in the simplest sense of that word, insofar as our actions don't take place in the proverbial void. They have a context. They have consequences. And as we shall see, the allotment gardening context – what we actually get up to on the plots – doesn't stop at the sheer pleasure to be had from growing things (and eating them) but carries on out from there into the wider world, linking up with a number of far broader issues. These concern such things as nutrition, health, resource use, pollution, recycling and the like. All of them touch, in whole or in part, on the natural environment, on our equivocal place within it, and on our equally equivocal attitudes towards it.

It's also "personal", first because I need to introduce myself and tell a little of what I was up to before I got the allotment, which is the main theme of this chapter and the first bit of the next. Second, because in this attempt to weigh my efforts in the balance I need something to put at the other end of the scales. How do we normally judge what we've done? Or failed to do? We use our past, our experience, as a measure, or else we use an external mark, something out there in the world. As every fool knows.

Several years ago I watched a television biography of Kenneth Tynan, the fabulously libertarian theatre critic, who's often best-remembered nowadays for introducing the national broadcast media to the more robust side of the English language. Tynan, who was born in 1927 and grew up in Birmingham, a "cemetery without walls" as he unfairly called it, felt that his life only began when he started as an undergraduate student at Oxford. At about 60 miles away, not so very far from Birmingham but, clearly, a town with a very different style. As for the first couple of decades of his life, Tynan forever afterwards thought of them as a waste. And as he first turned up at Magdalen College with his luggage – with the world just emerged from war – he was heard to instruct the porter: "Be careful with those trunks, my man, they are freighted with golden shirts!" The porter's reply isn't recorded, though in that vanished age, far more egalitarian and far less polarised than our own, one can quite easily imagine him telling the tyro Tynan cheerfully to fuck off.

My own "golden shirt" has been cut from a coarser bit of rag, a 16- by 8-yard patch of London clay, on the fringes of Highgate. When I first got the plot I was quite new to gardening of any kind, and as I started to dig over the ground and sow a first few seeds, many of which – to my astonishment – actually sprouted up, though I could hardly tell at this early stage what I'd sown from what was a weed, I soon found myself exhilarated by the experience, and the place rapidly captured most of my attention and much of what passes, with me, for imagination. As it has continued to do, without fail, ever since. There was something more to this than simply a falling away of my youth. Like Kenneth Tynan passing for the first time through the college gates, I felt at last that life had given me a break.

So, true to the spirit of intermittent biography mentioned above, time to fast-forward a quarter-century or so, from the crawling escapee I was in Totternhoe, to the new version of a crawling escapee that I'd become by 1992.

The late eighties and early nineties – the period during which all of the events recorded in the remainder of this chapter took place – caught me at something of a low ebb, so much so that even today I can't recall anything that happened to me in those years, whether good, bad or indifferent, without the memory being filtered through a fog of dread. Death had worked havoc amongst the members of my family, which was never a large one to begin with. One relationship had crashed, and another had failed to take off at all. In the former case, my ex-girlfriend had fled to the Hebrides, where she'd taken up a post as an inspector of fish farms, and in my more revolting moments of self-pity, I imagined this drastic change of career would test the limits of her idealism far more strenuously than anything I'd ever proposed. Or failed to propose. In the latter case, the failed take-off, well, I never did quite work that one out, but this was a woman who needed money, and on top of all this other grief I was broke, scraping one of those bare and frustrating livings, as a proofreader, that are often romantically called "freelance".

Whilst I felt there was little I could practicably do to ease the emotional side of this series of crises, except quietly ride the whole thing out, like a sick dog, I thought I'd do well to address the economic aspect. So I decided I'd acquire some better and more marketable skills, and enrolled on a course in book design and production, studying under the legendary Robbie Robinson at the London College of Printing & Distributive Trades, at Back Hill, in Clerkenwell, EC1.

What Robbie didn't know about book design would make a very slim volume. All the rest of it was covered in various of his own publications, and for a year I learnt a great deal about such things as hardback to paperback conversion, integrated text and illustration, and so on. Often these intensive learning sessions would be relieved at about 5 o'clock with a glass or two of Robbie's home-made wine, which was good stuff, although not so good as the home-made labels he put on the bottles, marking his new vintages, each one of which was a minor classic of ravishingly good typography. To say nothing of the splendid certificate we were awarded at the end of the course, typeset by Robbie himself in old-fashioned "hot metal" characters and beautifully printed on an antique press that was tucked up under the roof of the charmingly decrepit factory building in which we worked.

And therein, alas, lay the whole problem. Old-fashioned. Robbie wasn't too far off retirement, and the college's budget didn't stretch to computers, or desktop publishing to be more accurate. Our designs were all "scissors-and-paste", and as I set off back to the workaday world with my beautiful certificate and a heavy portfolio of meticulously glued-together pages, touring around any and all of the London publishing firms which expressed the least interest in seeing me, it didn't take a genius to work out what was up. The computer revolution. No less.

I quickly lost count of the number of office corridors stacked up with empty Apple Mac boxes, waiting for the bin men to take them away, with their shiny new contents – screens, scanners, keyboards and all the rest – emptied out onto a thousand cluttered desks like Christmas come too early. In the interviews that

I managed to wangle I always faced the same key questions, and they were all to do with software:

"Do you know Quark?" To which I answered, warily and softly, "No."

"Do you know PageMaker?" "No."

"Do you know any Quark?" "No."

"Do you know any PageMaker?" "No."

"Not even a little bit of Quark?" "Sorry."

"Not even a little bit of PageMaker?" etc., etc…

It became a kind of weird catechism, one that marked the long distance, I came to realise, by which I'd fallen short of my target of gainful employment. I had to shake my head so many times, whilst maintaining an outwardly cheerful and enthusiastic demeanour, I'd swear some days that by the time I got back home it was about to come unscrewed. Derangement lurked. Which was not aided by the fact that nobody else I met in these interviews knew Quark or PageMaker either. But unlike me they were already working, already in place. And each time, as I set out for the next interview, accompanied by a sense of doom which grew by several orders of magnitude over the weeks and months, it was as if that heavy portfolio I lugged around was full of blueprints for a hot-air balloon, which I was trying to pass off to NASA as the latest thing in intergalactic travel. It wasn't too many months before I'd gone through all the "space agencies" in town, and the interviews dried up, which was a curious relief, as at least I could keep the shit-eating grin off my face for long enough to regain a modicum of mental composure.

With full-time work thus a dim prospect, I continued to scrape romantically as a "freelance". And with an abundance of spare time at my disposal, thought it would be a good thing to devote myself wholeheartedly to a leisured mode of living, either to sport, or to the limp, spontaneous life of the artist.

First I considered taking up jogging, and pictured myself bouncing earnestly around the byways of Hampstead Heath in a vest and shorts, working up an honest sweat. But this vision of purposeful activity was quickly dashed when I remembered a conversation I'd once had with my mother, who'd died not long since. From something worse than a lack of exercise, I might add. "Why a woman would jog," she'd said, "I've no idea. But why a man jogs is simple. He's a rapist practising his getaway skills."

So out of respect for my mother's memory, or rather, her peculiar sense of style, I decided against jogging. By way of apology to those of you who do enjoy this particular form of healthful and inexpensive exercise, all I can do is point out that the old girl had always been fond of hyperbole. An inherited trait, though molecular biologists and others may deny it.

Instead, I took up swimming, and every day set off with my new trunks rolled up inside a towel to Swiss Cottage baths. Soon I was up to a mile on each visit, 40 lengths of that recently demolished pool, up and down, up and down. I've been quite short-sighted, as in myopic, for a long time, and a measure of my beginner's enthusiasm for these aquatic efforts can be noted in the poignant fact that I actually had a pair of swimming goggles made with corrective lenses in them. This meant that after every pair of laps I could check the clock that hung on the wall over the shallow end, and time my exertions to within a few seconds. As well, of course, as search for any stray man-eating crocodile that managed to make its way up the overflow pipe from the sewers of Hampstead. Not that I ever discovered one. Or anything else of interest for that matter.

What I *did* discover was the profound tedium of swimming endless laps, which has a kind of mindless, meditative quality. Not unpleasant, but hardly a thrill-a-minute; more a watery blankness, which induced – for just as long as I stayed in the pool – a deep hibernation of the brain. More than once, on emerging from this dreamless, thoughtless exercise, I would recall a novel that I'd read, years back, about a cargo ship, surviving a prolonged and furious storm. Or rather, one detail in that book, the title of which escapes me, concerning a Chinese member of the crew of the tempest-enduring ship, who as a boy had been made to sit and stare at the big toe of his left foot for 24 hours, without respite, as a lesson in patience.

One of my own big toes lost patience before the rest of me did, and responded by sprouting a sizeable verruca. Not to mention the host of other outrageous foot diseases that soon followed, as I coursed my barefoot way each day through the changing rooms, their floors awash with a thin slurry of septic filth, something the pool's management were none-too-careful about cleaning up. I battled these infections with various chemist's shop potions, not without success, but the verruca wouldn't shift, resisting every brand of flesh-eating gunk available over-the-counter, and it eventually grew large enough and painful enough to drive me to seek the advice of my local GP.

I was lucky enough never to have been a regular at Doctor Pawson's, and in fact usually tried to avoid the place, not least because the good doctor belonged to that class of wonderfully healthy sixty-somethings, tanned, slim, athletic, who still play squash thrice a week and have recently taken up the new challenge of windsurfing. Guaranteed on sight to make any of us lesser mortals feel ill, even if we didn't feel too bad to begin with.

His surgery was to be found, set well back from the world, in a quiet side street a few minutes limp away from the Finchley Road in East Kilburn, in a large and ornate late-Victorian residence. A house with the kind of high ceilings that can make you wonder, in an idle mood, if the late Victorians themselves hadn't been a race of giants. The lofty waiting room was hung with many drapes and lined with dark and heavy furniture, with more than one aspidistra filling the narrow gaps between the chairs. These were arranged around a large, oval table on which were neatly fanned out quantities of sales catalogues from the better auctioneers, as well as many copies of *Tatler* and *Fly Fisherman*. I happened to be the only patient, but as it was all so quiet I suspected I might be in for a long wait, and settled down with an armful of fishing magazines into a comfortably sponge-like leather armchair.

The silence was underlined – with a genuine touch of cliché – by the slow tick of a grandfather clock. Or rather tock. TOCK. TOCK. TOCK. All rather hypnotic. I began to doze off, although I'm quite certain that I didn't actually fall asleep, because I was halfway through reading a ninth or tenth feature about the same gigantic Norwegian salmon, when the receptionist called me through.

The dapper doctor was dressed with immaculate care, in a fawn-coloured three-piece suit which richly emphasised his windsurfer's tan, and he wore one of those ties with bold stripes that aristocrats put on for special occasions. This appeared discreetly to announce his membership of The Pony Club UK. He also sported a set of long, greyish sideburns of a sort which were last in vogue in the 1960s. Highly polished brown brogues adorned his feet. We first exchanged a few pleasantries on my general state of health, all of which, I suspected, were weighted on his part to confirm a pre-conceived notion that I was a pure-blooded Neanderthal. In poor shape, too, despite all my laps. After which I finally got to remove my own rough boot and holey sock, and raise my rank foot, replete with its verruca. He leaned forward, at an angle of faint disgust, for a closer look. "My goodness! The infected area is rather large," he said, "just wait there for a moment if you please". Then he got up and walked quickly out of the room.

I hardly had time to be puzzled by this sudden exit before he returned, and hadn't even lowered my bare foot. He seemed to be absent for about 30 seconds, but clearly wasn't, because during this interval the steady forward progress of chronological time had cracked/   /cracked with violent force! As I saw that the doctor had stripped off the fawn suit and was dressed as if for golf, in Burberry slacks, white-fringed shoes and an open-necked navy-blue shirt. He'd also managed to shave off the mad sideburns. I was so stunned by my sudden and unexpected plunge into this time-warp that, to begin with, I could barely move, or talk. Even my hearing seemed to be playing tricks as he sat down and leant forward again and repeated "Yes! The infected area is rather large." Before adding, "Liquid nitrogen – I don't keep any here!"

Well, after that I rallied round a bit and escaped as soon as I could. A thousand years might have passed, or less than a single nanosecond, as I found myself out of the tall house and scurrying as fast as I could manage, on one-and-a-half feet, down the doctor's long drive. At the far end of which the everyday noises of the street soon helped me to recover most of the rest of my wits.

It took five visits to a chiropodist and four freezing shots of liquid nitrogen, at £20 a go, before I was finally rid of the verruca. Soon after that I washed out my best pair of swimming trunks. When they were dry I stuck them in a jiffy bag. And late the next evening posted them, anonymously, through the letter box of the nearest Oxfam shop. The redundant goggles I hung on to, for no better reason than that they'd been expensive.

Most mysteries probably do have a resolution, though time and chance will need to coincide if you're to find it out. It was quite some years before I discovered that Doctor Pawson wasn't some latter-day Time Lord, though by then I'd moved flat, and with some relief had put myself beyond the range of his care. Fast-forward again several years to the allotments, and I'm talking to one of the plotholders who in his spare time also happens to be a GP, Philip Matthewman, telling him a bare bones version of the verruca story. Not long before I'd finished he began to chuckle: "No, dear chap. Not Doctor Pawson, Doc-*tors* Pawson. Quite good friends of mine actually. *Gemelli sine ulla discrepentia*. Note I don't say "gemini", which would be "balls" to you. Identical twins. Perfectly identical. Two brothers working in the same practice."

And here's the first in an occasional series of handy allotment gardening and related hints. When you're back home from the plot and about to peel your onions, or even worse, when grating fresh horseradish root, wear an old pair of swimming goggles. Just the thing to keep you from bursting into tears!

❖   ❖   ❖

Well, alright then, so my sporting career was a dead loss. But at least, I thought, I had the consolation of a creative life to look forward to. I began to cast around for a suitable medium through which to express myself, and started out painting with watercolours. The materials for this weren't cheap, all those little tubes of paint; although I loved the names, some of them quite beautiful: Scarlet Alizarin… Cerulean Blue… Gamboge Hue… Payne's Grey… Permanent Rose… Viridian. Not to mention the price of the paper, like thick blotting paper but vastly more expensive.

I learned in primary school that if you mix all the colours of the rainbow together you end up with white. So I mixed paint, time and again, from the dear little tubes, and what I invariably ended up with wasn't white at all, but shades of mud: Dull Brown… Dirty Tan… Khaki Sludge… Grubby Umber… Changing-Room Floor Grey… These I vigorously dolloped onto the thick blotting-type paper, though the effect hardly pleased the eye because every daub seemed to blur into every other, so it wasn't long before I began to worry that not merely was I short-sighted, but might also be colour blind.

In search of expert help, I showed some of my work to one of my downstairs neighbours, Cate, a recent graduate in Art History who was employed by one of the more futuristic art galleries in Cork Street, W1. It specialised in science fiction stuff, I believe. Up in my kitchen, Cate was quite happy to accept a cup of weak tea, although she turned down the plate of jam doughnuts I offered. She listened with patience as I expounded on the technical colouring problems I was experiencing, an explanation which, inevitably, developed into a wider diatribe covering many of the more general difficulties of my existence.

"Ah yes…" she said. "Yes." Tutting with an empathy that had me quietly moved. "Alienation. Considered by many to be a prerequisite for much of the twentieth-century's greatest art. Though not everyone agrees." She thumbed through my muddy paintings, some of which were by now picking up tea stains from the table top, not that this made them any worse. "I think you'd better try Soylent Green," she sighed.

Soon after, I went through every art materials supplier in the phone book. None of them stocked it. I was back at square one.

Glorious Mud. Daubs on pricey paper. Then one fine day, as I laboured over my easel, the sight of my latest dull dabblings set my blood racing. In a moment of blinding insight I *just knew* my true medium. Mud = Clay. I signed up for pottery lessons.

These were handily taught, in a ramshackle mansion known as the Camden Arts Centre, just a few doors down from the equally ramshackle mansion in which I was at the time living, in Arkwright Road, NW3. I am by the way aware that the Centre has recently had a major makeover, and now serves the finest sausage rolls in North London. But when I knew the place, turning up for my pottery classes, quite frankly it was a bit of a dump, well overdue for the refurbishment that it has since enjoyed.

On turning up for the first class I was firmly directed from the ground-floor reception desk down to the dusty basement, where the pottery rooms, or "studios" as they were grandly called, were to be found. What struck me immediately was that I might have enrolled, by mistake, on a course in basic car mechanics, because all the other students were women. Not a single bloke. The only other male in the room was the teacher, an extremely tall, lean and pallid Rastafarian, dressed all in a motley of red, yellow and green, traffic-light colours, with the most fantastical mullet of blonde, two-yard long dreadlocks I'd ever seen, escaping from underneath a big woolly hat. This was someone whom, whilst we'd never actually met, I had seen before, having spotted him several times scooting down Arkwright Road on a curious bicycle. Or rather tricycle, only in reverse, with two wheels on the front, which were separated by a large box for carrying stuff around in – a memorable sight indeed.

Once the class was all present, and settled, the teacher spoke up. "Welcome! You are all very welcome to Camden Arse Enter.

My narm is Ras Jurgen. I'm here to teach you pattree." He had the most beautiful voice, deep, mellow and measured. "I am from Danmark, a plass called Christiania, which is in Copenhagen. A very special plass, but… My spiritual home is Africa. Africa is the Cradle of my Soul. As it is, for all of Eye, and Eye." Here he paused, and gestured around to us with a pale, upturned, long-fingered hand.

His voice was beautiful indeed, but the accent I couldn't place. Or rather could, only it was coming from several places at once. Can you imagine one of Linton Kwesi Johnson's most powerful early poems, say, "Inglan Is A Bitch", recorded by a second Johnson, Boris, in the original heavy dub style? Then have the result redubbed by Bo' Selecta doing his Norske best? Well, maybe not. But if you can, that'll give you some idea.

Ras Jurgen went on to tell us, at some considerable length, that he'd just returned from a scholarship in Zimbabwe, a plass which he mistily recalled as a version of paradise.

I wouldn't like to create the impression that I'm not interested in Zimbabwe, but at the time, it's true to say, it wasn't high up on my list of cultural priorities. The reason for this is that I was developing my own conception of a perfect world, somewhat different from Ras Jurgen's. So I was impatient, full of pottish ideas, and couldn't wait to get started on the clay.

This impatience was entirely prompted by the fact that I'd just finished reading Robert Graves's *Seven Days in New Crete*, that weirdest of takes on the utopian society, mostly written in the waiting room of a Barcelona hospital. A tale in which we learn that we must "retrace our steps, or perish". A world where, once a day, smoking tobacco is encouraged. Where the cattle wear "wide leather shoes" so as not to churn up the pasture with their bare hooves, and are trained to defecate in specially dug latrines, to spare the ruin of the greensward with their "casual droppings" – all "charmingly scientific!" Yes, I had a mission. I was going to make pottery which would, I imagined, enhance the domestic lives and bring cheer to the noble citizens of New Crete!

Eventually, Ras Jurgen's Zimbabwean idyll ran through its per-oration and rumbled to a stop. And as soon thereafter as I could, I dived at the clay – to use a suitably outmoded and outlandish phrase – with gusto. And it wasn't too long before the pudgy and formless matrix in front of me on the table began to yield up the shapes of various items of New Cretan crockery.

Within a few short weeks, there were sets of lager cups, in the form of octagonal cones, mounted on elegant stems. Jugs from which to pour the lager. Also oil lamps, small globes held up on three hollow legs, which doubled as the apertures for a trio of lamp wicks. And bowls in the shape of fig leaves, each lobe of the leaf curled up and overlapped to form the required bowl-like shape. I cut out the clay for these using real fig leaves as tem-plates, and these I pinched from where they overhung into the street from a neighbour's garden – such were the lengths to which I was prepared to go in my sudden enthusiasm for the potter's art.

As my confidence grew I started on a series of coil-built amphorae, of increasing size and sculptural complexity – deep-bellied vessels with long, fat necks braced half-way or so along their length by elaborate handles, rising to hugely flaring rims or top-heavy spouts. All of this stuff was decorated with cameo work, medallions pressed from hand-carved plaster moulds, with motifs such as that of the Sun King, the two-headed swan, the gyrtrash, seahorses, dolphins, scallop shells and such like.

I can't say I wasn't enjoying all of this, in a frenetic fashion, and to be honest, got so carried away with myself that I didn't pay too much attention to what the other students were up to. What lit-tle I do remember of their work, I'm ashamed now to admit, I was ever-so-politely condescending about. Opposite are two examples.

There was a silent, dark-haired woman in dungarees, who made pod forms, which looked a bit like segments of giant conker husk. She had endless grief from the prickles breaking off, and when I suggested she might like to try strengthening these with unbent paper clips, she just glared at me, like the insufferable New Cretan snob I'd become, without saying a word.

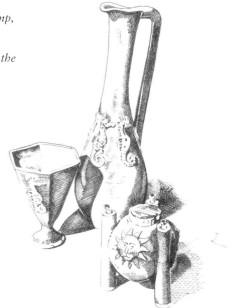

Pottery of New Crete: a lamp, lager flask and lager cup. I made masses of this stuff before being booted out of the studios.

Then there was the glamorous wife of a North American diplomat, who modelled figurines. A beggar woman and child. Two kittens playing with a ball of wool. Trying to render a reasonable simulacrum of cat fur and balls of wool, in clay, is no joke, but she tried her darndest, not – I snootily thought – without success. One day, I proudly showed off to her some of my own work, including my latest giant amphora. "O wow!" she cried, "O wow!" then burst into wild laughter…

"OK then, Ms Husk…"

"OK then, Mrs Walt Disney…"

I grimly thought to myself, "I'll show you!"

And so, back to the pug mill, for another slab of pudge.

Of course, all this messing about with clay wasn't really what put the "Art" into the Camden Arts Centre. Whatever the shenanigans down in the basement pottery studios, they were just a sideshow, probably no more than a means to secure community funds from the Council. The real business happened upstairs in the galleries, where the Centre had a proud record of putting on daring shows. This was *l'Art pour l'Art*, radical, conceptual – proper *épater* the *bourgeois* stuff. One of the most controversial exhibitions about this time was to do with Lorena Bobbitt, whose uncompromising commitment to the *avant garde* was revealed when she chopped off her husband's penis and threw it out of the window. That anyone could create an entire exhibition around such a small, painful and pitiful act was beyond the scope of my comprehension. But anyway, I thought, this was not the sort of thing the true New Cretan – inhabiting a world devoid of evil – should go and see.

There was another radical show at the Centre that year, put on by Michael Bracewell, the novelist and critic. And since I was aware that my low pottery wasn't really what proper art was all about, I thought I should go and have a look. Besides which, I had the perfect excuse to try to wheedle an invite to the opening night, because I'd met Michael a few times, some years before, when we were both studying English and American Literature at Nottingham University. He'd given me some good advice at the time, and also his copy of John Skelton's *Complete Poems 1460–1529*. We hadn't stayed in touch, and I'd not returned the book. So the thought occurred to me to turn up with it on the opening night, explain the situation and thus lever my way in amongst the free quiche and plonk.

John Skelton, court poet or laureate to Henries the VIIth and VIIIth, was a great favourite with Robert Graves, a strange coincidence indeed given my then-current obsession with the pottery styles of New Crete. Skelton wrote a lot of bawdy lyrics to do with beer-drinking and so on, but also kept running into trouble for carping at authority, provoking the dangerous rage of Cardinal Wolsey on more than one occasion, by writing rude poems about him and refusing to turn up at Wolsey's court at Hampton.

My name is Colin Clout.
I purpose to shake out
All my conning bag,
Like a clerkly hag.

…For as far as I can see,
It is wrong with each degree:
For the temporality
Accuseth the spirituality;

…The prelates ben so haut,
They say, and look so high,
As though they woulde fly
Above the starry sky.

So Skelton jogs on, in a jolly fashion, page after page. It's a wonder he wasn't hanged for it.

Well, the opening night of Michael's exhibition came along, and I duly turned up at the door with the Skelton book bound up in some old Christmas wrapping paper, which may have been a weak stab at artistic irony on my part, but was more probably due to the fact that I wasn't going to waste money on a sheet of something more secular. I began to expound my book-return alibi to the pair of black-clad doorpersons, but they were rather too busy to listen to it. "Go in! Go in !" they cried. So I did.

There was Michael, whom I still recognised, just, in the midst of a great white space, most of which was filled with a mêlée of fine art fans, dense, loud and heaving with an intimidating creativity. Obviously, it was his night as The Man, the centre of things. For a while I lurked on the fringes of the crowd, but gradually, with my courage fortified after the manner of the Dutch Masters with a glass or three of red wine, I began to press my way through it, clutching the Skelton and trying not to look too awkward, or to stumble into anyone more poised than myself – which, to be honest, must have been absolutely everyone else, gathered there under that high ceiling.

Eventually I was close enough to be within earshot of The Man, who was explaining to a couple of admirers what the show was about. Something Warholian. Out of *From A to B and Back Again* (the book that, amongst other things, invented the concept of "famous for fifteen minutes"). Suddenly the admiring pair vanished, and I found myself within the eye of the art hurricane, whirling all about. The Man turned towards me. "Don't I know you from somewhere?" he asked.

At this juncture I'd like to record my urbane and witty response, rekindling an old friendship, etc. But unfortunately, on this occasion, Life failed to imitate Art altogether.

I chickened out.

I blew it.

"No," I said. "Unless you've ever been downstairs. I'm doing pottery classes."

"No, I mean from some time ago." I could see that he was puzzled, but by then of course I'd made my play, and had to follow it through. "I don't think so", I lied.

"Weren't you at Nottingham?" asked The Man.

"Well, I've been through it on the train a few times, on my way to somewhere else…"

"Oh." He made once last effort to be sociable. "Is that for me?" he asked, in a jocular fashion, indicating the wrapped book.

"Er no… I'm Christmas shopping early this year…"

"Very commendable!" and with that he vanished into the crowd, relieved, no doubt, to be shot of the biggest bore in the room!

I wish I could come up with an explanation for my ridiculous behaviour on that occasion. But I can't. Was I myself one of Skelton's haughty prelates? Or else a version of honest Colin Clout, trembling at the knee before Michael Bracewell's Wolsey? Whatever. As the laureate himself succinctly wrote, "*smegma non est cinnamonum*". I came not to Court…

But, having turned my gaze from the High, for a while yet I

maintained an interest in my Low Art, and kept up the pottery classes. Not long afterwards, however, even this came to a thumping halt.

The problem was quite straightforward. Ras Jurgen had come to hate my guts. Which was hardly surprising, given all this honky New Cretan bullshit that I wouldn't stop banging on about. I must admit, the New Crete clay concept *was* all a bit esoteric, not to say unusual, and my enthusiasm for it could easily grate on the uninitiated, i.e. on anybody else but me. And I'm not really surprised, looking back, that the whole thing was offensive to Ras Jurgen's own adopted sensibilities, which he'd taken up wholeheartedly and sincerely, for reasons I never learnt, but which were probably as opaque as my own. There was, you might say, simply not enough common ground between us.

Anyway, he began to make his feelings known, first by accusing me of using up so much clay there was none left for the other students. Which, to be honest, was bollocks, there was plenty of clay about, all he had to do was shovel some more through the pug mill. When I pointed this out he was not best pleased. Other minor rows followed. In the end I appealed to the gallery dudes upstairs, but they were far too preoccupied in organising their latest conceptual assault to bother with something as dull as clay, and soon saw me politely off.

Then the kiln, the firing of which was Ras Jurgen's responsibility, started to play up, and each of my giant amphorae, one by one, was ruined. Either the temperature wasn't high enough to melt the glaze properly, so he told me, and they came out looking like they'd been dipped in something horrible – which wasn't *cinnamonum* – or else, he said, it was too high, and they actually melted, coming out from the firing drooped, cracked, slumped, useless. In this manner I lost weeks and weeks of work.

Too low. Too high. Never just right. After a while I began to disbelieve that these mis-firings had any true mechanical cause, and out of a mighty exasperation – as my handiwork was destroyed piecemeal – I'm sorry now to say that I provoked, deliberately, a full-on shouting match, in which I accused Ras Jurgen of outright sabotage. He was fully enraged, and in return accused me, amongst other things, of being akin to those racialist farmers who were deliberately holding back the development of the Zimbabwean economy and trampling underfoot the freedom and dignity of the people. Which I wasn't. Any more than he himself was President Robert Mugabe. But no prizes for guessing which of the two of us held the reins of power!

And that was it. I was banned. Barred. Something I'd never managed to achieve before, not even from a public house, let alone pottery lessons. A disaster. First my sporting debacle, now the door to the gilded world of art, whether High or Low, had slammed shut in my face. So I carried on with my scratchy, romantical "freelance" work, and when I wasn't doing that, which was often, I stayed mostly in bed. Dozing. I'd reached the lowest of ebbs, feeling that the tide of my fortunes had gone right out, if you see what I mean. Totternhoe was the dimmest of dim memories, but ever since then, so it seemed to me at the time, I'd gone precisely nowhere.

CHAPTER TWO

Cold Feet

S o there I found myself, one wintry morning near the end of 1992. I was lying, as they say in Glasgow, *in mah scratcher*. Several weeks had passed since I'd crashed out of pottery, and I was wondering about the little I had to do, how to somehow stretch out the two tasks on the day's agenda:

1. Polish boots.
2. Buy toothbrush.

Frankly, I couldn't quite see how I was going to make all this excitement last for the next 16 hours, before the next bedtime. Just then, there came a tapping, a tap-tap-tapping at my bedroom door. The sound had a quality of gentle persistence, and was one with which I'd become familiar over the past few weeks, announcing that it was Oz, the newest of my two flatmates, a beautiful expert in the food sciences recently arrived from Ankara. I was very impressed with Oz, not least because she could conjure a decent meal from three potatoes, a garlic clove, a dribble of oil and half a pot of plain yoghurt. She also had some endearing idiosyncrasies, including one about the mail. Under no circumstances should letters be left in a heap on the broken-down storage heater in the hallway, as had been the previous practice. Instead, immediately after the postman had dropped them through the letterbox onto the doormat, they should be passed on to whichever of the occupants of the flat they were addressed to.

Fine by me!

"Oz, good morning."

"Meek!" (This was Oz for "Mick".) "How do you know it is me?"

"By the quality of your knocking, Oz. You have a distinctive knock."

"Quality of what? My what?"

"Never mind, no matter. What is it?"

"Meek! There is a letter for you!"

A letter had become something of an event these days, particularly since my publishing interviews (or politely worded refusals to grant the same) had dried up. Even so, I feigned indifference.

"A letter?" I stifled through a fake yawn, "Does it look interesting?"

"No. It is quite boring, really. It is from the Camden Council."

"Oh. Well. (Sod it!) Can you lean it up against the bottom of the door?"

"No Meek, I don't think. It may be boring, but boring things are often most important. I will push it underneath."

"OK, Oz. But push it hard, or it will get jammed on the carpet."

"Yes. Yes. There. I have pushed it Meek. Now I am going to work. Byee!!"

"Thank you, Oz."

I was wondering just how far I could push it myself, meaning the unbearably crappy innuendo, before realising I would have to re-organise my list of tasks for the day ahead:

1. Open letter.
2. Polish boots.
3. Buy toothbrush.

Things were looking up! Soon I was out of bed and had made myself a mug of excellent coffee, something we weren't short of at the time, thanks to one of Oz's uncles in the Turkish wholesale

The infamous Fitzory map (shown without earwax), which has run through many photocopied generations, and has by now confused more than one generation of potential plotholders.

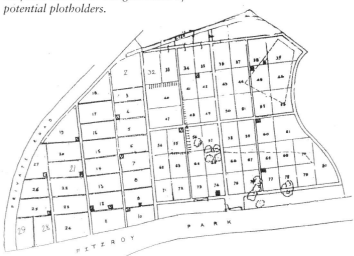

trade. A couple of genteel gulps and I began to properly come round. I sat down at the kitchen table and tore open the Council's brown envelope. Inside were two folded A4 sheets: a kind of *pro forma* letter, and also a mysterious map, which I looked at first. It was one of those umpteenth generation photocopies of photocopies, covered in black freckles, with heavily blurred and scarcely decipherable writing on it. And it was besmirched in places with what looked like earwax. Apart from the fact that it seemed to be divided into a kind of rough grid and there was no X-marks-the-spot, for all the sense it made I guessed that I could be looking at a map of Treasure Island. The letter, of course, soon cleared up this minor map mystery. I don't have the original, but this is roughly what it looked like, and roughly what it said:

London Borough of Camden
Leisure Services

Date   7 December 1992
Reference LS/ALLOT/VB

Dear Michael Rand

FITZROY PARK ALLOTMENTS

You are now close to the top of the waiting list
for an allotment plot in Camden. Therefore I have
pleasure in enclosing a plan on which the vacant
plots are highlighted in yellow (Nos. 3, 19 and
36). Plot Nos. 3 and 36 will be awfully hard work,
if you are interested in either of these there
would be no rental charge until April 1994.

The gates to the allotment site are locked (this is
to prevent unauthorised intrusion). If you wish to
inspect the vacant allotments, please contact this
office within TEN days and a key will be sent to
you.

Tenancy agreements will be drawn up if you decide
to go ahead and rent an allotment.

Yours sincerely,

etc., etc.

But having solved one puzzle, the letter immediately created another. Indeed, I read it with growing bewilderment and by the time I'd finished, was seriously confused. My mind jumped back to an occasion by now a few months old, to a small bar off New Oxford Street, W1, where an evening of hilarious and – inevitably – heavily phatic conversation, with a group of Icelandic tourists, had ended with the disappearance of my bag. Along with other props to my existence, this happened to contain my passport, and since neither the bag nor any of its contents had ever been handed in, my first thought was that this surely must be one of those cases of "identity theft". That some desperado, armed with my passport, was pretending to be me in order to swindle the Council out of one of its allotments. Strewth! Was there no sump of depravity, so foul, so noxious, that some despairing soul won't tumble into it? But then, aided by more swallows of coffee, the full gamut of memory returned for the day. With a minor start, I realised that once-upon-a-time I *had* applied for an allotment. But that had been at least four or five years ago, and somewhere during the tedious interim between then and now, I'd forgotten all about it.

A call to the number which was helpfully provided in the letter confirmed that my long-term memory was correct. According to the Council's records, so I was told, I had registered for an allotment and been put on the waiting list – which, yes, unfortunately was rather a long one – six years and eight months previously. But now that my name had risen to the top, did I think I still wanted one? I paused for a second or so before replying, thinking of my day's list of tasks, now reduced back to the original two.

"Yes," I said, "I suppose I do."

"Good," came the reply, "In that case we'll send you a key to the gate."

A week passed as I waited for the key to arrive. Meanwhile, I'd primed an old friend with the news of this sudden development, and she'd agreed to go to the allotments with me to help me have a look around. OK, so this sounds entirely feeble, but the truth was that with my complete lack of any kind of gardening experience, I'd had to own up to her that I was in a somewhat ambivalent position. A bit like that of a tremulous teenager, who really would prefer to go to the dentist on their own, but isn't quite old enough to handle the experience without a familiar adult standing by.

With the various emotional upheavals and shake-outs of recent years, my friendship with Theresa O'Neill was one of few that had stayed intact. Not something I could put down to any redeeming feature in my own character, but rather to the entirety of her own. Theresa was as resourceful a person as you would ever meet, and wise on an eclectic range of topics, from slip-cast porcelain to *les sans-papieres*. Two subjects which, come to think of it, might be vaguely related.

One quality which I had particular reason to value was her immunity to panic, not a surprise if you consider that she was raised, as the fourth in a family of 12 children, in Middlesbrough, that gritty palimpsest of large-scale industrial boom and bust. She'd once told me how, as kids, in the rare event that they ever had any pocket-money they wouldn't spend it on rubbish like sweets or comics, but head off to the shops for extra rations, usually bread and cheese. There was more than a touch of the Celt about Theresa, dark hair with blue eyes, slender, poetical – likewise she could be as tough as new leather, when the need arose. And she hasn't changed all that much, by the way!

"My name's come up for an allotment," I said to her then, feebly, over the phone.

"Well, we'll go and have a look at it," she replied. "Where is it?"

"A place called Fitzroy Park, I've never heard of it…"

"I know where that is. Highgate. Off Millfield Lane. Either that or Grove Road. We'll take the jeep…"

"But do you really want to…?"

She cut in: "Don't be such a drip. I was brought up on allotments. I know all about them."

This was news to me, but welcome. The vision flashed through my mind of a dozen wiry kids, sitting in a circle surrounded by verdant greenery, chewing on bread and cheese in quiet solidarity, waiting for the spuds to ripen, or whatever spuds did. It passed in a moment and I didn't try to communicate it to Theresa. Not quite the kind of whimsy she'd appreciate. Instead, we arranged to make a date to visit as soon as I'd got the key.

Thus was the die of my subsequent fortune cast, and I made my first trip to the site in quite some style, as a passenger in Theresa's bright yellow jeep. Weather for the day was mighty unpromising: cold, damp, gloomy, with the wake of the previous night's rain threatening frost over the next.

The jeep had a kind of canvas hood, which could be fixed down by various poppers and straps, but despite the lateness of the season and the morose weather, Theresa hadn't attached it yet. Forewarned of this I was clad in a couple of extra jackets and also a bobbleless bobble hat. Even so, by the time we'd skirted Hampstead Heath at high speed and lurched to a halt beside the allotment gates in Fitzroy Park, I was glowing very fresh in the face, with a numb and dripping nose, as well as lips frozen to my front teeth. Theresa, nonchalant and hatless in a thin jacket, was apparently immune to this soft grade of southern cold, so I thought I'd better keep quiet and tough it out.

I clambered purposefully out of the vehicle, walked over and leant on one of the double gates, in just the kind of pose I imagined a happy farmer, surveying his fruitful acres, might adopt. (In those days I was obviously quite innocent, imagining such a chimera might actually exist.) It wasn't actually a comfortable lean because the gates – in keeping with the rest of the allotment fence – were mostly vertical iron spikes, and the view over the plots from this particular vantage point was an indifferent one. But this last fact scarcely mattered, since, like the Martian who lands amongst the spectators at a cricket match, I hardly knew what I was supposed to be looking at.

There was nobody about, and little to be seen, except a bunch of half-dead and dripping grass, a few gimcrack huts and several other pointless-looking frame structures which seemed to be used for no better purpose than a failed effort to dry out a bunch of ragged fishing nets. I could also make out a row or two of what I definitely knew were cabbages, obviously a long-stalked variety. The fact that there was something I could actually recognise in this out-of-season scene of horticultural desolation was a minor encouragement.

"Well this is all very nice," I said. "There's some cabbages over there!" I looked back over my shoulder and there was Theresa, eyeing me with a cool gaze, and clutching a garden spade, which she must have pulled out from the back of the jeep. She'd also exchanged her driving shoes for a pair of deadly serious black wellie boots.

"They're sprouts," she replied. "As in Brussels. You might like to open the gate."

"Ah. Hah! Yes! The gate…". I fumbled in turn through each of the pockets in my many-layered togs, and wouldn't you know it? Out of a dozen or so pockets the gate key was in the very next to last one. By which time Theresa's cool look was beginning to take on a hint of the icily efficient ferocity with which she normally deals with cases of total incompetence. But we made it inside the gate eventually, and I pulled out the not-Treasure-Island map from between two layers of jacket without much further trouble.

"The plots on the map seem to be numbered," I pronounced, poring myopically over it, "but how that relates to what's actually on the ground – to coin a phrase! – I've nary a clue."

"Marker posts" she said, took a step and bumped her rubber boot against a short concrete post poking out of the ground alongside the path. "There's one here." A closer look revealed that the post did indeed have a number cast into it. What's more, after a bit of a cross-check I saw that the number on the post *really did* correspond to one on the map. Amazing-but-true! In attempting to explicate this remarkable correlation to Theresa I soon realised that what, to me, was a revelation of some significance, was to her mind a statement-of-the-obvious, so glaringly inane that it called for an incisive response.

"Look, I haven't got all day," she said. "I've got stuff to do. Give me the map and you take the spade." So we swapped, and she strode fleetly off, with my well-muffled self huffing in close pursuit. After a minute or so of walking right angles around the plots, checking concrete stumps along the way, we arrived at the first vacancy, number 36. At which point I decide to seize back the initiative, and so piped-up emphatically, "This all looks very pleasant, nice and peaceful and so forth..."

"No." said Theresa "No. No. No. No. NO! Too far from the gate. Also... (here she reached into her jacket and pulled out a small silver object, a magnetic compass, from which she took a quick bearing, then pointed an arm) ...as I thought. North is that way. What you've got here is almost exactly a north-facing slope. The sun can't reach it. Cold ground. It'll take forever to heat up in spring. And the angle must be all of 15 degrees. Far too steep. Open soil creeps down a slope – you'll spend half your time shovelling it back uphill. Quite apart from the Japanese Knotweed." She gestured towards a stand of six-foot, dried-up stems at the lower end of the plot.

"I'm not sure," I ventured. "Whatever it is, it looks well dead to me."

"Of course it is, it's winter!" came the exasperated reply. "All the energy is down in the roots. It'll shoot up again next year and you'll have a bloody horrible job getting rid of it."

"Oh!" was about all I could manage.

She took a quick peep at the map. "Let's have a look at 19." And off we went.

No. 19 was an odd shape, mostly triangular, where the grid of plots was obliquely cut across by the boundary of the site. Here, the metal railings were augmented by an overgrown hedge, out of which sprang a number of largish trees. I thought it wise to keep quiet this time and get the benefit of Theresa's knowledge, and I suppose that in resisting my constant urge to make crass remarks I managed to soothe her patience a tad, as she made her assessment. "This is better. Almost level. But it's too low, it's a good six inches lower than the one next door." (It was.) "Which means either somebody's been nicking the topsoil or else it's been too heavily cropped. You'll need tonnes and tonnes of shit to put that right. And it's waterlogged. Same problem as before – it won't warm up, especially if the spring's a wet one."

We both looked down at our feet, squelching on the low ground. Below the knee, my trousers were sodden from the wet grass we'd encountered. Water was pooling around the toes of my soaking, unpolished boots and my rapidly chilling feet, just as nicely as it was around Theresa's own rubberised tootsies, snug and dry. The contrast, needless to say, spoke a fat tome or two about our relative states of preparedness.

"We need a closer look," she said. "You can dig the test pit; it might help warm your feet up! A foot square and a foot deep will do." So, for the first time in a quarter of a century, since I was a child on holiday on some distant Cornish beach, I set to work with a spade. Soon, as a result of my lusty efforts, a small hole appeared in the plashy turf.

"That'll do," barked my foreperson after a bit, "now let's have a look. Not at the spoil heap! Look at the hole!" An existential moment passed, before I swung my attention around the right way, to the unspeakable reality of the face of the void I'd just created. "There, that dark layer at the top is obviously the topsoil, but see where beneath it starts to turn orange? That's your subsoil. If you were lucky, very lucky, you might get a foot of the dark stuff, but here you've only got four or five inches – it's badly degraded. There's something else as well," she said, raising her eyes from the pit to the line of sporting vegetation on the boundary. "The hedge. Privet. The roots go for miles and it sucks all the goodness out of the ground. And they should never have let those sycamores get so big. The biggest weeds in the world. You can't see it now but there'll be too much shade when they come into leaf – you'd be lucky to grow anything at all along that side. Plus, unless you want to start up a sycamore farm, you'll be pulling up seedling trees all year round."

By now I was entering into the spirit of this, and poor No. 19, which might have seemed good enough to the ignorant eye, we both now gazed upon with something of the harsh pity of shrewd and hard-bitten gardeners, nodding our heads over it in sage agreement. As if the plot were some ghastly tract of sterile tundra, fit for nothing but the last port-of-call for a tribe of deluded and famished lemmings. Which left us, after I'd backfilled the small pit, with one last chance, plot No. 3.

Just as I was beginning to pick up on this old-time gardeners' shrewdness – which in my case, of course, was faked – I also began to feel a touch of Theresa's sense of urgency. As far as I knew, urgency was a constant factor in her waking life. But at that particular moment in my own, it was a thing propelled by a creeping sensation of frostbite in the lower extremities. Which probably wasn't helped, I guessed, by the fact that my feet still hadn't completely got over their trip several months back to the time-warping medicine man.

Play up, and play the game! I thought, as I began to stumble lamely and gamely along in Theresa's wake, bound for Depot No. 3, imagining myself, loyal to the last, as one of Apsley Cherry-Garrard's companions in *The Worst Journey in The World*, his epic account of Captain Scott's final attempt on the South Pole. "This sterile quest", as Winston Churchill was later to call it. Undertaken by a generation of heroes, possessed of a fanatical courage, which was disguised by an exquisite politeness as they endured – without a murmur of complaint – unexplored extremes of frigidity, eating poor food, clad in inadequate clothing, lumbered with primitive equipment. Men of ice, shuddering in freezing agony in a thin tent, which did little to keep out the hellish blizzard howling all around:

"Blast! That's the last of my frosty fingers gone. Would you mind awfully, old chap, stepping outside and checking on the emperor penguin eggs?"

"I can think of nothing I'd be more delighted to accomplish on your behalf, my dear fellow, but unfortunately both of my scurvied legs have just frozen orff…"

"Not day-dreaming, are you?" said Theresa.

"Absolutely not, my dear chap, nothing could possibly be further from the truth," I murmured. Then more loudly, "No! I mean No!"

"Good. I hope not. Because this is Plot 3. I think this one'll have to do you."

We did a quick survey. Dug another little hole. The topsoil seemed thick enough. The aspect wasn't ideal, just north of west. But the slope was moderate, and at the same time, sufficient to ensure free drainage. What I chiefly remember is the sizeable extent of dark green ivy, creeping over the top third of the plot in search of a tree to climb. Which, so Theresa told me, showed that that part of the plot can't have been dug over for several years at least. No knotweed. No greedy hedge. Sycamores fairly distant. So I backfilled again, then we both backpeddled several right angles, out of the gate and into the jeep, for a bit of a conference.

"Hobson's choice…" said Theresa, as she changed back out of her wellies, kindly lending me the thick socks which went with them, which did a little to quell my lurid fantasies of The Pole. Not that I'd dared to mention such thoughts. Improper whimsy once again. She wouldn't approve. I was to make sure I washed them out *thoroughly* before handing them back. Meaning the socks, obviously.

"…meaning a choice of one. Plot 3. The others are crap. But all of them are too far from the gates. And the paths are poor."

"But it might be more peaceful further from the gate. More restful." So said I.

"Sod restful! You need access, need to get stuff in."

"What kinds of stuff?"

"For a start, you need a shed. You don't drive. So you can't sit in the car when it rains. There's manure to bring in. Materials. All kinds of things. Tools to store. You'll want a fruit cage…"

"A what?!" Thus it was that I found out what the fishnet drying-rack structures were really for.

"Also, you'll need to dig a pond."

"No I won't!"

"But you are going to be organic, aren't you?"

"As in 'no chemicals'?" (I knew that much!)

"No. As in 'gardening to the sound of church music.' What do you think I mean?"

"Well I hadn't thought…"

"*Well.* You'll have to get used to the idea. If you want to take it on. Number 3. Running a plot successfully is just as much about brains as brawn. And it's not as if you're doing much these days. What happened to the pottery?" (Being aware of Theresa's interest in all things ceramic, I'd given her a New Cretan lamp for her last birthday.)

"I'd rather not talk about pottery," I said, as the memory of the enraged Ras Jurgen rose up briefly to trouble my thoughts.

"So you might as well take it. OK. But there's no point in doing it if you're not going to be organic. Otherwise you might as well not grow anything and keep going to Tesco's." (Bear in mind this was as long ago as 1992, before the supermarket giants had wised-up to the lucrative potential of organic produce.)

"OK, so, praise be!" I said ironically, "I'm organic."

"Then you'll need a pond. Lots of nice frogs to come out at night and eat up your slugs…"

And so forth. Clearly, there was a lot to think about, and even more to do. We kept up this "meretricious persiflage" for a while longer. My brain ached to take it all in. And, of course, I hadn't brought a notebook along to jot down the gist of Theresa's wisdom. Meanwhile, despite having put on her thick socks over my own thin wet ones, my toes weren't getting all that less cool. Far from it. Although I continued to tough it out, in the true spirit of early polar exploration.

Eventually, she announced my time was up and that she had to leave, because there was a meeting of her *sans-papieres* support group she needed to go to. "You'll have to walk back over the Heath," she said. "Think you can do it without getting lost?"

"I'm quite sure I can," I replied.

Theresa must have detected the trace of doubt in my tone.

"Here, you can borrow this." She pressed a small object into my palm. It was the silver compass. "Just keep pointing the needle west and keep walking. Sooner or later you'll hit some place you recognise," she said, revving-up the jeep's engine as, once again, I clambered out.

"Well, thanks," I said. "For everything. And the compass. I'll bring it back next week. With the socks."

"Think nothing of it, old bean!" said Theresa, as she revved-up again and roared away, laughing her head off. She really said that. *Old Bean*. It was *uncanny*.

I made it back across the wild wastes of Hampstead Heath. Guided by unerring magnetism. Later rather than sooner. By the time I was back indoors the frost that had threatened all day was coming on, and the gloom had turned to thorough dark. Oz was in a breezy and cheerful mood, blistering aubergines and red peppers on the naked flame of the cooker. Which was a favourite style of cooking for her, albeit one I'd never seen before myself. Being somewhat fatigued, I pleaded not hungry. Rolling the idea of "roasted red peppers" briefly around my drained brain failed to turn up a single smutty pun or solitary innuendo. A shame. Or maybe not. So I went back from the kitchen to my room and flopped, three jackets, bobbleless hat and yet-damp borrowed socks and all, on to *mah scratcher*. I needed time to think. But instead, I fell asleep.

I pieced my tentative thoughts together over the next few days. On balance, I decided to give allotment gardening a punt. In making this decision, I wish I could say that I was inspired by a burning idealism. But it wasn't really that, because although at this very early stage I was certainly curious about the plot and its potentialities, I was starting from a very long way back so far as information was concerned. More important at the time was the fact that I was bored and, crucially, broke. Remembering the letter from the Council ("`...no rental charge until`

`April 1994...`"), I knew that for more than a year the plot would be free. So it wasn't as if I'd end up much out-of-pocket if the whole enterprise was as complete a flop as my last few projects had turned out to be.

Looking back, I've found no reason to call Theresa's judgement on that day into question. I took on Plot 3. The extent of my success, or lack of it, can be discovered in what follows. As for the low and waterlogged Plot 19, she was quite right, because it's languished over the last dozen and more years under five different tenants, and each one of them has – after a year, or a couple of years or so – given up in disgust. As for No. 36, the steep one with a terrible aspect, that did eventually get taken in hand, in a rather spectacular and successful fashion, but that's a story told in a later chapter, Black Gold.

Anyway, if – like I was – you're an allotment neophyte, and can't find your own Theresa to hold your hand, lend you her socks, compass, and so on, here's a long-winded summary of my advice on what to look out for when first inspecting the plots. I've added a bit to what Theresa and I discussed, in the light of my subsequent experience. Old allotment lags, as well as new hands who've already made up their mind, won't of course have any use for such patronising stuff, so can skip the lot.

Location In urban zones, allotment sites are notorious for being squeezed into marginal locations, where no better use for the land that they occupy could be found – whatever "better" might mean. Such locations include alongside railway lines, or adjacent to main roads, etc. If you have the luxury of avoiding the worst of such sites, its no bad thing, because apart from reduced airborne pollution, especially from busy roads, your sense of bucolic pleasure on the plot will be vastly enhanced by a maximum of peace and quiet.

Aspect/slope Assuming the site itself passes muster, and that you're offered a choice of plots rather than just one, this is the next thing to consider. If the site slopes at all, stand at the highest point on the edge of your possible plot and imagine rolling a ball down it. That's the direction of your slope, i.e. *aspect*. And unless you have an internal compass as accurate as that possessed by Chingachgook, the last of the Mohicans, take along a mechanical magnetic one. A south-facing aspect is best, making most use of whatever sunshine there is around, which is particularly important in the spring, when the sun is still at a low angle relative to the horizon and is struggling to warm your soil.

This applies throughout the UK. Conditions in other places, whether on the shores of the far Horican or anywhere else, are of course well outside of my parochial experience.

The flipside of this is to try to avoid north-facing aspects, which have least in the way of direct sunshine, and are more exposed to frigid winds blowing down from northerly latitudes. Anything else is OK, and even north needn't be a complete disaster, if not too steep. Frequently-dug soils, such as those found on allotments, have a terrific tendency to slump downhill, a phenomenon known as "soil creep". So steepness can be a problem, whatever your aspect. As far as this last point is concerned, less than eight degrees of slope is fine, though you'll need to borrow a geographer's clinometer to put an actual figure on it. Failing which, use common sense, and steer away from anything precipitous. Unless you fancy making terraces.

Access By access, I mean distance and ease-of-travel within your site. If it has no track for motor vehicles, or if you aren't going to drive to it, either from choice or out of necessity, bear in mind the distance to your plot from the nearest gate or dropping-off point, for taking any deliveries. Shifting a ton or more of manure a distance of 20 as against 200 yards, means all the difference between a cushy job and an exhausting one.

An obvious point, which can often get overlooked, is the deleterious effect upon your strength of fighting against gravity on repeat journeys. Inward journeys (gate-to-plot) which are uphill are far, far more physically wearing than downhill ones. The reverse doesn't apply, because if your new plot has loads of rubbish on it to be taken off before you move in, the site owner should take care of this. Paths between the plots should all (ideally) be navigable by wheelbarrow, without jumps, jolts or swerves, all of which can easily cause a loaded barrow to tip over.

Shelter If possible, avoid plots that are too windswept, although you'll probably find little real difference in shelter between any one part of your site and any other, unless it has an alarming topographical diversity, which on UK allotments is thankfully rare. Obviously, further down a slope is likely to be more sheltered than further up. But at the same time it's probably best to avoid low-lying hollows, where you might encounter excessive frost, or shade, or poor drainage. See below, for more on the last two of these. So far as the first is concerned, freezing air is reputed to roll down a slope on a cold night and collect in hollows or "frost pockets". Since I've no personal knowledge of such a phenomenon, to my mind "frost pockets" are best lumped together with UFOs, abominable snowmen and the Loch Ness Monster. The fact that nobody's ever seen any of them is no guarantee that they don't actually exist.

Shade I can't think of any food plants which I've tried to grow which actually *require* shade. Unlike, for instance, crazy things such as ferns, which have an intermediate or thalloid stage of growth, one that's destroyed by desiccation, in direct sunlight. Most of the things that you plant to eat will flourish in a good level of direct light and fail to do so in constant shade. So avoid the proximity of large trees, especially forest species which, as has often been pointed out but bears repetition, have as little value on a decent allotment site as they do in the small- to average-sized garden. In either place, even if they do no specific harm they'll never do you any good. If you suffer from the shade of overhanging trees the effect can be fairly disastrous, and it may well be beyond your powers, whether physical or legal, to put right, apart from trying to negotiate a discount in allotment rent covering the unusable portion of your plot.

Similarly, try to keep clear of overgrown boundary or other hedges, unless you plan (and can get permission!) to give them a savage haircut. Huge trees and hedges will also hog for themselves a lot of the nutrients in your soil, which if you're planning a well-cropped allotment, you can ill-afford to lose.

Vandalism It's always worth asking other plotholders about this, no matter how civilised a corner of the world your plots appear to occupy. Allotments provide a plethora of opportunities for petty pilfering, vandalism, etc. and can therefore be a magnet to bored and frustrated teenagers, a species which, somewhat like dandelions, can turn up almost anywhere. In the worst cases, the depredations of idle youth can leave a site untenable.

The unhappiest instance I've encountered of this was at the Forest Farm Allotments in Hainault, IG6, London Borough of Redbridge. This is, or was, an excellent site of about 100 large plots, with decent facilities, which in recent years has been completely ruined by destructive juveniles. The conflict between them and the plotholders has obscure origins, something to do with shortcuts and rights of way. But it has developed into something serious enough to bleed the place of almost all of its tenants, leaving – on my last visit – just two plots still occupied, both under siege conditions, and the rest of the site a vast wilderness of brambles.

I spoke to one of the pair of survivors of this massacre, a pugnacious East Ender who wasn't about to be driven off his ground by any 'orrible bleedin' yoofs. His willingness to row with them had ultimately sparked a minor riot, when they called for reinforcements by mobile phone, and thoroughly trashed his plot, whilst he took cover in an abandoned shed. Eventually he escaped to his van, driving off under a shower of rocks. Nowadays he leaves the plot wrecked – nothing left worth smashing up. It was a very sorry sight.

To my way of thinking, it seems pointless in such situations to challenge such naughty scamps, since it's unreasonable to expect their burgeoning feelings of anger at the futility and injustice of life to be tempered by any understanding of its subtlety. And since degrees of anger frequently work in inverse proportion to experience, you risk turning *yourself* into a target. So unless you fancy a social-work challenge type of role, avoid vandal-knackered sites like the plague.

Weeds When starting out on your allotment it's best to be wary of the more fashionable stuff you might read or hear about the "enjoyment" of weeds. If your interest is in growing food, which of course is mainly what allotments are for, you need to discriminate between plant heroes and villains in a fairly brutal fashion – we're not talking about letting Nature have a free hand. Later on, perhaps, you may reach a level of horticultural sophistication in which your carrots will co-exist in a state of happy symbiosis in the middle of a nettlebed. Though I doubt it. So at first, avoid as many and as much of the following as you can:

As well as Japanese knotweed (*Fallopia japonica*), there's your horsetail (*Equisetum arvense*). Then there's couch or twitch grass (*Agropyrum repens*). There's large or common bindweed ("granny-pop-out-of-bed", when I was a kid, also known as *Calystegia silvatica*). Also ground elder (*Aegopodium podagraria*), which was apparently introduced to this country by the Romans, to bung in their soup – the mad fools! There's creeping thistle (*Cirsium arvense*), ditto creeping buttercup (*Ranunculus repens*), stinging nettles (*Urtica dioica*) and brambles (*Rubus fruticosus*). According to the American gardening writer Michael Pollan, this last used to be known in the United States as the "blasphemy vine". Once you've ripped your paws a few times trying to pull it out, you'll soon dream up some choice terms of abuse for it of your own.

All of these species are extremely widespread and persistent, tending to become rampant, even ubiquitous, in formerly dug ground which has fallen into disuse. So that neglected allotments can provide such villains with ideal growing conditions. But if you can't avoid these or other unwelcome plants, don't by any means be put off. Determined physical effort and a modicum of ingenuity will soon sort out even the worst. Rope your friends in to help if at all possible.

Soils and drainage If you can, keep clear of any plots which look "sunken" compared with those adjacent to them – it's a sure sign of past bad practice, which in all likelihood will mean problems with soil fertility, and possibly with the soil structure itself, which will at least be horribly lacking in organic matter. There's more on this theme in the Black Gold chapter.

It's worth the trouble of digging small test pits, as Theresa and I did, on any plots that you're offered. All other things being equal, choose the plot which looks as if its got the deepest topsoil. A shortage of the same can badly retard drainage, on clay soils especially, by which I mean soils overlying a clay substrate or "bedrock". This problem is at its worst in winter or early spring, because the solid clay beneath the soil layer forms an impermeable barrier to rainfall over the colder and wetter months, and can result in semi-permanent flood conditions on low and/or level sites. There's nothing strictly unnatural about such a process, but if prolonged by foul weather it becomes inimical to intensive horticulture of the allotment type, and can take a lot of hard effort to get around, involving ditching cuts, lashings of manure, importing topsoil, making raised beds and the like.

So if your site is on clay, try to avoid those parts that are either at the bottom of a slope or are completely flat, and if in doubt, ask somebody who already knows the place. Having scared everybody with this, it's worth mentioning that it may well be that your entire site has had land drains installed in the past. These often take the form of deep-cut ditches, filled with coarse gravel and hidden by the soil put back on top. This is certainly the case on many of the larger allotment sites I've visited around London, although many plotholders I've spoken to aren't aware that they exist. But neither have they mentioned poor drainage problems!

A last point here is that it's fruitless trying to dig a soaking-wet clay soil, at any time of the year, because apart from slithering about all over the place, risking a nasty groin strain, you'll "poach" the ground by squelching and compacting it with your feet. Keep yer plates off it until it dries out a bit (as I was once advised). Which brings me to the final item on this list…

Feet This doesn't belong here at all, but I feel so strongly about it that I'm moved to repeat it regardless. One of the main things I learnt on my first visit with Theresa O'Neill to Fitzroy Park allotments, and have confirmed on subsequent occasions since, is as follows. Wet feet are safe enough in a heat wave. In any other type of weather, Wet Feet mean Cold Feet. So remember what Oliver Cromwell really said to his Roundheads as they were about to carry out an attack on the Cavaliers by wading across a river: "In All Things TRUST to GOD. But keep your *FEET* DRY!"

CHAPTER THREE

Rustic Hyperbole

Like the bashful newly-wed, a creature that in truth is probably extinct outside of the repertoire of a handful of badly outmoded comedians, when it came to getting started on Plot 3, I began with a case of "first-night nerves". Sheer lust to plant my seeds wasn't enough to rush me through the courtship preliminaries: clearing, weeding, digging, hoeing and so on. But I'd hesitate to stretch the metaphor too far, because – as anybody who has ever bothered to compare these two pleasurably unhygienic activities will tell you – sex and gardening aren't quite the same thing. Despite what some of the current crop of TV-personality gardeners appear to imply. In either case, *enthusiasm* is a great enhancement to *experience*, but no substitute for it, and without the latter, the former may have come and gone before you know it. Ideally, of course, you need both qualities in balance. That's about as far as it goes, because in serious gardening you have to keep at least some of your clobber on, including a decent pair of waterproof boots, whereas in serious lovemaking, *of course*, you need to discard the boots and put on an Hawaiian shirt over a hired gorilla suit. And wear a surgical mask. On all five elbows.

Given such complexities, it's hardly surprising that I was slow to get going on the plot, but it was after all the middle of winter, early in 1993, by the time I'd signed a tenancy agreement and thereby got permanently to keep the key to the gate. However, as the weather warmed up a touch, so did I, and by March I'd started to make the regular visits to Fitzroy Park which I've kept up ever since. My first move was to actually work out a route, since, not being a driver, I couldn't simply jump in the wagon and whizz off from flat to plot.

The balkanisation of North London is often said, in these parts, to be nowhere more brutally expressed than between Hampstead, where I was then living, and Highgate, where the allotments are to be found. The reasons for this are a can of quasi-intellectual worms, which I'd prefer not to open, because the issue has always seemed to me, more than anything else, to be a case of "like poles repel". You can spend forever highlighting non-existent differences, but for present purposes I'd rather get straight to the point by highlighting instead one of the most striking physical aspects of the Hampstead/Highgate repulsion, which is that there's no direct bus service between the two places. This is all the more peculiar if you consider that they're only a mile apart.

The 210 route makes a brave stab at it, passing on its westbound leg the length of Highgate High Street, then along Hampstead Lane, through the old toll gate at The Spaniards Inn and along Spaniards Road. But just before what should be its triumphant descent down Heath Street into Hampstead proper, all bells ringing, it mysteriously doubles back at the Whitestone Pond and slopes off down North End Way, towards the delights of Golders Green. A bit like a racehorse refusing a fence, you might say.

Nevertheless, since the 210 goes *nearly* all the way, I made the best of it and incorporated the bus into my manoeuvrings, making the first mile of the journey on foot. This took me the length of the curiously named lane known as Frognal, up to Branch Hill, after which it was a short hop up a set of steps and track known as The Judge's Walk, before I reached the bus stop by the Whitestone Pond where the bus did, and does, its about-face. Assuming there actually were any 210s about – as it's always been a rare species in the bus genus – the rest of the journey was straightforward. Half a dozen stops whisked me to Highgate, to the end of The Grove, with Fitzroy Park being a pleasant down-hill stroll from off of that noble thoroughfare.

What's chiefly remarkable about this journey is that it took me through some of the highest-quality and most expensive urban space on Earth. Is this a boast? Not really – I never belonged to it, or felt that the least part of it belonged to me. Until, that is, I arrived at those allotment gates. So I'm not about to drone on in the manner of a fawning guidebook, about "the beauties of Hampstead", etc., apart from noting that its loveliness is much appreciated by many of those who truly feel at home there. At Branch Hill Mews, for instance, lived two characters I knew from my then local pub, the Coach and Horses on Heath Street, a pair of jovial cab drivers: "Branch 'ill? Larvely! What we call the Poshest Carnsell Estate in England!" – so one of them once told me…

Hampstead Heath itself, however, is well worth a mention, not least because it's still there at all, 800 acres of precious wide-open space, a green island in an ocean of urban concrete, tarmac and brickwork. Also, for present purposes, as it forms the wider land-scape setting, or context, for the Fitzroy plots. They didn't get there by accident! So how did they? In order to find this out, rather than jump straight off the 210 and rush down Fitzroy Park, spade in hand, time to freeze-frame, and pursue the following digression, some spadework of a different order into the history of the local landscape, and one or two associated themes.

The preservation of Hampstead Heath makes a fascinating story, but it's also a hugely complex one. So, at the risk of provoking the dismay of our many, many local historians, whether professional or amateur, I have here reduced it to its bare essentials. Basically this is a tale of two Heath halves, West and East. To the west, which I'll describe first, lies the Heath proper. The contiguous lands to the east have a somewhat different tale to tell, and are dealt with separately.

The proximity of both Hampstead and Highgate to the Heath has in recent times become their chief attraction, although this wasn't always so. Before the nineteenth century, the customary view amongst polite society was that any heath or woodland or similar ground was simply "waste", the haunt of squatters, rustic dolts, perverts and other idling types, where no civilised person would care to venture.

But with the unprecedented speed of London's expansion, cotinuing throughout the Victorian era, this view began to be superseded by a more practical one, which said that – however noxious and unregenerate the character of their inbred inhabitants might be – it would be a good idea to "conserve" at least some of the remaining open areas between the huge acreage of new streets, to help prevent everyone, whether posh or pauper, from choking to death on a surfeit of coal smoke.

In a series of fiercely fought legal battles between various developers and these early conservationists, drawn out over half a century from the 1820s to 1870s, and during the course of which the fate of the *western* half of today's Heath was determined, the conservation cause was helped by the long-standing designation of much of that area as common land. The people of Hampstead and its environs had the usual commoners' rights over the Heath's meagre resources, such as collecting turf, sand and firewood, or for grazing their animals, but since those who exercised these ancient communal rights didn't actually own the acres on which they exercised them, they couldn't be straightforwardly paid-off by developers. The matter of ownership here was never a simple one, and many efforts to build on the west Heath during these years foundered on complex legal arguments over the limits, if any, placed on the rights of private property by the rights of common which were exercised over the disputed tracts.

Like all good Victorian melodramas, this one has a dastardly villain! Step forward, if you please, Sir Thomas Maryon Wilson, Colonel of the West Kent Militia, and *lifelong bachelor* (boo, hiss, etc.).

In 1821 Sir Thomas became the largest landowner in the area, through inheritance from his father, with extensive landholdings on either side of the Heath, as well as certain customary and ill-defined rights over the Heath itself, which were attached to one of his new titles, that of Lord of the Manor of Hampstead.

Since the concept didn't exist during his lifetime, it's no doubt churlish to accuse Sir Thomas of being backward in public relations. Nevertheless, it seems, that in his many attempts to secure the legal permission he needed to build over his lands he remained ever constant to the Spirit of True Villainy, conducting himself throughout in a most satisfyingly vicious, devious, arrogant, inconsistent, destructive and petulant manner. The Heath became a bargaining chip in his machinations, as time and again – whenever his applications to develop his other lands were obstructed by the Court – he threatened to destroy the place, and even made efforts to have it physically removed, through having it quarried up and carted away. And so, apart from a handful of aristocratic relatives who were honour-bound to take his side, he upset just about everyone else who took an interest – in short, he became the man they all "loved to hate".

And as you might expect in that age of virile religiosity, Almighty Jove himself was enlisted in the struggle against Maryon Wilson's monster of Mammon, as, for example, when Sir Thomas was accused in the *Morning Herald* of trying "…to shut out the free air of Heaven from the toiling mechanic and feeble invalid, by covering Hampstead-heath with bricks and mortar…" Here, with that brand of high-toned criticism characteristic of its age, the journalist has mingled and mangled Hampstead with Heaven. Before stuffing this hybrid paradise with the exhausted and the sick. Ouch!

Few could resist joining in the fun. Charles Dickens himself weighed in alongside the growing band of the righteous, in his popular periodical, *Household Words*. Doubtless, his fame allowed him to be somewhat less circumspect than the *Herald*'s relatively unknown correspondent. Sir Thomas, declared Dickens, was "…some half-fledged baronet… who… fancied that no title at all might suffice for appropriating that of the public… may nightmare tread with donkey hoofs on his chest, and… scald his brain with weak tea!"

Half-fledged? Donkeys hoofs? Weak tea?!

It's ferocious stuff. But, in his determination to turn a profit, Sir Thomas was unfazed by Dickens and all the rest, to the last, and it became clear to the multitude of his opponents that there could be no victory this side of the grave. Many were the sighs of relief, politely suppressed, when he finally obliged them all by dropping dead in 1869.

The various lands and land rights passed to his brother, Sir John, a much more affable fellow with no interest in these ghastly disputes. Within two years he had sold the manorial rights to the Metropolitan Board of Works, for a little over 200 pounds the acre. A bargain price. Thus were the squatters, rustic dolts and perverts – or to be more precise, their descendants – left to what remained of their natural habitat, and the west side of Hampstead Heath was saved in perpetuity.

What of the *east* side of the Heath, as it survives today? The first thing to point out is that there's no record of it ever having been actual "heath" at all. The available evidence, whether on the ground, as we shall see in the next chapter, or in those few antique documents that still survive, show that it was ordinary farmland, fields and hedges, private as opposed to communal property. The basic reason for this is a matter of geology, as most of the east side lies off the comparatively barren sands of the hilltops, which were too infertile to ever be worth the trouble of agricultural enclosure.

Much of this eastern farmland was saved from being built over through its conversion to "landscape" in the 1700s. This story somewhat resembles our widespread modern myth, that whenever we're on holiday down in the Mediterranean, we can never get up early enough to beat the Germans to the best part of the beach. In this case, however, it's a matter of *class* rather than *nationality*, because the early birds here were a certain fraction of the new

British aristocracy of that thrusting eighteenth century, who took over the east Heath some years before the majority of their more slow-witted and plebeian countrymen had realised the advantages of the place, and decided to follow suit.

To our new eighteenth-century aristocrats – fashionable, rich, talented and energetic – the immediate advantages were obvious. By moving to the northern heights, which, at the time, lay well outside of the physical boundaries of the capital, they could escape its clamour, crime and unhealthy stinks. (This latter including, of course, coal smoke – they were just as ahead of the game on this as on everything else!) At the same time, being located a mere four to five miles distant from the Cities of Westminster and of London, they could conveniently travel down to where all the action was, whenever needful, by private coach.

In other words, this was rural bliss, but handy enough to tap into the real sources of power and wealth. And at this stage in the nation's history both of these desirable commodities had come, more than at any time since that of the Romans, to rely on the metropolis, on its networks of industry, trade, investment and patronage. Which was something far more sophisticated than the simple possession of wheat or cattle to send to market. Indeed, looking forward to our own times, our eighteenth-century "new Augustans" were proto-yuppies, setting an example which much of the country has, in modified form, followed ever since.

We're often told, after all, that in social matters we're most commonly inclined to ape our betters. Furthermore, that such an inclination works itself out not only through the single lifetime but, frequently, through generations.

When it comes to our modern social geography there may well be quite a bit of truth in this, because in the process of moving outwards from the capital, our eighteenth-century urban-fringe aristocrats did much to initiate, and to promulgate to the wider world, the parable that sets "town" and "country" in opposition. Versions of this story have crept down the social scale, over the decades, over *centuries*, with what seems to be a relentless force, until nowadays they've gained enough in strength and popularity to dictate the pace and movement of untold millions of British lives, and in the process, have taken on an ever more schizoid slant.

The most usual modern version of the town versus country parable runs as follows: that in order to live well, we have to be near enough to the town to get our money from it, and at the same time, need to find a place to live at a safe distance from its inevitable contaminations. Hopefully, this will take us to some untouched rural corner, not too far away, one that nobody else knows about. Where we can pretend, at least during our leisure hours, that the town doesn't actually exist, and that, in spite of all our industrial luxuries, at heart we're a nation of stout and honest country folk.

Which is the main reason, I suppose, why a miserable and antiquated hovel in North Essex, built in a swampy hole, will cost you half a million quid. Just as long as its off the main road and has a fire hazard roof, i.e. one covered in thatch.

If you bother to scratch at it somewhat, our latest version of the myth soon emerges as far more weird than it appears on its surface. We think we belong to the land. But we don't. We think we're close to it. We're not. Where that leaves belonging and closeness in human terms is a theme largely beyond the scope of these jottings. Except to bear in mind that the way we organise our physical space is a paradigm for the organisation of our social space. So that a desire for bucolic exclusivity, it seems, forms an uneasy foundation for our acceptance of social division. A somewhat unnerving thought.

Not – to return to our main theme – that our eighteenth-century betters would be satisfied with a hovel in a swampy hole. No! There was a bit more to it than merely getting out of town. They needed a slope, because without a slope you couldn't get a view, and without a view, you couldn't properly do your landscaping. A question, then, of finding suitable topography, since most of old London lies on land which is as flat as a fart.

Travelling northward from the Thames it's not until you reach the heights such as those found around Hampstead and Highgate, that you'll find a natural prospect worthy of the name.

To the best of these prospects repaired William Murray, the first Earl of Mansfield, Lord Chief Justice, wit, and wizard of the new commercial law, when in 1754 he bought Kenwood House. Which he had rebuilt by the best architect of his day, fellow Scotsman Robert Adam, between 1764 and 1779. The first Earl also began the landscaping of the grounds, in proper Capability Brown fashion.

Both the building works and landscaping were then continued by David Murray, a career diplomat and the second Earl, though by all accounts a far more dour character than the first, his uncle, from whom he inherited the estate in 1793.

In contrast to the early documentation regarding the house itself, so far as the landscaping is concerned, surviving records are quite thin on the ground. So when it comes to discovering which out of the two Earls was responsible for which bit, much of the minor detail is lost. This has been the cause of polite quibbles amongst recent historians of Kenwood and its environs. But for our purposes, it hardly matters, since our first two Mansfields were certainly of one mind in carrying out these works, and it's enough to note, that shortly before the turn of the nineteenth century, they were largely complete.

Kenwood House lies on the northern fringe of today's Hampstead Heath, and it's the south-facing prospect from the rear of the house, which looks out from the heights over the Heath's broad acres towards the centre of the capital, that concerns us here. Much as it did the Mansfields. To quote from one of our most distinguished guidebooks:

> Standing on the southern terrace, with our backs towards Adam's graceful stucco, we can still trace many of the lineaments of the original landscape perspective, albeit more overgrown than would originally have been the case.

A dramatic opening is contrived, as the foreground falls abruptly away in the steep pitch formed by the embankment to the terrace, which after a matter of a few yards alters its angle to a much gentler downward slope, dropping through a parkland scene, a wide meadow with a diversity of trees, both native and exotic, scattered thinly over the expanse of close-cut turf. Many of the trees appear to be of comparatively recent growth, though there are one or two ancients, including a stately pollard and a big maiden oak.

At the foot of this falling slope, the central focus, the middle ground, is formed by a pair of ornamental lakes, the near banks of which are marked by a sparse veil of swamp cypress and other thinly umbrageous specimens, through which the surface of the waters is glimpsed, quiet and reflective, although enlivened from time-to-time by the squabbling of ducks and other buoyant fowl. To the left, the far bank is indicated by the pale dash of a modest folly known as "the sham bridge". And rising up athwart this background, but held at bay by the far shore of the lakes, springs the dark palisade of Caen Wood, the remnant of primary forest from which the house derives its name.

The sides of this vista are both framed by rising ground and by planting designed to direct the wandering gaze back towards the centre. To the east, a blinker of laurel and sombre hollyoak tops out the ridge, while to the west a wedge of oak and birch marks the course of a tiny stream, one of a number feeding the lakes, pointing down towards them in an emphatic diagonal.

Actually, this isn't out of a guidebook – I just made it up. But still, it's all quite magnificent, a classic landscape of its type, in which existing elements of a panoramic scene have been subtly manipulated to emphasise its natural beauty, and to create a sense of expansiveness, with all mundane and artificial impediments, such as hedges and boundaries and – God forbid! – the sight of neighbouring dwellings, either swept away or concealed. A kind of rustic hyperbole.

❖ ❖ ❖

Why is such a landscape valued in the first place? Why go to all the trouble and expense of preserving, not to say enhancing, its qualities? Our first two Earls, who of course carried out the preservation and enhancement, would no doubt have said it's all a matter of good taste – but is it only this? Whilst the sense of aesthetic pleasure in the scene supplies a superficial answer, one which might easily satisfy the unenquiring mind, we might well go on to ask, where does that aesthetic sense itself come from? What prompts it? Thanks to the work of Professor Jay Appleton at the University of Hull, we're beginning now to realise that there's something far more animalistic involved.

This is "Prospect/Refuge Theory", and if you've not heard of it before, don't be put off by the clunky title, because the theory supplies a persuasive framework for interpreting the evolution of our shared human psychology, through its intimate relationship with the very land in which it developed, during those long ages when human existence was a more beastly business than it is these days.

It goes more or less like this: our distant ancestors, whether human or hominid (i.e. pre-human), spent several million years traipsing about in the open savannahs of central and eastern Africa. This is the environment in which the human species began, to which its faculties are most attuned and where, until comparatively recently, it has passed most of its time. Untold generations scavenged for a living over the grass and through the scattered woods, travelling in small groups, subsisting on leaves, termites and similar poor fare, dodging giant sabre-toothed cats and other carnivores. To begin with, as a rare treat, they got to bicker over the leavings of suchlike ravenous beasts.

Ages rolled by, whilst in slow increments our forebears developed their social and technical skills: language, tool-making, the controlled use of fire and the like. Eventually these skills grew to such a pitch of sophistication that our desultory scavengers turned into efficient hunters – they became ever more deadly – mob-handed, they could even take on the sabre-tooth moggy! Ultimately, this transformation launched them (by now, I should really say "us") out of the African niche on a path towards domination over the natural resources of the entire planet. A dominance which, with its dire ramifications for most other forms of life, has only recently been achieved.

The crux of the theory is that throughout this long process of development, whether hunter or prey, our ancestors lived the lives of animals. Like any other species, in order to survive, their main requirement was to *see*, yet *not be seen*. So, when it was time to rest, they would instinctively seek out a campsite that was both "prospect" and "refuge". A shady clump of trees or rocky outcrop on the crest of a hill, commanding a view over an open scene, rich in food and other resources, was ideal.

These places were highly prized and at times, no doubt, were fought over with other animals or competing human groups. So they played a key part in our ancestor's growing perception of value in the landscape and of their enjoyment of it. Whether simply optimising survival chances or ultimately, perhaps, sacred, such sites possessed special qualities. Through long usage, an appreciation of these qualities became hard-wired into the collective human psyche, and this knowledge was carried along when *Homo sapien*s eventually rolled out of Africa and spread around the world.

Thus, the theory claims, an image of the ideal human landscape is deeply imprinted in all of our minds. We're most at ease with a good view, over a scene which is extensive and open but at the same time, full of natural detail. Having acquired this mental model over several million years we haven't lost it just because most of us now live in cities, which are no more than the blink of an eye, given the timescales involved. And there's no reason to think that we'll lose it in the future.

What an insight! If there's any truth to it, the theory would indeed explain a great deal about our attitudes and behaviour towards the natural world, whether sublime or ridiculous. To pick a few examples at random:

– *feng shui*: the sophisticated eastern method for working out, *inter alia*, the best spot for your tomb or temple;

– English landscaping: including the close correspondence between *feng shui* values and those of our home grown landscape tradition, Brown, Repton, Don, et al;

– picnics: our modern predilection for parking as near to the top of the hill as we can get, then eating our sandwiches *without even bothering to leave the vehicle*;

– maybe, even, the rationale behind the half-million pound hovel in a hole that I was moaning about earlier. Well, maybe not the prospect but at least the refuge part. Perhaps I shouldn't have been so nasty about it;

– last, but not least, as many of you will by now have guessed: Prospect/Refuge Theory explains the saving of the East Heath!

Because, having got up to Kenwood "first", thereby securing their prospect/refuge, and having had it done up at great expense into a decent facsimile of the human landscape ideal, the Earls of Mansfield needed to protect it from those deadly predators who trailed them north from old London town, whose mundane and artificial villas threatened to encroach on to the sacred land.

This meant that preserving Kenwood was not only about looking after the house itself, but about maintaining its natural setting and in particular, the views to be had from it towards the south. This was achieved through that favourite expedient of the person of means: land purchase. There were many such acquisitions over the years, the two largest being also the most important.

In 1789 the first Earl bought up Millfield Farm, 90 acres lying below Kenwood House, previously let to the Hampstead Water Company, which managed a string of ponds within the property to supply drinking water to those areas of North London immediately downstream. Nowadays these ponds are used for bathing, very popular in summer. In fact, many of my friends on the plots, particularly women plotholders, combine gardening with swimming in the warmer months.

When I told them that I was going to mention the ponds in my book, they were at first curiously silent, then after a pause, took great pains to point out that the water is fantastically polluted. That, in fact, only a hardened dog could swallow it and suffer no ill effects. Also, apparently, several mutant alligators have recently been spotted lurking in the reeds. So it's at considerable personal risk that you go swimming there at all. And there's a perfectly good lido not far away, at Gospel Oak, if you're really desperate for a cooling plunge.

Anyway, to clamber out of these fetid wallows and get back to our subject: in the 1840s, the Fitzroy Estate to the east of Kenwood came up for sale. This was about 100 acres, property of the Earls of Southampton. The Mansfields stepped in again, and most of the Fitzroy land was preserved from being built over, although parts of the enlarged estate furthest away from Kenwood were sold on, including several parcels of ground in the area where the allotments are to be found today. These sales no doubt defrayed much of the purchase price for the whole 100 acres. Several large villas were soon put up, but at the same time, there were various "no-build" covenants attached to many parts of these land sales – it's clear that whilst the Earls accepted they'd have to put up with *some* new neighbours, they didn't want too many of them! This last point is worth bearing in mind in the next chapter, when it comes to looking at the specific location of our allotments.

But at this present moment our narrative byway reaches an emphatic fork. In securing the extensive lands, as mentioned above, and other bits and pieces, the Earls of Mansfield happily preserved the greater part of the remaining open space. In doing so they helped to save much of the diversity of wildlife for which – although both the land itself and the many species it supports have since been much knocked-about and altered – Hampstead Heath is still prized today.

This topic, unfortunately, is a path that will have to remain untrodden. Instead, having laid out the bare bones of our historical landscape context, time to unfreeze the frame and focus back in on the plots.

So, there I was, back in the spring of 1993, jumping off that 210 bus in Hampstead Lane to head down Fitzroy Park, spade in hand. I can't say that I kicked off gardening with any great ceremony, by cracking a bottle of champers over the first inverted sod, or performing any similar atavistic rite. Perhaps I should have done! Instead, what I did do very early on was to start an allotment diary, at whose prompting – if anyone's – I can't now remember, in which I noted down with the true pedant's energy every last detail of my activities either on, or for, the plot. This I kept up for about three years before suddenly stopping it, for no better reason than that I'd filled up all the pages in the notebook I was using. By then, I guess, it had served its main purpose, to help me clamber over that first hurdle, *complete ignorance*, with which I couldn't help but approach the whole matter of fruit and vegetable growing.

Having recently read back over some of this diary, I can detect something frenetic, almost compulsive, between its lines of puerile and ragged prose, a sharp chord of overexcitement, one which leaves me now, it's a relief to say, more amused than uneasy about it. But whatever the diary's literary qualities, or rather the absence thereof, the thought occurs to me that it's just as well I kept one, because otherwise I could hardly begin to recall, nowadays, How It Was I Lost My Allotment Virginity.

From my allotment neighbours I soon learned something of Plot 3's previous tenant. Quite a character, by all accounts. Since taking on the plot a number of seasons before, he'd made just a token effort to grow something, setting out a couple of rows of runner beans only, each year, which he'd then make no serious attempt to harvest when they were ready. Eventually, even this meagre effort proved to be incompatible with his principle passion, which was for booze. So the plot came to serve no better purpose than as a crash-pad on warm and dry weekend afternoons in the summer, when he and his muckers would lurch down the hill from a lunchtime session at one or more of Highgate's hostelries and drop off to sleep in a litter of emptied beer cans, amongst the burgeoning weeds. Several years had passed in this way before the Council finally booted off his dipsomaniacal carcase and re-let the plot to me.

You might think that my judgement of this character comes over as too harsh. But the reality is that "Use it or Lose it" applies to allotments, and with good reason in areas like this, where they're in such short supply. Because not using the land for its intended purpose is simply to withhold it from somebody who would. Maybe for years.

Anyway, as well as dozens of mouldering beer cans, he'd left me with plenty of clearance of unproductive vegetation to be done. This being a task which I tackled with alacrity, by dividing the plot lengthways into three long strips, clearing each one in turn, planting as I went along. One aspect of this that I do remember well was getting shot of the considerable quantity of ivy that Theresa and I had noticed on our first visit, its many creeping stems having formed, in parts, a kind of dense latticework over the surface of the soil. Since this was too tough to be chopped through with a spade, I soon discovered the pleasure to be had in its destruction by swinging at it with a long-handled mattock, and whilst I've had little serious work for this implement to do, following those initial months of clearing the plot, it's remained one of my favourite tools to use.

I also became a student of vegetable-growing literature, mostly the kind that's found on the back of seed packets. It took me a while to figure out those little colour-coded charts which are designed to make sowing, planting-out and likely harvest times completely idiot-proof, but once I'd mastered the code I began to sow thick and fast, in greedy anticipation of all the free grub that I'd soon be able to pick. Within a short time, my "first-night nerves" had gone entirely as I piled broad bean, radish, parsnip, carrot and not-a-few other seeds into the hastily-dug ground.

However, it wasn't as if I was actually working on an empty stomach, and having just mentioned *greed*, perhaps I should point out that there was a further element to my eagerness than outright gluttony. What I found was that allotment gardening answered to a hunger that was just as much mental as physical, and that the many satisfactions to be had from it were both more nebulous, and more profound, than I'd expected. To be honest, I've not tried too hard over the years to render such sensations into words. Which you might well be glad to hear, since one theory of the prospect/refuge sort per chapter is no doubt enough. But out of the turned-over soil I'd conjured a strange, green ghost, and fallen in love with it. It was this, as much as anything else – greed included – that propelled these initial efforts. As it still does. Weird love, indeed.

And so… more sowing. Next came peas, lettuce, beetroot, french beans, all in rough rows across the cleared strip of ground. Not to mention onion sets. And seed potatoes, an authentic "Dig-for-Victory" variety called "Home Guard". These I remember in particular because when they first sprouted out of the soil, amidst the copious other growth that poked up beside them, I didn't know what the "haulm", or potato foliage, actually looked like. I was on the point of weeding them out when a timely bit of advice, from one of the other plotholders, showed me the difference between what was a spud and what was a dud.

Alongside all this sowing and planting activity I began to work on the plot's structure, by which I mean all those basic contrivances used on allotments to furnish a measure of ease and variety to the gardener's work. These contraptions included a shed, fruit cage, cloches and cold frames, brick paths and so on, with most of the materials being found as chuck-outs from skips and similar sources. Also, partly prompted by Theresa's early insistence, though I wanted one anyway, pond construction.

The tenth of May, 1993, was a momentous day. Crucial enough, at least, to rate an entire page of my diary. I got to eat my first home-grown produce: four entire radishes, which had managed to escape notice by the riotous mob of slugs and snails that my efforts seemed to have unleashed. Not that they had really, of course; the slimy chancers were there already, hidden in huge numbers in the grass and other rank vegetation where they'd been undisturbed for quite some time, and I was obviously improving their diet as well as my own.

It's curious to think, in fact, that growing food for yourself can provide an improved diet, in particular a more varied one, almost by default. The failure, if you can call it such, lies in planting first, asking questions later. This is an important point, easily overlooked, but it's proved I would say by my first tiny radish harvest. To put it plainly, I've never gone into a shop for a bunch of radishes; they're a type of vegetable about which I've always been somewhat equivocal, as to my taste there's always the suspicion of bilge water beneath their peppery tang. So that whilst I wouldn't *buy* them to eat, if I can *grow* them I will, and having grown them, feel I can't just chuck them away. The same goes for quite a number of other fruit and vegetable types, which if displayed in a shop rather than sprouting in my own soil, I'd probably not even notice were there.

How I tackled the different aspects of fruit and vegetable growing and my experiences on the plots are laid out in upcoming chapters. The table of Contents at the start of the book gives a rough-and-ready guide to what was involved, for anyone looking out for a particular theme.

To sum up these early digging days: they mapped out the boundaries of my obsession. I was fascinated by the place, and by its varied potentialities, and as this fascination developed I soon found that many aspects of my previous sense of failure and frustration began to diminish in importance. I was getting back on top of events, not simply being ridden by them. And was meeting new people – some of whom make an appearance in what follows. A generous, thoughtful and patient bunch for the most part, as committed gardeners need to be. And even when I didn't agree with their growing methods, on any specific point, I still had something to learn from them.

Also, I've since realised, there was something more to it than this. Because the seeds I began to sow and to nurture in those early days also stand for the start of whatever sense of belonging to somewhere – anywhere – that I've managed in my life to acquire. Sometimes I suspect that this isn't quite normal. But whether it is or not is beyond my understanding, and definitely beyond the scope of any enquiries I'd care to make in the hope of extending it.

CHAPTER FOUR

The Oomygooley Bird

So, to employ a bang-up-to-the-minute locution, within a few weeks I'd become "energised" – no less! – by Plot Number 3, and had started to put the best part of my spare time into it.

I'd regularly leap off that 210 bus looking forward to the day's work, feeling as lithe and indestructible as the hero of one of those kung-fu-bungee-jumping films: *Crouching Gardener, Hidden Horticulturalist*. That kind of thing. And in bouncing hugely along the road, plot-bound, I'd often gratefully experience a touch of what the Lords Mansfield had spent a fortune to pre-serve. To be clear of all the traffic, which is raucous and honking around here for at least 16 hours out of every 24, is a privilege, and to saunter down Fitzroy Park between the mighty chestnuts and limes that line the way is to stroll down what's still a country lane. Much the same route, so I've since found out, that was fol-lowed in the past by John Keats and other legendary figures of the Romantic movement, who'd often come this way, on purpose, to listen to the nightingales. Once past the plots, Fitzroy Park runs down to Millfield Lane. Here's a coeval comment from the critic and essayist James Leigh Hunt, taken from his 1828 memoir *Lord Byron and some of his Contemporaries*:

> If the admirer of Mr. Keats's poetry does not know the lane in ques-tion, he ought to become acquainted with it… It has been also paced by Mr. Lamb and Mr. Hazlitt, and frequented like the rest of the beautiful neighbourhood by Mr. Coleridge, so that instead of

Millfield Lane, which is the name it is known by on earth, it has sometimes been called *Poet's Lane*, which is an appellation it richly deserves... running through trees and sloping meadows, and being rich in the botany for which this part of the neighbourhood of London has always been celebrated.

Not that I've ever heard a nightingale here myself, they're as long gone, no doubt, as the poets hereabouts. But still, even today it's hard to imagine, amidst such happy vestiges of rural charm that still remain, that you're a within five miles of St Paul's. Not proper allotment territory at all, I supposed at first, since whatever else in general allotments were meant to be, they surely belonged to urban margins, odd corners of leftover land fit for no better purpose. Some pestilential and hopeless ground, crammed next to the old gasworks, or squeezed down by the railway.

As I've since discovered, this ain't necessarily so. Over the last decade or so I've turned into quite a kernosser-of-plots, and in various travels about the place have found that there are plenty of pleasant allotment sites dotted about, some in splendid locations. And if you're wondering where the world's most dramatically beautiful allotments can be found, here's a subtle hint, from the indefatigable William McGonagall:

> Beautiful Ancient City of Perth,
> One of the fairest on the earth,
> With your stately mansions and scenery most fine,
> Which seems very beautiful in the summer time;
> And the beautiful silvery Tay,
> Rolling smoothly on its way,
> And glittering like silver in the sunshine –
> And the Railway Bridge across it is really sublime...

Cross on the walkway beside the tracks of that sublime bridge, halfway over the River Tay from the Perth shore, and you're there. You've reached the fabulous Moncrieffe Island. Most of it is a golf course, obviously not such a surprise in Scotland, but the narrower top end is given over to allotments, some 70 plots which are managed by the Perth Working Men's Garden Association. From here it's only a few steps to the riverbank, and mind you'll need to buy a permit, but if you have one, and if you're handy with a fly rod, you've a fair chance of catching a proper wild salmon to go with your kale and tatties.

The natural setting here has an inspiring grandeur, of a quality which is only to be found – throughout the length and breadth of the UK – amongst the ancient hard rocks of the north. Moncrieffe is a low-lying island set in an authentically mighty river, with the steep wooded ramparts of Kinnoull Hill towering overhead to the east. The island's soil is blackly fertile, a dark and peaty alluvium, enriched by winter floods. The Tay can be as ferocious, at such times, as William McGonagall would have it smoothly rolling in the summer months, since it can discharge more water than any other river in Europe, and heavy rainfall, a frequent occurrence up in the vast area of the Highlands which it drains, can turn it within hours into an awesome torrent. I spoke recently to an old friend of mine who'd seen the worst flooding in memory, back in the early 1990s. Derek Guild is a renowned artist, the best of his generation. He grew up in Perth, and the soul of the Tay often flows, with a potent symbolism, through his work – no wonder! – as he told me:

> I went down with my father to watch, by what we call the lower bridge, not the railway bridge. The level was above the arches and was flowing over the top of the roadway. Actually *over* the top of the bridge! Twenty feet above the usual. All that gravity, running away with itself, totally out of control... the town was flooded, the river was like boiling mud soup, full of peat, with sixty-foot tree trunks rushing down with it, looking like twigs in all the expanse of water, churning away... frightening. Incredible! When the floods went down we were surprised to see that Moncrieffe Island was still there at all.

When I spoke to Matt Young of the Perth Association he too had good reason to remember this event; "1993 was quite a spate. The allotments were completely submerged. That was the year we found that we'd rabbits could climb trees!"

Well, when it comes to allotment gardening, there's obviously down by the railway, then there's **DOWN BY THE RAILWAY!!**, as Moncrieffe Island proves. I don't doubt its wild beauty for a minute, having seen it for myself, but I'm as partial as anyone and so I'm sure that in allotment terms, Fitzroy Park comes a close second to Moncrieffe. It doesn't have the drama but it does enjoy certain advantages of a more mellow sort, since unlike Perthshire, it doesn't get frosts in the middle of June. Something of a relief to all softie Sassenach gardeners like myself, whose natures yearn forever southward, so long as the thermometer remains frigidly below 10°C. Not that we cease to function, but we don't exactly flourish. A bit like plants, in fact.

Anyway, there you have it – north or south, there are some lovely allotment sites about. Yet by the time I'd started to put myself straight on the point, it had already sparked in my brain a sense of fascination for the history of the Fitzroy plots. And there was something else that I hadn't cottoned on to right away, but found out over the course of time, that my enthusiastic excavations on Plot 3 were already casting-up a number of historical clues. Or – to be exact – *archaeological* clues.

Just as the litter of mouldering beer cans that was lying about the place when I first arrived there indicated Plot 3's immediate previous role as a slob's paradise, so my digging began to unearth some earlier evidence of land use. Much of it was obvious, like rusting old tools: trowels, fork heads, with or without bits of rotting handle attached, also a number of old milk bottles, from many a bygone tea break of yesteryear. I was quite amazed just how much of this sub-archaeological grunge came to light, and being a hoarder I'd soon built up a fair collection of it. This was evidence, where obviously none was required, of the allotments being… well… being allotments!

But there was older stuff still than this, mixed amongst it in the soil. In particular, clay pipes, mostly bits of pipe stem but also a few pipe bowls, the equivalent from previous centuries of cigarette butts, though unlike modern ones, almost indestructible. Soon I'd saved an entire antique milk bottle full of them.

Allotment archaeology in action – some of the clay pipe bowls dug up from Plot 3 at Fitzroy Park. The presence of these ancient "cigarette butts" in the soil is frequently an indication of a previous type of land use.

These pipe fragments tell a specific tale of a former use to which this stretch of land had been put. This runs as follows. Under the usual practice of old-fashioned "mixed" agriculture, with corn and cattle of equal importance to the farm, the cows would often be kept indoors in the winter months, where they'd be fed on hay and turnips, and other stored crops.

The reason why this was done was a bit more involved than simply to shield them from the travails of freezing weather. Quite as important as protecting the beasts was protecting the soil itself. This was especially the case on clay soils, like those found here, which during winter would have little enough grass growing on them anyway and would invariably be cold and waterlogged for weeks or months on end, and whilst in this sorry state would be vulnerable to squelching and compaction by heavy hoofs. The technical term for this being "poaching". So the cows would be herded inside into stalls, which served the dual purpose of preserving them from the extreme misery of constantly wet feet, an affliction that's apparently just as bad for the morale of cattle as it is for human beings, as well as saving the sodden turf from ruin.

Here, the wayward thought strikes me – though I've no great desire to remind myself of my pottery days – that for those of you who can remember as far back as the first chapter, and have read your Robert Graves, this need to protect the structure of the soil was what was in the back of his mind when he had his utopian cows wear "wide leather shoes"! Though whether the soils as far south as Crete get waterlogged in winter is a doubtful proposition, albeit one excused, I suppose, within the fuzzy parameters of artistic licence. But anyway, enough of this. My New Cretan potting days being well past. If nothing else, getting the allotment put at end to all that.

So, to bring the story back nearer home, here we have a barnful of snug overwintering cattle, with all their shite and bemerded straw bedding regularly flung out into the farmyard, which after a few months would amass a heap of useful dung. This was casually supplemented by all manner of normal farm rubbish: kitchen peelings, boiled bones and pisspot slops, also hearth ashes, defunct boots, toe rags, fur, hair, occasional discephalated teeth, offal too putrid even for the hogs, odd broken crocks and kitten cadavers. And by many discarded "cigarette butts" in the shape of busted clay pipes.

In the spring, before the wheat, barley, rye, etc. were sown, all this valuable muck would be shovelled into carts, carried out to the arable fields and spread about to fertilise the soil. Most of it, thankfully, would decay to nothing in a year. But not all. The point being, that whether in your own garden – unless it's a very long-established one – or on your plot, wherever you dig up a goodly number of clay pipe fragments you can say, with a moderate level of certainty, that the land has a long previous history of arable use. You're standing in an old corn field.

So, in the case of Fitzroy Park, this bit of evidence confirms the documentary record that this part of the old Fitzroy estate alongside Hampstead Heath was not itself classic heathland but had been ploughed up for several hundred years at least – it was farmland. Not quite earth-shattering news, I'll admit. But I think its fair to conclude that if you look at it carefully enough, such apparently slight and trivial evidence gives you an intriguing peep into the past. Several such evidential strands, considered together, can broaden out this view and start to provide you with more detailed answers, and this is what happened next on Plot 3, when my digging turned up two further clues, with a convenience which would seem to me now quite ridiculous, had I not discovered them myself.

Exhibit 1 is a lump of rough-cast concrete, 3 feet long by 1 foot square. I dug this out, along with yet more milk bottles, much broken window glass and the remains of a hobnail boot, when excavating just above the top of the plot to make a level space for my shed. (More as to which, see the later chapter, Design and the Broken Man.) To put it kindly, it's quite a crude object, and was perhaps used as the step for a previous shed that was put up on the spot, a shed that has long since collapsed and rotted to oblivion.

Whatever its original use, there was nothing at all remarkable about such a lump at first glance, but since I vaguely thought at the time that I might re-use it for something or other, I cleaned off its coat of soil with a broom. In so doing, I found that some anonymous gardener from a previous generation had gone to the trouble of roughly carving a few numbers into it. This is a rubbing of the same, which I did later on, once I had found a soft pencil:

This rubbing shows a momentous date, scratched into a rough lump of concrete, which I've since called "the 1939 stone". These scratchings provided me with a not-after date for the founding of the Fitzroy Park allotment.

1939. A momentous year. On 29th April, Portsmouth beat Wolves 4-1 in the FA Cup. Later, in August, Joachim von Ribbentrop and Vyacheslav Molotov signed the Nazi–Soviet pact, which was followed in September by Hitler's invasion of Poland and with Britain and France declaring war two days later. Thus, a second generation of Britons was cordially invited over the Channel to defend the ever-waning prestige of our Gallic cousins.

Exhibit **2** is a slightly less unsightly object. A stoneware bottle, eight inches tall – including its original screw-top lid – which once contained ginger beer, a refreshing brew very popular during those parched Victorian and Edwardian summers. A sketch of it is shown opposite.

I found the bottle at the other end of the plot from the "1939 stone", when I was remaking the path with a collection of old bricks I'd gathered together. To bed these into the ground properly, I'd scraped off the rough grass and dug down through a thin layer of cinders, as well as a further layer consisting of compacted clay-with-stones, a common type of path-making stuff, that

The mysterious Idris ginger beer bottle of prophecy. Once I'd found out the date of its manufacture, I had the not-before date for the plots.

when I was a boy we called "hoggin". The bottle was beneath the hoggin, which (the same goes for many another allotment project in those early days) I'd been attacking with more energy than skill. It lay in plain topsoil, and actually came up wedged tight between the tines of my fork. I'd failed to smash it simply by chance, and felt at the time as pleased as Little Jack Horner to retrieve such a plum, for my burgeoning museum of allotment detritus.

In terms of actual information, so I came to realise, what's important here isn't the mere handsomeness of this stoneware bottle – with its cursive script, strangely like the Coca-Cola one – but precisely *where* it was found. Here, we need to invoke that strange incantation known as "The Law of Superposition", a magnificent title for what nowadays we'd think of as a blindingly obvious fact. Although not always so obvious, it seems, since the law wasn't even dreamed up until as late as the seventeenth century, by the Danish doctor turned part-time geologist, Nicolaus Steno. So, what does it say? "Whatever lies beneath is (usually) older than what lies on top".

Later, this fundamental principle of sedimentary geology was pinched by archaeologists to describe the chronological sequence of the (man-made) strata that their own scrapings revealed. Scientific proof, indeed, that amongst our many fields of learning, geology is older than archaeology! But strictly in terms of the Idris bottle, found lying beneath the allotment path, Steno's Law tells us that – out of these two features – the bottle must have got there first.

When it came to researching this chapter, many years of course after the bottle's discovery, the obvious thing to do was to put a date on it. Which proved somewhat more irksome than I'd anticipated, with much anxious twitching, on one end of the phone. The worst part of this being an hour of my time wasted, going round and round the tele-non-communications loop at Burton-upon-Trent's biggest tourist attraction, the Coors' Visitor Center (formerly The Bass Museum), which runs one of those robotic, recorded switchboards, devoid of all human intervention or sense. All well and good, I suppose, if you happen to be one of our national utilities companies, or else one of the larger bilking societies, but unworthy of a decent museum.

So, spurning such pointless and infuriating technology, I went back to basics, and got hold of a very informative book, *Miller's Bottles & Pot Lids – A Collector's Guide*, written by Alan Blakeman. As well as being full of handy information this is an enjoyable read in itself, for the specialist and non-specialist alike. One of those slim labour-of-love volumes without which our culture would be a far poorer thing than it already is. Out of the pages at the back I got the number of a reputable specialist firm, BBR Auctioneers of Barnsley, South Yorks., and called them up to explain my business. This time around, thank heavens, the real live human switchboard operator was very pleasant, and didn't think my request was at all odd, putting me through straightaway to their bottle expert, who asked me to describe the item. Which I did, and also happened to mention where I'd got their phone number from.

"Yes", he said, "I think I know that particular bottle, but what you have to bear in mind is there were ten to fifteen *thousand* ginger-beer makers in Victorian Britain. What's the stamp on the back? That'll confirm it."

I hadn't even known there was one, but found it soon enough, a tiny imperfect impression near the base, which I duly and laboriously spelled out, my eyeballs refulgent with the effort: "...something T, something F, F. Then on the line below that there's something M, B, something, something H..."

"Oh yes. I do know the one. Made by STIFF of LAMBETH. Idris were a London firm back then. The bottle dates to 1910, though I can't be any more accurate than that."

I was so pleased to get this crucial bit of information that I actually became somewhat effusive, mentioning how I'd found the bottle and why I wanted it dated, because it was for my allotment book, and would the expert mind if I mentioned him on the acknowledgements page?

"Not at all," he said, "My name's Alan Blakeman – I wrote the *Miller's Guide* you just mentioned!"

Well... if you've never heard of serendipity before, there's a great example...

The point is that between the stoneware bottle and the 1939 stone I'd managed to dig up a date range for the establishment of the Fitzroy plots. But having said as much, to be scrupulously and archaeologically impartial, I need to mention that I'm making here a trio of assumptions, as follows:

Ass. 1: That the allotment paths were laid at the same time the plots were first marked out. Which seems to me a fair conclusion.

Ass. 2: That neither object was "curated", i.e. kept for generations as some kind of totemic object, before being dumped. Unlikely in the case of the 1939 stone. It's not exactly an object of beauty, and weighs about half a ton, so I can't believe its ever moved far from where it was made. Unlikely, too, in the case of the Idris bottle, particularly if you consider the kind of reasoning that any "curator" might have to come up with, in order to explain their behaviour:

> Oh yes, that's great-great-grandma's old stoneware ginger beer flask. We'd never chuck it away. It talks. It knows stuff. It has powers to *foretell the future*. Why, in the early 1960s, for instance, it predicted that we'd land on the moon within ten years. At the time we all scoffed, of course, but then look what happened... in July 1969, Neil Armstrong stepped out of the Eagle Lunar Module on to the smooth surface of the Mare Tranquillitatis...

No, surely not! With ginger beer being fairly perishable stuff, the bottle had to have been emptied, then thrown away, soon after it was used for its mundane original purpose. Besides which, what kind of lunatic would be barking enough to "curate" such an object anyway, whatever their crackpot reason for doing so?

Ass. 3: That the marks on the 1939 stone were made that same year, and not by someone either looking backwards or forwards to it, from another. And definitely not by a Portsmouth fan, a vanishingly remote chance in this part of the world which has long been completely overrun by Gooners. So the immediate outbreak of the Second World War was surely in our amateur stonemason's mind, and the date was recorded accordingly.

If we accept these assumptions, there's our Fitzroy Park allotments founding dates: not *before* 1910, not *after* 1939.

Such being the type of basic information which, if you're lucky, can be gleaned from dug-up clues. But a word of caution is in order here. If you're determined as I was to become your own amateur archaeologist, whatever else you do, confine your excavations to somewhere like the allotment where you can't do damage to any *real* archaeological strata, and if you want to do really serious Time Team-type stuff, join your local archaeology society first!

So much for the evidence on the ground. Or under it. But I was yet more curious about the Fitzroy plots' past, and realised that so far I had only a fragment of the story. It wasn't enough. Time for some *historical* input into the tale.

For this, I first took "the line of least resistance" – better known as "the idle route" – and consulted our unofficial allotment historian, Michael Grice, a retired architect, now into his ninth decade. Whilst he certainly won't thank me for saying so, Michael is a remarkable man, the nearest thing we've got around here to the Renaissance Ideal. Like many architects – of what must by now be called "the old school" – he has an acute fascination for the world and all its workings, a catholic interest of long standing, which has rendered his mind well-informed and eloquent on almost any subject that comes up during our frequent and overlong tea breaks on the plots, whether it's how to get the best out of your raspberry canes, or less workaday stuff: art, books, music and so on.

Not just classical music, either; for some reason, Michael is a connoisseur of punk rock, the proper 1970s stuff. The Damned. The Jam. The Clash. The Buzzcocks. Not, as he's mentioned more than once, the derivative rubbish still put out nowadays by a few die-hard bands. Whilst at the same time an original like John Lydon uses up the last vestiges of his "street cred" – the one true measure of punkhood – by disporting himself on television. With sharks, with *insects*! And free Sex Pistols CDs are given away with *The Evening Standard*. An outrage, Sir!

I'm not quite sure where Michael's love of punk comes from,

though he has met Sting on a number of occasions. "Not my greatest claim-to-fame by a long chalk," he told me. "That was when I bumped into Robert Graves, in the urinals at Palma airport, back in 1966!"

When Michael first vouchsafed this snippet to me, out of nowhere in particular, I was somehow vaguely shocked, as with *déjà vu*. Once again, the dim and darkling ghost of New Cretan pottery reared up to assault my thoughts... "Get thee behind me, Ras Jurgen!" I murmured, mentally lashing out at his shade with my wide leather boot. But I actually said, out loud, rather nervously and stupidly: "Well I never! Old Bobby Graves, eh? So what did the two of you find to talk about?"

"We conversed freely," replied Michael, with a note of irritation for once creeping into his normally well-measured tone of voice, "as I recall, about which out of the two of us held in his mitt the most stupendous wanger! What do you bloody well think we talked about? What do any two men talk about in a *pissoir*, unless they're after one another? Nothing! We remained silent, of course!"

"Hmmm! point taken..." I thought, but held my peace, as the conversation drifted off to less emotive territory. Best practice in manuring asparagus, I think it was...

Michael was one of the founders of the Architects Co-Partnership (ACP), which he helped set up along with ten other graduates of the Architectural Association school just before the Second World War. Most of them soon got called-up, so that was it for "the duration". But, after the survivors of the original group had returned from their various military duties, ACP was refounded and, as pioneering architects of the Modern Movement, designed such projects as Essex University and the St Paul's Choir School, as well as the magnificent, but ill-fated, Brynmawr Rubber Factory. This building was at the time much praised for its beautiful concrete-shell roofs, later emulated in structures such as the Sydney Opera House. The design of the Brynmawr works was as much a matter of post-war austerity as of pure aesthetics, since at the time the country was short of construction-grade steel, so the roof coverings soaring over the broad factory floor spaces – lacking metal reinforcement – had to be arched rather than flat to carry their own weight.

ACP was one of the first British architectural practices to look for work overseas and the first to open an office in Nigeria, in 1955, where it designed the Volta River Dam Project and several dozen schools, in Lagos and elsewhere. Michael has asked me not to mention here the many hair-raising adventures that he had during those years, as he jetted off to Africa and Arabia aboard screaming Vickers VC-10s, in search of commissions, although I am allowed to say that on one such occasion, in order to conform with local dress code requirements, he once went to meet the Nigerian Minister of Education rigged out in a cape and hat made of zebra skin!

Nor am I supposed to mention, since Michael assures me there's not one jot or tittle of truth in it, the famous rumour that he once felled flat his fellow Modernist, Ernö Goldfinger, with a single blow from an anglepoise lamp. During an argument over the decorative potential of rolled-steel joists. This is a pity, since it seems to me a far more instantly gratifying form of revenge upon that ferocious genius than that exacted some years later by Ian Fleming, who was for a long time Goldfinger's neighbour in Willow Road, Hampstead, NW3. But that, as they say, is another story…

Anyway, according to Michael's account, the Fitzroy allotments were created at some time back "between the wars". Which, I was relieved to note, appeared to confirm my date range, derived from the Idris bottle and the 1939 stone. Their creation was due to a benefactor, a generous chap called Appleby, who'd made his fortune – like many another wealthy Londoner over the years, not least our first Earl of Mansfield – by taking to the law. Appleby, by the way, at Michael's insistence, shouldn't be pronounced as if compounded of the eponymous fruit and insect, i.e. APPLE-BEE. Absolutely not! The stress is firmly on the middle syllable and the first is almost silent: a-PELL-by.

Mr Appleby lived in The Elms, a large house situated on the north side of Fitzroy Park, a couple of hundred yards up from the allotments. This being originally one of the upper-crust dwellings built after the 1840s when portions on the fringes of the Fitzroy estate were flogged off by the Earls, as we saw in the last chapter. It is still a substantial property and has recently been acquired by a Russian titan of industry for a cool £17 million. The grounds of Appleby's property originally extended downslope to what's now the lower boundary of the allotments, and it was this lower portion of his land that he gifted to the local borough, "for the use and benefit of its citizens". The Borough Council were naturally very grateful, and decided that the best use for their new freebie acquisition would be to turn it into allotments for the benefit of the labouring poor. Which they accordingly did.

So, the Fitzroy Park allotments were created out of the philanthropic concern of a generous gentleman for the welfare of his poorer neighbours.

How true is this charming tale? As my Trotskyite snowboarding buddies might say, does it *rock*, or does it *suck*? Determined to find out, to put the last piece of the allotment story into place, I thought I'd better check Michael's oral history against the version to be found in the records. This turned out to be, somewhat as I'd expected, "the line of maximum resistance", which involved several gruelling days spent rummaging around in Camden Council's Local Studies and Archives Centre in Theobald's Road, WC1.

Archival research is a bit like old-time panning for gold, or at least what I imagine this to have been like: swilling around hundreds-weight of worthless fragments; hours of strenuous and tedious effort for a few valuable grains of dust or a tiny glowing nugget. This, in spite of the inexhaustible patience and resourcefulness of the archivists themselves, who are amongst the most considerate and generous people on Earth, always ready to suggest new leads, and then retrieve the appropriate dusty scrolls.

Well, not quite scrolls! Before it counted as part of Camden, the relevant local authority for this part of Highgate was St Pancras. After many a false start, I eventually found myself panning through the many volumes of the *St Pancras Borough Council Minute Books 1914–1960*. Occupying a whole nine yards of bookshelf space. Every single item of business to fall within the purview of the Council's committees is there, in full and fluent English, an entire lost world of municipal trivia, bound in solid leather, in varying states of decay, although curiously enough the older volumes have survived in better shape than the more recent. Every faulty streetlamp. Every disorderly house. Every discovery and report of a new nest of rats. Every blocked drain. As well as every tosheroon spent on repairing, surveying, murdering or disgorging the same. And amongst all this, there is to be found, the True History of the Fitzroy Plots.

You'll no doubt be relieved to hear, that just for once I've edited what I found out down to its bare bones. So far as I'm able. What *really* happened was as follows:

By about 1920, the many "emergency" allotment sites in the area that had been carved out during the First World War, from the lower slopes of Primrose Hill, Parliament Hill Fields and elsewhere – to help sustain an ill-fed and increasingly bereaved local populace – had been returned once more to grass. But this minor consequence of the outbreak of peace left "hundreds" of dispossessed allotment tenants clamouring for new sites. So, as part of a wider effort to increase the amount of public open space, in 1921 the Council used its statutory powers to serve a Compulsory Lease Order under the Small Holdings and Allotments Acts 1908–1919, on no less a local worthy than Alan David Murray, the sixth Earl of Mansfield, who still owned the great bulk of the Kenwood Estate. They wanted 14 acres, for the express purpose of turning the land over to allotment use.

Whether due to this process of municipal arm-twisting or to financial retrenchment, or both, or neither, it appears that the sixth Earl was prepared to relinquish the Kenwood Estate in its entirety, as long as he was paid a decent price for it and – true to the spirit of his ancestors – as long as it was largely kept from being built on.

So the Estate was made over to a Trust, the Ken Wood Preservation Council. Some bits and pieces were again sold off, including more parcels of the old Fitzroy land, once again with "no-build" covenants over many of these, to spike the advance of the villas. Somehow, whilst the various legal niceties involved were being discussed, the Council's requested allotment acreage was whittled down from 14 to a meagre 1.3. This being a puzzle that I didn't solve. But, in 1924, by an Indenture, the Trust permanently made over these 1.3 acres, a "triangular field", to the Mayor, Aldermen and Councillors of the Metropolitan Borough of St Pancras. The cost was £1,755. By this point, 27 plots had already been laid out on the available space.

Perhaps, by the time all of this had been worked out, many of the "hundreds" queuing for allotments had got tired of it all, since there's nothing in the records to suggest a public outcry over this much-reduced provision. Although I guess that such a lack of protest, or of any evidence for it, could be explained by the amazingly high degree of deference that's said to comprise one of the cornerstones of our culture. Such part of it, that is, as ever gets put into Minute Books. The plots of the triangular field form the lower part of today's site.

What of the top half of the plots? Demand was clearly still there because in 1929 it was minuted that the land lying next to the existing site would be ideal, since as well as being adjacent, it was known to be one of those areas covered by a covenant, so couldn't be built upon. The owner was asked to consider letting out the ground, but was having none of it.

After that, the Minute Book stream appears panned-out. In some years, provision of more space gets raised, but without much enthusiasm. The Council pleads a lack of available land within its boundaries and the issue is let go – most years there's no mention at all.

The Second World War was much like the First, with sudden necessity providing an instant upswing in interest. New plots were created all over, even in the back gardens of bombed-out buildings, provided the rubble layer wasn't too deep. In 1942 the Borough had almost 1,800 temporary plots, and "Dig for Victory" prizes were offered to the best. But by 1944, with the tide of war on the turn, there was little sustained interest on the Council's part in retaining any of these "emergency" sites any longer than absolutely necessary.

But – behind the committee scenes – somebody, or some bodies, were obviously still badgering away. Reaching 1947, and having almost abandoned my archive stake, I found my first real nugget since way back: compulsory purchase powers were sought "in regard to land adjacent to the Fitzroy Park allotments, and opposite to the house known as 'Hillside', for allotment purposes". A Compulsory Purchase Order was served that same year, although once again there were various legal rows, which weren't sorted out until as late as 1953, when the land in question, 2.16 acres, was bought for the final knock-down price of £900, with a massive £80 of legal costs attesting to the fury of the struggle over its fate. This area made some 40 additional plots and established both the current boundaries and internal layout of the site.

And that, roughly speaking, accounts for the founding of the Fitzroy Park plots. Much as we saw in the last chapter with the preservation of Hampstead Heath, our allotment story is a tale of two halves, a compulsory lease and an indenture for the lower half, dating back to 1921, and compulsory purchase finally pushed through in 1953, for the upper.

In terms of extent: after several decades had gone by, the original 14 acres applied for were pared down to 3.5, making some 70 plots, not enough space for the hundreds of applicants for which the Minute Books periodically claim there was a need. There were plenty of other land-use pressures most of the time, not least for more housing, and the Council underwent various mood-swings along the way. Such, in the end, was the local compromise. A hero's welcome was no doubt given to all those returning out of the shambles of the World Wars. But if, around here, any of the freshly demobbed of two generations sought a personal peace in their own spud patch, they probably had to wait a long time to get it.

Not all that much has changed, in fact, since the 1950s. Our twenty-first-century Camden Council, which has the best pro-allotment will in the world, can still provide only one plot per thousand people in the Borough. There are 400 on the current list of applicants, with the average waiting time gone up from the six years and eight months that I had to kick my heels, to more than eight. Not for the first time, the message is – napoo plots.

What's worse, so it seems to me, is that the Council's legal ability to create new allotment space has gone. So far as the central boroughs are concerned, the London Government Act 1963 did away with the powers of previous legislation, particularly the compulsory powers of the 1908 Act. So the vanished 10.5 acres of the 1920s are an opportunity lost forever, much to the disadvantage of each of today's potential plotholders, who are made to hang around for years, just as their predecessors were. Whether the burgeoning interest in organic growing will have any effect on this state of affairs, even over the long term, seems doubtful, as it's as still as crowded around here as ever, and the old conflicting land-use pressures recorded in the Minute Books remain the same.

A further point concerns the non-appearance in the historical record of that enigmatic friend of the people, Mr Appleby, folklore's fairy plot-father. The person on whom the Compulsory Purchase Order was served in the 1950s isn't named in the minutes, so as a last resort I looked up the title in the Land Registry. The name Goodison crops up. Living at Hillside. The no-build covenant is listed as dating back to 1841 – this was part of the fringes of the Fitzroy land sold off by the Mansfields to help pay for the entire estate. No Appleby of The Elms. And no gift to the poor.

So the real story, unfortunately, doesn't contain any philanthropy at all. It's about politics. Meaning it's about the law, and about the law's division of power amongst competing social classes, as well as the rights of individuals versus groups: wealthy landowners, municipal socialism, legal compulsion, etc. All played out in a framework of fierce competition for a limited amount of space. Nothing to do with the milk of human kindness, which, anyway, has never been one of London's most treasured commodities. Mr Appleby, so it turns out, not only didn't *rock*, he wasn't even in the frame, and you don't have to be a Trotskyite snowboarder to appreciate this particular irony.

I haven't yet dared pass this last bit of information on to Michael Grice. In the unlikely event that he ever reads this book, I'm hoping that his justifiable rage at all the other liberties I've taken with his character and his experience will serve to obscure the phantom status of our kindly benefactor, although I do suspect that one way or another I'll have to spend the rest of my days looking back over my shoulder, in dread of the sudden descending rush of the anglepoise of vengeance.

Something that did become clear concerns the question I put at the start of this chapter, about why the Fitzroy plots are found in such a pleasant locale. It turns out, of course, that whilst not quite as dire as being stuck next to the gasworks or the railway, this was marginal land all along. Marginal, that is, to the magnificent prospect and refuge created at Kenwood by the Earls of Mansfield, and kept intact by them more than a century and a half as London boomed – at arm's length – all around. And likewise marginal to those that followed them, with the various covenants to frustrate the speculative villa builders. We might also remember here the stupendous Moncrieffe Island, with its mighty river and raging floods. What's that if not **MARGINAL**? The real question concerns the quality of the margin, not whether or not it actually exists.

Readers with total recall will remember that I began this book with some notes on landscape history. These last two chapters demonstrate, in passing, the basic sources for any similar investigation, whether the evidence sought is physical, conjectural or historical. All three are needed if you want to do a thorough job. And don't worry if, in the process, you create as I've done something less worthy of the Owl of Minerva than of the Oomygooley Bird, the fabled creature that flies around in ever-decreasing circles, until it finally disappears up its own arse. Because the fact that this stuff is deeply, deeply parochial is precisely what makes it interesting.

My final historical footnote concerns the fact that the Fitzroy plots were created in two halves, lower being earlier and upper, later, with 30 years between them. The weird truth is that even today there's a division between the two sides. Upper/later plotholders are known on the site as "uppies": these are the theorists, the ones who sit on the allotment committee – such as it is – forming discussion groups, focus groups and the like. By contrast: lower/earlier types (where my allotment is situated, proving incidentally that the 1939 stone is the real McCoy) are known as "downies", who by and large spurn the committee and the group stuff, theorise less, dig more, and generally make a clean sweep of the Best Kept Allotment prizes generously given out each year by the Council.

Can this, I wonder, really be the vestige of an ancient rivalry stretching back half a century and more, to past generations of plotholders who are almost – although not quite – as lost to us today as are the Tribes of the Stone Age?

Who knows? I'll bet the Idris bottle knows, what with its mystical powers and all, but to be honest it hasn't been saying much recently and I'm thinking of reburying it.

CHAPTER FIVE

Blue Murder

"There's no point in doing it if you're not going to be organic. Otherwise you might as well not grow anything and keep going to Tesco's."

Once again, my wholesale apologies to all of our supermarket giants. Theresa's words, flapping around in my skull when I first got the plot in 1992 and was squaring-up to the "organic-or-not?" question, do obviously date back to that strange era, the time before our country's leading food retailers carried the wide range of organic produce for which they're nowadays renowned. Now that's what I call progress.

Over much this same time period I've made a certain amount of progress of my own, so far as gardening experience goes. Not such a massive feat if you consider just how far back I had to start. This chapter concerns some of what I've learnt, and continue to learn, about growing organically. In particular, it looks at the kinds of choices you might face when attempting to deal with the more common plant pests and diseases found on the plot.

To throw yourself into the pro- and anti-organic debate, these days, can be somewhat like jumping the gunwale of your bark, deliberately, into a raging sea. Once floundering in this vast foam of words, you may regret making the leap, because the very best you can hope for is to be eventually washed up, exhausted and concussed, on to some unknown and rocky shore.

How much more pleasant, then, to stay safe and dry in your cabin, and contemplate finer subjects, such as the visual arts. For instance, what's the world's greatest ever painting? Is it, perhaps, Constable's *The Hay Wain*? Picasso's *Guernica*? Van Gogh's *Sunflowers*? My own contender for the world's greatest art prize, since my tastes aren't exactly cutting edge, would have to be Leonardo da Vinci's *Mona Lisa*. Here's my version of it:

The Mona Lisa. Well, my attempt at it. Not quite the genuine article.

I pride myself in this work of homage on having captured La Giocondor's enigmatic grin rather well, as I'm sure you will agree. Indeed, you might even say that my version of da Vinci's masterpiece lacks very little of either the beauty or the subtlety of the original.

No?

And that's about all I've got to say, for the moment, concerning whether to grow organically or not. If you choose *not*, and decide to load up your allotment with chemicals – herbicides, pesticides, artificial fertilisers, etc. – as do quite a number of plotholders of my acquaintance, you'll end up with a lame sketch. A mockery. A crude and insipid facsimile of something beautiful.

In this chapter, for the most part, I've kept my mind close to the garden scale, where we have the luxury, the pleasure, of being able to attend to our plants as individuals. On the larger scale, this same luxury isn't of course a realistic approach for a farmer, but apart from noting this fact I'm not qualified for further comment.

And since I'm avoiding farming here, I'm also going to duck out of the debate about genetic modification of crop plants (GM) at this particular point. Not that I don't know some of the history – crown gall virus, *Agrobacterium tumifaciens* – and all that, but it's just too boring and too desolate a topic.

The genetically modified "Flavr Savr" tomatoes do rate a mention in a following chapter, Six of the Best. But for the moment, let me put it like this. If you know nothing at all about GM and want to get a vague sense of what it's all about, you're more than welcome to "improve" my Mona Lisa sketch with your own graffiti. Give the old girl, e.g., some donkey's ears, an elephant's trunk, teeth, a few pimples. Take something that's already horribly crude and turn it into a hybridised abomination worthy of H.G. Wells's *The Island of Dr Moreau*. Such a sacrilege having just occurred to me, in fact, I thought I'd actually commit it, as shown below.

This, to me, sums up the very soul of GM and its relationship to industrialised farming. Where food production is the issue, GM is not "the only way forward", as its sponsors often claim, any more than it's the only kind of useable science.

The GMona Lisa. The crude and insipid turned truly freakish.

So far as trouncing nature on the plots is concerned, during my early days at Fitzroy Park I was surprised, at times, by just how entrenched in allotment practice was the casual use of extreme chemical "remedies". In fact, some of the older chaps turned out to be a lot less like The Victorian Kitchen Gardener, and more like The Chemical Brothers.

Two instances stand out in my memory, brief details of which are given below. In both cases, for once, I've left out the names, though whether from polite circumspection or plain cowardice, I couldn't say.

On the first occasion I was admiring this ancient fellow's tip-top Brussels Sprouts, which stood to attention each winter in straight and upright ranks, very much – in that apt, if weary simile – like soldiers on parade. Their old colonel was more than glad to explain his success:

> You sow these in four-inch pots, with fresh potting compost packed down hard. When it comes to planting them out, when they're about nine inches or a foot tall, you sink a same-sized pot into the soil for each plant and again, pack the earth down firm around it. This is for a mould – when you hoick out this pot, it leaves you with the exact size and shape hole in the ground to drop your plant in. But before you do that, you get a couple of gallons of strong Jeyes Fluid mixed up for each hole, and you water in it and all round, a good drench. This kills off all the insects and bugs and any other stuff that might damage the roots...

The idea that you need to actually *disinfect* the ground in this fashion, with such a concoction of killer tar acids as Jeyes', seemed to me quite insane, treating your soil less like your most precious asset, and more like the sanitary ware of some fetid shit-house. The man's mad, I thought. But I was wrong, at least so far as doubting his sanity was concerned, because the Jeyes Fluid trick turned out to be a perfectly respectable and widespread habit amongst many of the longer-standing plotholders, whenever it came to brassica planting-out time.

Still, to me it has always been a loathsome idea. And, for the record, if you didn't already know, Jeyes Fluid is now banned for pesticide purposes under the EU rules. This means that you can't use it to sterilise the soil. Nor to kill off mosses, lichens and algae growing in soil contexts. But you *can* still use it to swab the same kind of stuff from the glass in your greenhouse (should you have one), because entirely different sets of regulations govern pesticides and disinfectants. This farcical state of affairs will doubtless persist into the future.

My second chemistry lesson is yet more crazy still. Here's a gentleman for whom I have a great deal of respect, and who by no means disrespects his earth, having piled a tonne or two of manure and top quality compost into it each year, for at least a couple of decades. A large part of his plot is a permanent bed for onions and garlic, so I asked him once if he ever had any problems with white rot, that nasty fungal scourge of all the Alliums. He replied much as follows:

> Never a problem... I had a puffer... A thing with a rubber bulb. When I was planting out the onion sets I'd puff some of this powder into each slit in the ground before sticking in the set. Mercury oxide or mercury something or other. Always worked a treat! Banned years back, I ran out of it some time ago. But I suppose there's plenty of it left in the soil to keep working...

On hearing this, I was amazed that he could "keep working" himself, and I looked at him somewhat asquint. He showed no signs of staggering or trembling, no obvious brain damage or incoherence, paralysis or convulsions. None of the classic symptoms of mercury poisoning at all. That he'd avoided this seemed a miracle, though doubtless a proper explanation lies in the minutiae of soil chemistry. Either that, or in the fact that most of his excellent-looking, disease-free onions get done up in plaits each year, and given away as presents to family and friends. And enemies too, hopefully.

Between these two – mercury oxide and Jeyes Fluid – there's a list of similar chemicals, now banned from the garden, that's longer than your arm. These are so many and so dangerous, indeed, that a toxic waste disposal organisation has been set up, which can help you to deal with them. So, if you're worried about that near-antique tin or bottle of nameless gunk that's been lurking, for time beyond recall, in the back of your shed – bearing in mind it won't necessarily be marked with the skull and crossbones, but could still be deadly – go to the internet, and look up:

pesticidedisposal.org

which is part of the PAN UK network.

At one stage of writing this chapter I thought it would be a good idea to draw up a list of all these prohibited products, but it was a hopeless task, like something out of one of the more autistically inspired passages in a Georges Perec novel. This is the author, you may remember, who once managed to list in one of his books every single thing that he'd eaten or drunk over the course of an entire year. Which is child's play, compared with my unfinished catalogue of banned garden chemicals. So, the two examples I've already mentioned will have to stand in for all the rest.

It's pointless being critical towards these chemically inclined old fellows. They're no different from any other generation, in the sense that they're men of their own time. Meaning, in this particular case, a relatively brief historical moment – from the 1940s to as late as the 1980s – during which, whatever else was afoot, heavy usage of dangerous chemicals in garden-scale horticulture was not only very widely accepted, but positively encouraged. This by industry, and by various departments of government. It's a supremely crass remark to say that such fashions are bound to change. But, where the spread of organic growing methods is concerned, such a change is driven by much deeper concerns than caprice, or whimsy, as man-made poisons continue rapidly to pile up in our environment, and more and more people seek to escape from them.

An unquestioning belief in scientific progress – that formerly glorious one-way ticket to a material utopia for all – has given way to a more nuanced view, one which starts from a healthy scepticism towards the Emperor's splendid clothes. This new attitude by no means attempts to reject science in its entirety, which in any event is a naïve impossibility, but amongst other things is marked by a readiness to examine each matter on its merits, and not to take the whole job-lot on trust at the behest of some officially-labelled "authority". It's approach is holistic, in so far as it attempts to look at the whole picture, not just at the individual objects in it but how they're connected. If such new thinking does add up, in the end, to a sea-change in our outlook, it's one that many believe is overdue.

❖ ❖ ❖

When it comes to organic methods for dealing with pests and diseases, the range of possible tactics, and scope for innovation of your own, is almost unlimited. So at this point it's probably a good idea if I resist my normal instinct to ramble all over the place, and confine myself to my personal experience of the more frequently encountered hazards, for as much as possible of what follows. Well, not totally confine myself, but even covering the basics leaves quite a bit to be said.

In discussing disease and pest problems generally, the first point to make about them is – **DON'T PANIC**. If your soil is in good heart (as to which, see in particular the following chapters, Compost Canards and Black Gold), and if your seed is also good, for most of the time you can still commit all manner of gardening infelicities, without your beloved plants crashing suddenly dead to the ground, all at once – in the Miltonic manner – as thick as autumn leaves that strow the brooks in Vallambrose.

Working with the everyday resilience of nature is one of the great joys of any sort of gardening. Plants are deeply vital things, and they generally don't collapse when least expected, but wait until they're good and ready to do so, i.e. when they've completed their full life-cycle. Not that we always let them get that far. But this quality, nonetheless, makes them very unlike, say, household appliances, modes of transport, clothing, furniture, model aircraft kits or human love affairs, when it comes to prematurely falling to pieces.

Having said as much, there are certain exceptions in the way of common diseases and pesky pests, to watch out for on the plot. The ones that I've had to deal with most often are as follows:

Blight (*Phytopthera infestans*) is a revolting fungus which destroys its victims from the inside by invading their vascular systems. This makes it a fast killer. And as its principal vector is the air, if conditions are right for it you're very likely to find not just the odd instance of the disease – on a spud plant here or on a tomato plant there – but mass destruction of the lot. Blight's favoured conditions for airborne attack are "Smith periods", which are defined officially, if I recall correctly, as two episodes of longer than 11 hours' duration of greater than 95% atmospheric humidity over any 48-hour period. The technically inclined will need to confirm this independently, but basically we're talking about consecutive warm, damp days and nights in late summer and autumn.

This means that the best way to avoid the blight, for potatoes, is to plant early maturing varieties and get them into the ground as quick as you like in the spring. I usually stick my seed potatoes in three weeks or even a month earlier than exactly what it says on the tin, and in the interim, cover the ground over them with cloches. A tinge of frost, knocking back the first shoots into the light, isn't generally fatal, and is far preferable to total blight obliteration if you're running late in a bad autumn. Allowing for a bit of luck at both ends of the season, weather-wise, your spuds will be done growing and ready for excavation in good time (four to six months after planting, depending on what type they are), before the blight can get to them.

If you're habitually nervous, it's really *not* worth remembering that the "burnt-thumb print" on leaf margins, which is often the first sign of blight, can also be caused by many of the myriad other diseases to which potato plants are prone, also by senescence, i.e. old age. The first sure sign of attack is wilting at the tips, though by then, the entire plant can already be a bit far gone. Such diagnostic hazards can make each autumn a game of chicken for the keen spud person. In any event, if you have planted your potatoes out early, be ready to chicken out early, as smaller healthy spuds are much to be preferred to larger ones which, having already acquired the disease, are then destroyed by it in storage.

In terms of timing, look out for signs of blight attack on other people's plots, or in any neighbouring vegetable gardens, because in purely statistical terms, you're unlikely to be the first victim. As soon as you see it, move fast. Make every effort to warn the affected party and then cut your own spud foliage right down, bagged it, burnt it, or both. Then leave your actual tubers in the soil for three weeks before digging them out, during which time any blight spores lying on the surface of the soil will hopefully have perished. The spores don't survive too long on their own, without something suitable to bite on.

Certain copper compound sprays can be used under current organic practice, though at the time of writing, won't be for much longer. They work on the prophylaxis principle, so there's no point in spraying after you've diagnosed the blight, you'll only be shutting the door after the horse has already got into the stable, as it were.

A further tip when planting seed potatoes is to avoid using your home-made compost in the trench, unless you can cast-iron guarantee to yourself that it never had the least fragment of potato or tomato in it. Blight will often overwinter on any such stuff in the compost heap, and if you then plant your spuds in it you're courting tragedy from the ground up. Use your oldest leaf mould or manure instead.

To conclude, if you can get your earlies in early, most years you'll be fine, even if the blight's rampant.

Tomatoes, which are of course close relatives to spuds and equally prone to attack, are a bit more tricky. Unless you can grow them in a greenhouse or a polytunnel, it's difficult, given the UK's present climate, to steal a march on the seasons. Grown outside, they'll be pushing it to ripen before those damp autumn days come round.

Still, presuming that you've got a cold frame, it is worth sowing your tomato seeds under it as early in the year as you dare risk, for later transplant to the open air. Tomatoes have no frostbite resistance to speak of, but the cold frame will help a little bit (not much!) and the seed itself is optimistic, germinating almost as well at low as higher temperatures. So if lukewarm fortune smiles on you, early in the year, your efforts won't be for naught. In my part of the world, this means sowing in mid-March.

Ideally, I'd grow tomatoes completely under cover, but at Fitzroy Park, greenhouses and polytunnels are classed by the Council as structures which require planning permission, which means, in reality, *sie sind immer verboten*. So the plants go outside, but with a kind of supporting frame, which can be quickly covered with a polythene roof, if blight looms o'er the horizon (see illustration overleaf).

The point of this is to let in light and air, but to keep the foliage dry, which prevents blight spores being washed into the leaves by raindrops. For the same reason, if watering is required I'll spurn the sprinkler, which rains "upwards" as well as down, and let the hose trickle straight on to the ground at the base of the plants.

The M. Rand Patent Tomato Support with Polythene Roof. Such a lash-up as this might just prevent, or at least delay, the onset of late blight among your tomatoes, by protecting their foliage from drenching rain, which washes blight spores onto their leaves.

Does this krazy kontraption work? Last year was moderately rotten for blight, boosted by a rainy August, but under their flimsy roof my tomatoes copped it later than anyone else's on the plots. I was lucky enough, unlike most of my neighbours, to get off a good tomato crop before their day of fungal doom inevitably came around, and I'd like to think this was down to polythene more than chance.

Clubroot (*Plasmodiophora brassicae*), lasting in the soil for years, is a fungally derived canker which affects hapless cabbages and their relatives. By causing their roots to ball-up into morbid lesions, it prevents nutrient uptake and curtails leaf growth and development, on a scale ranging from slight to savagely stunted. Preventing clubroot was probably what the Jeyes Fluid thing was all about. And since this disease is quite common on my allotment, my own practice is to follow the old sprout hero's advice to the letter – but to stop short of swilling on the disinfectant.

Cabbages, apparently, are the only crop plant that the cold north has contributed to world agriculture. Certain headlands on the Scottish west coast, too precipitous for sheep, are said to still harbour the "landrace", the ur-kale from which all the great variety of cabbage cultivars have, over the centuries, been bred. Which, if true, makes this a real wonder, a vegetable "hobbit of Flores", surviving in remotest isolation, from antiquity to the present. I've sworn to myself that one fine day I'll pirate a vessel and go and find it.

And my trusty crew of Flores hobbits have promised to stand with me on this bold adventure, shoulder to bellybutton.

The real point being that, given their northerly origin, cabbages need to work quickly over a relatively short growing season, and so the better fed they are, the better they'll crack on with it, clubroot and all other risks notwithstanding.

So, as previously advised, I'll plant my brassica seed in those same four-inch pots, in clean potting compost, stiffened up with a quarter sand. Then once they're through at three or four leaves, feed the seedlings fairly regularly with a liquid lunch, usually seaweed extract. The idea being to get a strong and healthy plant, grown as far along as possible, prior to planting out.

Before this happens I'll dig in as much manure or leafmould as is handy, as long as it's old, contains nothing brown, but is rotted to a decent shade of black. Plus, with leafmould, a scoop of chicken-poop granules for the extra nitrogen. Also, in either case, the real trick is powdered lime. A small handful per planting hole is essential, certainly on my plot, and if you can do no more in the way of practical measures, if clubroot is present or even suspected, always stick the lime in. It can work wonders, allowing decent brassicas to grow where none could do so previously.

I'll generally space the plants out half as much again as recommended on the seed packet. This way, I hope for fewer, bigger brassicas and less spread of the disease. With all this elaborate preparation and heavy manuring on their side, they'll usually race ahead and outpace the virus.

But if any look stunted, as sometimes still happens, a touch of garden archaeology at the base of each stem will show up signs of advanced canker, in which case the whole thing gets carefully uprooted, with the stump, root and surrounding soil cast into the purifying maw of my next bonfire. It's all quite a lot of bother, but I've had some cheering results on account of it, particularly with purple sprouting broccoli. The sight of this, in winter, is a five-foot tall promise of better days ahead.

White rot or **Storage rot** (*Sclerotium cepivorum*) is a fungus that is fatal to the onion family, and is truly a curse, since (similar to clubroot) white rot spores can lie hidden in the soil for donkey's years until something suitably oniony comes their way, to trigger them off. In this sense it's even worse than blight, which doesn't have the same powers of dormancy. This is just as well, because if it did, potatoes and tomatoes would soon both become extinct.

Common practice is to grow onions from "sets", i.e. tiny bulbs of a year's growth, which is a bit like buying piglets to fatten them up. Since this is usually done over the winter, and since the white rot fungus is inactive at a soil temperature below 10°C, autumn-sown sets will generally fare well until the following May or June. At which point the soil warms up sufficiently for the disease to get going and your onions to start to succumb to it, with their roots rotting off at the base of the actual bulb, which at this stage of their life cycle – invariably – will only be half formed.

Waiting for your onions to topple, whilst praying that they'll all be finished into fully-formed bulbs before this happens, is a tense business, and it's always mightily demoralising when the first one falls.

The best advice that I was given, which in view of the severity of the disease ain't saying much, was that once the first onion goes over, you should dig them all out at once. Which I would always do, and for several years even tried "sterilising" the base and roots of each dug-out half-bulb by splashing on a bit of boiling water. This never seemed to work, and for all I know may even have made matters worse. Anyway, I'd plait them into the usual onion ropes and hope for the best. Which I never got.

The fungus would complete its merry work in the plaits (hence, of course, "storage rot"), turning most of the onions into useless husks of powdery black spores, like overlarge puffballs.

There's no organically acceptable chemical cure for this. In fact, I don't think there's any cure *whatever*, these days, not so far as allotment gardening goes, beyond which I've never looked. Although I once read that you could properly "sterilise" an onion bed – not with anything so simple as boiling water! – but by soaking the whole area, thoroughly, with formaldehyde.

This seemed on a toxic par with the above-mentioned and long-banned mercury, but, because the recommendation was made in what was ostensibly a book about organic growing (albeit one of 1970s vintage), I did once half-heartedly get on the phone to pursue the matter. Several people at the other end had never heard of such a thing, but each knew somebody that might. So I was passed along the telephone line until I finally got through to a scientific researcher employed by one of the giant chemical firms.

So far as curing white rot in the soil was concerned, she was just as bemused as the others I'd spoken to, but was at least able to confirm that formaldehyde had been discovered, some years back, to be a potent carcinogen. And as such was no longer on sale to the general public. Which, to be honest, I was quite relieved to hear, because I didn't really want the choice of trying it out.

Not even several years later, when, finally sickened at the sight of my plaits of "puffballs", I gave up growing onions altogether. Yes... once and only once have I been beat on the plots... and this was it! So, for the last three years I've made do with leeks, which can also be attacked by white rot but are able to see it off.

Then, just a-twelve month past, I read a letter published in an organic gardening magazine about the need to keep the base of your onions dry over the critical May/June period, when they're at bulb-forming stage and the fungus is gearing up for its seasonal attack. Combining this intriguing snippet with another, about onions thriving in a sandy, well-drained soil, my brain came up with the following – a contraption more elaborate, indeed, than the tomato frame – which I then knocked together. It's basically a wooden box, with no base but with a roof, and also an under-the-soil watering device (see illustration opposite). The box is filled up with the following:

60% alluvial soil	*from*	a gardening job I did down at The Oval – no onions grown in it in living memory.
20% sieved leafmould	*from*	you'll have to read ahead – see the Black Gold chapter!
20% sharp sand	*from*	sandbags, kindly donated by Mr Murphy, who's famous around here for digging many holes in the road and forgetting to fill half of them in.

As in the tomato gizmo, there's a polythene roof to let in light but keep off the rain. At the time of writing (January) the onion piglets are in and are well established. They may even be a shade more leafy than some of the sets on neighbouring plots. I haven't fitted the polythene yet.

The underground watering "system" is two bits of old hosepipe, each sealed at the far end, with a row of tiny holes drilled along the length, and with the near ends, on coming out of the ground, joined together and attached to a 10-gallon tank. The idea being that from next April the onions will get roofed over – to keep the soil surface dry – and if need be, I'll water them from underneath.

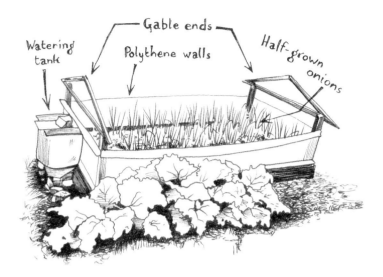

The M. Rand Patent Onion Bed with Roof and Underground Watering System. This shows the contraption before its roof went on, an affair of wires and polythene strung between the two "gable ends". All very elaborate, but if it works, it'll be worth it, meaning I can once again grow onions without having them all succumb to disease.

Of course, I've no idea yet whether this thing will work. By the time I do, these scribblings will be at the printers and it'll be too late to let you know. But if it proves to be no good, Plan B involves raising the roof a few feet and attaching polythene walls as well as roof, which will turn the whole thing into a greenhouse for growing tomatoes. And *Scheiße* to the Council's planning department.*

---

* Last-minute note here. I harvested these onions at the end of June. Not a single case of whiterot – a result! Whether this continues in future years is, of course, a different matter altogether…

Insect pests As mentioned in my opening remarks to this chapter, on the garden as opposed to the commercial scale, there's really no need for pesticides at all. Pick over each of your plants in turn. Remove and/or squash anything that's giving them grief.

Aphids (Aphididae) can be a particular problem, since, given an unlimited supply of whichever plant sap they feed upon, they happily get on with cloning themselves, what's known as asexual reproduction. This means that at any given moment there are several generations each queuing up, one inside the other, to be born. This weird state of perpetual pregnancy being vaguely reminiscent of those sets of nested wooden dolls which – along with furry hats and enamel badges of V. I. Lenin – used to be the only things that tourists were allowed to take out of the old USSR.

What this means, aphidly speaking, is that reproduction is amazingly rapid. In fact, statisticians have recently proved that if each and every member of all the aphid generations born over a single year on Planet Earth were to survive, and to reproduce in their turn, the resulting ball of aphid biomass would be large enough to gag a black hole.

Fortunately, of course, most of them don't survive. But still, this leaves plenty to damage the new growth on broad beans, brassicas, current bushes, fruit trees, etc. With a small amount of patience and careful hand-squidging you'll solve the problem. Look over your plants carefully, starting with the new growth in spring. You won't kill all of your aphids in this way, but the sludge of crushed corpses acts as a great deterrent to the survivors, most of which will be nabbed later on by ladybirds and suchlike.

Asparagus beetle (*Crioceris asparagi*) In the adult form, these are decorative little characters, about 6 or 7 millimetres long. They're readily identified by the three white stripes on each wing carapace, and by the simple fact that – no real surprise here – you'll probably never see one except on the asparagus bed, where they congregate from late spring or early summer for a lusty, ongoing bonk-fest. They are persistent, and will keep on reproducing so long as there's asparagus to chew on.

Their eggs are often found in neat little rows, up and down the stems. Both adults and grubs are what's known as obligate feeders – i.e. they can't stomach anything but asparagus. The grubs are as dull as their parents are colourful, a kind of olive drab colour, and often plentiful. Left to their own devices they can strip all the green outer growth from a stem in a few days, leaving behind its dead skeleton and moving on to the next. Insect piranhas.

So, you don't want them to get the upper hand, even though squashing your way through them all can be a time-consuming activity, if your asparagus bed is a large one, and will give you a whole new insight into the meaning of "green fingers".

However, as always, persistence pays, and in my experience it's best to avoid even organically tolerated sprays, like natural pyrethrum. The reason for this is that I've sometimes noticed a tiny insect, maybe a type of parasitic wasp, which *looks* as if it is laying its eggs within those of the asparagus beetle. Unfortunately, this happens on such a minuscule scale that even my short sight isn't up to the task of seeing what's really going on. But the *possibility* that such a natural control exists, which would be damaged by a spray, means that I don't use one.

Cabbage white butterfly The caterpillars which actually do the damage aren't themselves white, of course: those of the Large (*Pieris brassicae*) are yellow with black dots and a bit hairy looking, while the Small's (*P. rapae*) are smooth and cabbage-coloured for camouflage. Identification isn't so important, though, because *any* caterpillar on your brassicas will be after a free dinner – hopefully, a whole caterpillar lifetime's free dinners – so should be picked off. Likewise, squash anything tiny, bright yellow and egg-like, attached in clusters to the leaves. Protecting your crops with butterfly-proof netting (1 centimetre guage, or smaller), and planting early-maturing stuff, will also be a great help.

Though many gardeners won't have been as fortunate, I've never had a brassica attack that was bad enough to warrant any more radical method than hand-picking. Since this is the case, and since I'm as fond of butterflies as anyone – even if they are only boring old cabbage whites – I tend to take quite a relaxed view on this one. I've even toyed with the idea of growing a few "sacrificial" cabbages for the caterpillars to munch away at, but haven't yet dared to do so, for fear of attracting the scorn of other plotholders. Talking of which…

Cabbage whitefly (*Aleyrodes proletella*), **flea beetle** (*Phyllotreta species*) and anything else which is too tiny, too fast, too numerous, or all three, to remove by hand. Use a rechargeable vacuum cleaner, the type meant for sucking car interiors. With a little practice this works amazingly well. So the various jibes and guffaws of any onlookers, as you "hoover" your plants, may easily be shrugged off.

In concluding this brief list of common insect pests, my earlier appeal – **DON'T PANIC** – especially applies. All the types of pest discussed above have predators of one sort or another, and if these happen to be other insects, as is often the case, sprays will usually cause as much damage to predator as to prey. And don't try telling me that ladybirds are "immune" to pyrethrum – they're not! It's a grievous sin to damage a ladybird, and besides which, in any such instance you'll often be shooting yourself in the foot.

The reason for this is that it's a fundamental law of ecology that prey species bounce back from disaster far more quickly than their predators. They're more numerous and multiply faster, and also *sooner*, because there's always a time lag between the restoration of prey/food supply, and predator reproduction. Spraying is therefore often counterproductive, as it allows the creatures doing damage to your plants to return more strongly than ever, before their predators can "catch up".

❖ ❖ ❖

As noted, all of the above pests can be dealt with quite easily on the plot. But…

…and it's a big but…

…if you decide to go totally organic, the worst problem you'll face – worst of the worst – is how to deal successfully with the Blinking Bogies of Beelzebub, those slow, slimy, terrestrial members of the Mollusca phylum. Also known, as a Class, as the Gastropods, or "gastros" for short, that hell-spawned brood, in the Spenserian mode: immoueable, resisteless and withouten end.

Alright then – I may as well spit it out – slugs and snails.

It hardly needs saying that these furtive and sticky monsters can play an easy havoc with the organic grower's best efforts, particularly in the sowing season, a time when even a single slithering individual, the most pusillanimous of its tribe, will make a short night's work of a row of emergent lettuce or carrot seedlings. "Night's work", obviously, because both gastro types are usually as nocturnal as bats. So under normal circumstances, i.e. daylight, you won't witness their depredations. Only the consequences of same. Which can be such a wipe-out as to leave you with nothing whatever, as if you'd never sown your seeds in the first place.

If you're not organic, no problem… *pas de probleme… problemo nullo*! Reach for the pellets, those little blue pills which are irresistible to gastros of all colours, containing something or other which tickles their palates, with whatever it is disguising a lethal dose of metaldehyde, a substance which poisons them by dehydration and who knows what else. Just one decent sprinkling of these viciously effective jack-and-jills and it's gastropod game over.

The organic grower has no such luxury. Whilst the EU Organic Standards reluctantly allow their use, to the purist the pellets are out, because poisoned gastros don't make it back to their daytime bunkers. So that their dying bodies can be picked up and eaten by other animals, which are poisoned in their turn. Pets can fall victim, as can wild birds, hedgehogs, and (in all likelihood) frogs and toads. So, no cushy pellet option for thoroughly determined organic types like myself. Ahem. Cough, cough.

Just how effective slug pellets can be was demonstrated to me in a most horribly dramatic fashion on the first (and I wish I could say only) occasion I ever used the things. This was two or three years after I'd first got the allotment, and I'd built a fairly large fruit cage down at the lower end of it. This, you might remember, being one of the things that Theresa insisted I'd need when we first looked the plot over. It turned out that I didn't have the heart to disagree with her, and the finished item was an elegant construction, even if I do say so myself. A bit too elegant, in fact, as the wood that I'd made it from – which was planed one-by-one inch sticks from a local timber merchant – was on the thin side for the task, and it didn't last too many years before the whole structure rotted and collapsed. But at the time in question, I'd just finished putting it up, and amongst other mail-order purchases had bought a load of raspberry canes to plant inside.

Posted raspberry canes, particularly those delivered in bare-rooted form, do seem to suffer something cruel in the mail. Probably it's too hot in the sorting office and the postie's van. So anyway, after planting-out, a lot of my canes failed to sprout, and whilst pondering my next Rubus move, I'd pulled out the duff ones and planted, as a stop-gap, a long row of lettuces in their stead.

After a month or three these were a fine sight, a big healthy rank of crunchy salad, a pleasure to behold. Then, on arriving at the plot one morning, I noticed that a single lettuce on one end of the row had vanished. At first I thought someone had gone into the cage and pinched it, but a closer look showed that the plant had been chewed down, *in situ*, to almost nothing, a stumpy green nubbin being all that remained.

The next night saw the demise of the next lettuce in the row, in the same fashion, leaving a second nubbin. Then another the night following. And another. And so on. Within a week less than half the row was left. Courtesy of my unfriendly neighbourhood gastros, I was clearly on the lettuce road to nowhere.

I got angry. I was in the cage, gazing in dismay at the last few of my fine lettuces. In the cage. IN THE CAGE! To which, as it suddenly dawned on me, no pet, bird, hedgehog, frog or toad could possibly gain access...

You've guessed it. I scrounged a handful of deadly blue pellets from one of the other plotholders and sprinkled them carefully, guiltily, up and down the remains of the row, concentrating on the gap between the untouched plants and the adjacent stumps of their rasped-to-zero fellows, this being the most obvious direction of the gastropod assault. Then walked out of the cage, shut its door and scurried away home, head down, without looking back.

Being quite freaked-out by the enormity of what I'd just done – because I knew it would be sheer blue murder – I didn't dare return to the plot for a few days. When I finally did so, I picked my way cautiously along the path towards the cage. Somewhat, I suppose, like the first witness to approach the scene of a disaster, a kind of "approaching-the-train-crash" scenario, one in which the mind readily supplies clichéd images of horror, whilst at the same moment knowing full well that they're about to be shockingly eclipsed in the presence of the real thing.

I wasn't disappointed.

Once back inside the cage, what I found there, was this. All around the lettuce row and for square metres of ground round and about, the *entire surface* of the soil, with not a square inch uncovered, was bright with a coat of slime, exuded in their death-throes by dozens and dozens of snails and slugs, gone – foot, stomach and all – up to gastropod heaven. Just one vast glistening slimy sheet of death, littered with corpses, like the aftermath of a ghastly chemical warfare attack. Which of course is precisely what it was.

I was revolted. Genuinely so. Also shocked. And, also, although I hardly dare admit to it even these many years later...

Exhilarated. I felt like... God. On the gastro scale, that is.

"Now I am become Death, the destroyer of worlds," I muttered to myself – somewhat self-consciously – knowing these to be the same words out of Hindu scripture uttered by Robert Oppenheimer, el head honcho at Los Alamos nuclear research facility, as he witnessed the first atom bomb that he and his pals had constructed go up successfully in a gigantic ball of fire. July 16, 1945. Something new, under the sun. Well, OK, it's a long way from Los Alamos to Fitzroy Park, but whilst the scale isn't comparable, the emotion's the same. Of that, you can be assured.

In the light of this, if you can call it "light", it'll come as no surprise to you to hear that my subsequent attitude *vis-à-vis* the slug pellet question has been ever vexed, to say the least. One such disgusting massacre per gardening lifetime is already one too many, and the truth is, I don't actually detest the garden gastropods sufficiently to want to repeat the slaughter.

Indeed, though it mayn't seem credible in view of my past record, over the course of time I've actually grown quite fond, if not quite of slugs, certainly of the common or garden snail (*Helix aspersa*). This is more than partly due to this beast being called – amongst many other vernacular names – the "dodman", or "hoddy-man-dodd", on account of it being the symbol of those mysterious surveyors who first set out the ley-lines of ancient Britain, back in prehistoric times.

In carrying, in a shell, all its house on its back, and with a pair of eyes-raised-on-stalks representing the surveyor's pair of sacred sighting rods, it's easy to see how the snail, in folklore at least, has come to stand in for the human ley-line-makers of long ago. Easy to see, that is, if you can stretch your credulity far enough to give credit to the eccentric researches of Alfred Watkins, who certainly rates as one of the strangest and most original characters ever to have traversed the land.

In his youth, during the 1870s, Alfred Watkins was employed by his father, who was a brewer, as an "outrider", what nowadays we'd call a salesperson. This job involved much trotting on horseback about the lanes of rural Herefordshire – between some of the many and various alehouses dotted about that diverse and noble county – drumming up sales. A barrel here, two barrels there, and so on.

What young Alfred was the first to notice, or at least, the first to record, during the course of his peripatetic sales trips, was that various common topographical features to be seen in the countryside, whether natural or man-made, happened to line up. They made straight lines. And once he got this linear bit between his teeth – with the help of various Ordnance Survey maps – suddenly straight lines jumped out of the landscape everywhere. Extrapolating this phenomenon became his life's work. As he was later to put it, in his seminal book, *The Old Straight Track*, first published in 1925: "…mounds, moats, beacons and mark-stones fall into straight lines throughout Britain…"

Thus, were ley-lines conceived. Or, if you prefer, rediscovered.

Despite making it into print, Watkins' ideas weren't widely taken up for another 40-odd years, until the 1960s, when ley-lines became a mystical rage, turning somehow, in the process, into strange and potent earth-energy forces, buzzing and sparking away beneath the ground like perished power cables. Cool! I mean, so what if you were just another stoned long-hair crashing in a Camden Town squat? If your crash-pad was on a ley-line, as such places inevitably were, well hey! That like, meant something, maaaaan! And, of course, in much the same mystical guise, ley-lines still find favour with New Age Folk to this very day.

This meaning wasn't quite what Watkins himself had originally proposed. *His* ley-lines were unhippily utilitarian, first marked out, so he thought, with mounds, beacons and all, as trade routes for the portage of salt, flint, maybe later for metals. They were pathways through a sparsely populated land, following the shortest possible line between fixed points, a bit like prehistoric motorways, in fact. Sure. Cool. Maybe.

What to make of all this? On the main subject, i.e. the plausibility of Watkins' ley-line theory, I've no idea. But I have come to two ancillary conclusions:

(a) The beer salesperson's role is bound to involve a modicum of product sampling. Any pre-motorised salesperson, negotiating the highways and byways on horseback from one public house to the next, perforce inhabited a seriously meandering universe, and can surely be forgiven for developing a profound psychological need for a straight line.

(b) Whether "dodman" symbol or not, for any normal person, simply having heard of the connection makes a lifelong hatred of snails unsustainable.

So, how then do we deal with them, and their sluggish cousins, in a scrupulously fair and organic way, one which must needs avoid the demon blue tablets?

Ale is said to be much weaker now than it was in Watkins' day, but whether this statement is accurate or not, in the garden or on the plot you can still try "slug beer", which works as follows.

Go to a supermarket or off-licence and buy as many cans as you can carry of strong beer or lager. Always get the cheap and nasty stuff, because slug beer works by strength, not by quality. Take the cans up to the plot and find a strong chair to sit in.

Now comes the tricky bit. What you need to do is place a quantity of this cheap booze into your stomach. Through a process of trial and error, I've discovered that the best way of achieving this is to crack open one of the cans, place the open end as close to your chops as possible, then rotate both can, and your head, in a kind of backwards fashion, whilst at the same time swallowing vigorously. This takes a little bit of getting used to but it usually works.

Repeat this exercise every five minutes or so, flinging the empty cans into the recycling bin, which, with forethought, you'll already have placed close to where you're sitting. After approximately 20 minutes or a half-hour or so, you'll start to notice the slug beer take effect, as summarised below:

118

T + x* Result

20   You don't really mind slugs and snails all that much – they're
      alright – no, really.

30   They have a tough life, the poor darlings, anyway, who'd
      begrudge them a little bit of cabbage?

60   They've got *rights*. Just like us. Believe me. At the end of the
      day, I know what I'm talking about. It's typical sheer bloody
      human arrogance when we say we're better than them.

>60 Snells… Slush… warraboutem?

*Time from commencement of exercise in minutes (approx.)

Carry on for long enough, and apart from actually making
yourself ill, you might even catch a glimpse of that ley-line you've
always suspected was there, that potent line of earth-mother energy sparking away beneath the plot, the one with the herd of pink
elephants skating down it…

This, in my view, is how slug beer works best. Although you
can of course always go the more traditional route, by putting
down some shallow bowls or dishes between your plants, and
pouring the beer into them. In this way you can top hundreds of
woodlice, beetles and other innocent insects, maybe even the odd
slug or two. Sad to say, this really has been my experience with
slug beer. Yes, it will take out a proportion of your target gastropods, but with far too much "collateral damage", too many
victims of "friendly fire". Because slugs and snails are by no
means the only creatures on the plot with the tendency for one-
stop alcoholic suicide, and in this sense at least, slug beer isn't all
that much better than poison pellets.

"Barrier methods" might be worth trying. Broken-up eggshell.
Ground-up charcoal. Coffee grounds. Whatever. Sprinkled liber-
ally at the base of each of your vulnerable plants. None of them

that I've tried ever did any good, because most gastros are able to pick their way across, with no more difficulty than you or I might find in walking across a ploughed field rather than along a decent path. That's to say, we might be slowed down a bit, but if we've got any determination whatsoever, the rougher surface won't stop us getting where we want to go.

The only barrier that does seem to work, though not invariably, is a ring cut from a plastic bottle, placed around each seedling plant, with the lower end pressed firmly into the soil, and the top end smeared around with a generous gobbet of that famously effective cure for a blocked nose, Vicks VapoRub.

The medicinal cocktail reek of menthol, camphor and eucalyptus does seem to have a deterrent effect, although do bear in mind that repeat trips to the same pharmacy for pots and pots more VapoRub can lead to embarrassingly probing questions from the scrupulous pharmacist, and you might end up with some explaining to do: "More Vicks? Yes, but... Hahahahaha! It's not for me, you understand, it's for my slugs... Teeheehee!" Try toughing your way out of that one without a red nose!

Other organically acceptable methods for dealing with the gastropodal menace are many and varied. These range from upside-down oranges, with or without – which seems to me a fantastically unreal idea – mushed-up Weetabix shovelled underneath, or other such versions of the "humane trap". All the way up to the most technical and least humane, which is probably nematode worms, horribly expensive and besides, of doubtful efficacy outside of the controlled environment of the laboratory.

Digging a pond is always a good idea. In fact, pond construction was one of the first things I did on Plot 3 (thanks to that Theresa again). It's a good idea for all sorts of fascinating reasons. Just as long as you realise than none of them have anything to do with keeping down the gastro population on your plot. Don't for a moment kid yourself that simple possession of a pond will mean disciplined frog-squads jumping out of it at night to scarf up every slug within half a mile. Or even half a yard. This is a fantasy, one worthy of the Brothers Grimm, or whoever else writes fairytales, since it occupies that same outer realm of probability in which kissing frogs instantly produces heirs to the throne.

Then, of course, given their supposed dietary preferences, there's always the old three-legged hedgehog caper. This is sometimes said to work, although it isn't exactly a sure-fire thing, as shown by the following attempt made by a friend's father, Todd James, a retired musician.

Several years back, when he finally hung up his trumpet, Todd moved to Bridport, Devon, to an ancient townhouse with a walled garden. He's long been an enthusiastic gardener and was an early convert to doing things organically. He happened to notice one year that his garden was sustaining more gastro damage than usual, so he acquired a peg-legged hedgehog from a local animal rescue centre, where the poor creature was making a good recovery from the amputation of one of its front feet. By assuring the rescuers that he'd provide a good and secure home within his walls, by making a small donation, and by taking on board a great deal of useful advice about the care of pedally impeded tiddy-hoggies, Todd thought he'd obtained the ideal living (and organic!) slug hoover. After all, it wasn't going to go far on only three feet. Also, he hoped, it would soon realise which side its bread was buttered – as it were – and would settle down without qualm into its safe new abode.

So he took the hedgehog home and let it go up the back of the garden. Every evening, following the instructions he'd been given by the centre, Todd put out a small dish of cat food, to supplement its hoped-for diet of slugs and snails, and whilst he never actually saw the hedgehog again, at least he knew it was still there because each morning the cat food dish was empty.

Over the next few weeks, judging by the unabated level of damage to his hostas and other favourite flowers, it seemed that the hedgehog's effect on the gastro population in Todd's garden was – effectively – nil. Then, rising far earlier than usual one day, he looked out of the window to see the previous evening's dole of cat food being snaffled up by a small and chubby cat – a creature which he recognised at once, as being notionally attached to the household of his next door neighbour.

It seemed that the hedgehog had done a runner – or more likely a "limper" – probably, so Todd concluded, that very same night after he'd brought it back from the rescue centre. Hedgehogs, like most wild animals, being far tougher than we might think and obviously – in the case of hedgehogs in particular – possessed of an irascible and bloody-minded temperament. You just can't keep them, it seems, where they don't want to be. Anyway, apparently it was gone, though leaving behind it just enough doubt in Todd's mind, that he continued to put out the cat food every evening.

Which is how, after a while, he found himself the unwitting companion of the small chubby cat, which decided to move in permanently from next door. The neighbours didn't mind – they had pussies galore. Nor, quite clearly, did the cat itself. But, as might be expected, it showed no more interest in chewing on slugs than would any other well-adjusted member of its kind. In spite of this, or maybe because of it, the cat was eventually awarded a new name: Mrs Tiggy Winkle.

This goes to show, I suppose, that our great British tradition of irony – often said to be on its last legs – is alive and kicking in Bridport.

Despite being a complete flop, this hedgehog experiment does in fact provide a pointer as to the best method, without breaking the rules of the organic game, for dealing with our slithering foes. Forget hedgehogs, full complement of limbs or not, and likewise forget any other such non-reliable animal with a will of its own. To properly deal with snails and slugs the only truly reliable predator is *yourself*.

Putting this realisation into practice may not suit everyone, because for a start you obviously have to go nocturnal. It is, however, the only effective method that I've managed to discover. Each spring, armed with the weaponry of the chase – which consists of a powerful strap-on-the-head torch, a pair of rubber gloves and an empty plastic milk bottle – I make my way up to the happy hunting grounds of Plot Number 3. Lucky for me, since the service has been upgraded, there are plenty of night buses around these parts. And it's not unknown that I might swallow some "slug beer" before setting off, what with the street lighting in Fitzroy Park itself being non-existent; it's pitch black along there and a bit scary, even with the torch strapped on, thus furnishing me with a ready excuse to imbibe some Dutch courage.

Equipped with my various and vicious armaments, I go over the entire plot with what is often referred to these days as *a fine toothcomb*. By which is meant – amongst those of us who've been known to clean our teeth with a small brush once in a while but have never yet combed them – *a fine-toothed comb*.

Any and all gastros revealed in the light of my headlamp get picked up and rudely stuffed into the plastic milk bottle. This is where you need the gloves, because the slimy coat of some slug types will stick to your fingers as well as any superglue. While the bottle fills up, no doubt its prisoners suffer some intensely uncomfortable moments of overcrowding – thus far, at least, I am pitiless. But their suffering is soon over. I keep the hunt as brief as I can and then head back down the lane to the bus stop at the foot of the hill. Halfway down, there's a certain clump of bushes which I shove the bottle well under, out of sight, having of course first taken off the top. Thus its sweating captives can crawl to freedom in a relative degree of safety. Also, this means I can't be accused of littering. In fact its often a case of simultaneously picking up the last bottle from my previous visit, which is always, unsurprisingly, empty.

How often to repeat these night-time manoeuvres is a matter of chance. Slug and snail numbers seem to fluctuate wildly, year-by-year, but I'll generally carry out this exercise once or twice a week, from the start of April, until there's fewer than about a dozen captives to be found on the entire plot. Then in the summer I'll repeat the exercise for the benefit of new arrivals, although in a sporadic fashion, usually when we're out late on the plots during the barbecue season, i.e. no special trip needed.

I'll admit, the very concept of the gastropod hunt, as described, may seem to many people to require an effort way out of proportion to its intended results – even, perhaps, to be tinged with fanaticism – but the crucial thing is that it *works*. And if I'm ever tempting into backsliding, on some dark, wet spring evening, the memory of the lettuce-row massacre of long ago still remains sharp enough to carry me through with the job.

And I'll further admit that, yes, my one concession to not being organic is that I do sometimes still use slug pellets, in either of two specific circumstances:

(a) in spring, under the cold frame. That is, if some stray slug starts to chomp its way through my seedlings, and if I can't find and remove it by searching between the pots. Five or six strategically-placed pellets will off it. In this situation, no bigger creature can get under the glass and poison itself by eating the corpse.

(b) as a second line of defence, within the "Vicked-up" plastic rings already described. If any seedling planted out within one of the rings shows serious signs of damage, or is destroyed, and again, if I can't find the culprit after a thorough search, three or four pellets placed within the ring will usually sort the problem out. In this case, I'll cover the whole area with a bit of netting so that, as under the frame, nothing can get to the poisoned corpse.

The point here is that I'm on the hunt for recalcitrant individuals, not pursuing gastro apocalypse.

There are certain other circumstances in which pellets would be useful, but where the kind of precautions outlined above can't be practically put into effect. Such was the case this last year, when for the first time ever I tried to grow trench celery, i.e. the non-self-blanching kind. This did well to begin with, but once the trench was filled and the stems were covered around with earth, the tops began to show signs of leaf damage. I suspected the worst, and indeed on digging the celery up found that the heart of every single plant had been chewed to bits by an infestation of those little wedge-tailed slug bastards known as "keelbacks". But this wasn't a safe pellet situation, so the whole lot ended up on the compost heap, not a stick of it fit for human consumption, and for the moment my only answer to this particular problem is that I won't be growing any more trench celery in the future.

Similarly, I tend to avoid growing too much of anything that isn't open-leaved, since plants with closed heads, like many types of lettuce or cabbage, can suffer horribly once the slugs have chewed their way inside, into a cushy and impregnable berth.

Well, enough gastros. In a way, I'm sorry to go on about them for so long. These things get compulsive at times, as I guess you'll appreciate. The whole pellet issue is a fraught one, and in my defence I can do little more than repeat what I mentioned earlier about judging each matter on its merits. Personally speaking, I'm not a purist. If you decide in favour of blue murder, to your entirely organic neighbours on the plots you'll always be damned when you do. They'll scream it at you. But in terms of *results*, my trench celery being just one example, you'll frequently be damned when you don't. And there's no reconciling the two, not that I know of.* So the choice, as they say, is entirely yours. Whichever way you go, keep those rubber gloves on. And your life jacket.

All of the above comprises only one part of the organic story. Where pests and diseases are concerned, the general moral, so far as there can ever be one, is that prevention is always better than cure. The next three chapters touch on what, to me, is an issue both more fundamental and more fascinating – soil fertility.

---

*Another stop press here. As I write this, in the summer of 2005, a new type of slug pellet has just come onto the market, made of ferric phosphate, i.e. iron and phosphorus. These pellets are said to be completely environmentally friendly in that they aren't poisonous to anything except slugs and snails. Let's hope they work, even if it means that most of what I've written about gastropods will become rapidly out-of-date.

CHAPTER SIX

Compost Canards

First, let's sort out a problem of nomenclature:

Grasshopper: "Master, what is 'brock'? Is it a firework? Is it a badger?"

Master (the one with the scraggy white beard and ping-pong ball eyes): "It is neither, Grasshopper. Brock is the name which we give to any material that the ancient sages judged once – and for all future time – as suitable to put on to the compost heap."

When I first sat down to write a chapter about compost, sitting at home one frosty winter's evening with broken central heating, and nothing for company but an overlarge bottle of parsnip wine, I must confess to feeling almost crushed by the enormity of the task ahead. So much has already been written and continues to be written on the compost theme, which after all is a key part of organic growing, that in terms of the total expenditure of energy over the course of, say, a single year, you can easily imagine that there are more human calories burned up in writing about it than are expended in actually making the stuff. Or indeed, more than there are decaying vegetable calories, released to the atmosphere over that same time period, from the numberless warm and effulgent heaps scattered in gardens and allotments across the nation.

Compost is food for the soil, which, when dug back into it, and fully decayed, becomes food for your plants. Decay is vital to any natural system, whether a simple garden or something as complex as a giant rainforest. In all cases, plant nutrients are recycled over and over, through life and death, through all life forms, over the ages. Thus, to give just one example, your bones will inevitably contain calcium that once formed the bones of dinosaurs.

Strictly in horticultural terms, compost making is about giving nature a boost, by the *concentration* and *acceleration* of its normal recycling processes.

There's no definitive brock list for the garden or allotment compost heap, since individual tastes will always play a part. My own practice is to use whatever organic material I can get hold of, with a few commonsensical exceptions. This means:

(a) avoiding anything that will cause an unpleasant stink, especially animal or fish remains;

(b) steering away from man-made products, even where the materials are entirely natural, i.e. wool, cotton, leather. There are too many chemical "unknowns" in dyes, inks, tanning treatments, fire- and moth-proofing, etc.

Not everyone, of course, would agree with these exceptions. More detail on various of them can be found throughout this chapter.

We've no long tradition of compost-making in the UK, having been at it for about a century. Contrast this with the Chinese, who've been turning out the fertile gunk for four thousand years and more. Thus, along with such other rudiments of civilisation as writing, printing, gunpowder, the wheelbarrow, and the volume manufacture of training shoes, we have China to thank for both inventing, and perfecting, the compost-maker's art. Meanwhile, in this country, in the years BC – Before Compost – we made do with the artless muck-heap or midden, a seriously unstructured pile of waste matter onto which all manner of stuff was cast, willy-nilly, as noted in a previous chapter. We also had more bizarre and revolting methods of maintaining soil fertility, one or two of which are touched upon below.

Despite being relative compost novices, it's remarkable the enthusiasm with which many modern British gardeners have embraced the compost heap. People love the stuff, and the most singular aspect of this, so it strikes me, is the leading role that local government has recently adopted in encouraging such affection. Local councils, at least in urban areas, seem ready to fall over one another in their desire to encourage their citizens to turn their kitchen peelings and garden trimmings into food for the soil. Untold light-hearted pamphlets of the "how-to-do-it" sort have lately been turned out by enthusiastic local bureaucracies, which have also spent a fortune providing subsidised or even free compost bins, for those of their residents who need them. These are usually of the plastic "armless Dalek" variety, which do at least have the virtue of neatness in the garden. I have to admit, though, that the cynical hemisphere of my brain can't help but think that – even a single generation ago – all of this government involvement would have been regarded as a scandalous waste of ratepayers' money. Or Poll Tax. Or whatever else it was we were paying way back then.

For our present purposes, this same cynical hemisphere of the mind informs me that there's also bound to be an element of futility in any written attempt of how to make compost, since if, on the one mucky hand you're an experienced gardener, you'll have already worked out your own best practice, according to the amount of time and the quantity and/or type of brock you have available – so for all practical purposes there's not much, if anything at all, to be learnt. Whilst on the other hand (the clean one), if you happen to be a newcomer to the task, the range of putative advice is so vast that you can easily find yourself in the same position as that of the five blind persons who met an elephant. Here's G. K. Chesterton's version of this wise oriental fable:

> One of them seized its trunk, and asserted that an elephant was a kind of serpent; another embraced its leg, and was ready to die for the belief that an elephant was a kind of tree. In the same way to the man who leaned against its side it was a wall; to the man who had hold of its tail a rope; and to the man who ran upon its tusk a particularly unpleasant kind of spear.

You can't help but wonder what the elephant thought, subject to all this impolite groping, but whatever it thought, it was, of course – despite being all things to all gropers – always an elephant. Just as a compost heap is always… well, *what actually is it*?

In order to answer this question, it seems to me that we need first to know what compost *actually isn't*. After all, there are very many methods of enhancing soil fertility, most of which nowadays, as everybody knows, are chemical. But how about the pre-chemical era? To what extremes would old-time gardeners go – lacking a handy chemical fix – to ensure the continuing fertility of their soil? This takes us in one brief hop from live elephant to dead horse, with the following zany tale, which has been passed down through my family for several generations.

One of my great-great-(not-sure-how-many-greats)-grandfathers was employed as a gardener at Hampton Court Palace, and amongst his duties was caring for the famous Hampton Court vine, that most tremendous of plants, flourishing since 1768 and still producing 300-odd kilogrammes of grapes each year.

Manuring this beautiful monster was a task as elaborate as it was arduous. On the appointed day, my great^{n}-grandaddy and his doughty comrades would assemble with mattocks, shovels and any other necessary gear and – starting some distance away from the giant vine to minimise disturbance – commence digging a tunnel just beneath its roots. This took several weeks, but when the tunnel was finished, a fresh dead horse would be fetched from the local knacker's yard, dragged underground and manoeuvred into place. The excavation would then be laboriously backfilled, to reduce the likelihood of subsidence. Thus ensuring the vine's continuing fecundity for many years to come.

A likely story! Needless to say, when I checked its veracity with the present Vine Keeper at Hampton Court, the word came back that she had "no knowledge of anything like this having taken place". Just as well. Probably.

The least you can say, I suppose, is that my ancestor and his pals would surely have been better off keeping their poor nag alive, on some peaceful and forgotten corner of Hampton Court's extensive pastures, and applying its excrement to the vine as a surface mulch, instead of its dead body, dragged under it. But, who really knows? What do we know, today, about the motives of those sage ones who first decided the Apocrypha? And there may well be some mysterious fruitful connection between grapes and corpses, or at least grapes and hide, as Ford Maddox Ford once pointed out, having nourished a vine, with great success, using several drawers full of old leather gloves abandoned at his house by the family of the artist Walter Crane.

Certainly, those pre-chemical growers weren't always averse to what we might now call Extreme Composting. A second robust manuring method, one far better attested to than the Dead Horse Story, was rotten fish, known to have been popular amongst eighteenth- and nineteenth-century soil fertility fanatics, and explored recently both in books and on the television. Here's Jim Crace, from his brilliant historical novel *Signals of Distress*, first published in 1994. His hero, Aymer Smith, is wandering at dusk in the fields behind Wherrytown, not long after the town's annual pilchard hunt:

> He focused on the smell, before he focused on the ground. He knew it well. The field was full of fish. The sea was taking everyone away, and putting fish on land. There were no leaves or lakes or broaches, just one star-gazy pie with a four-acre crust of earth and a shoal of pilchards staring at the moon, their eyes as dead as flint, their scales like beaten tin, their frayed fins and tails like frost, their flesh composting for the next year's crop. The field was absolutely still. The fastest movements were the snails and slugs which were enamelling the fleshy silverwork with their saliva trails.

Manuring with fish... familiar practice, I've no doubt, for the pre-modern farmer living near to the coast, with occasional access to a big surplus catch. No big deal at all. But at the hands of a post-modern author, like Jim Crace, positively transformed into something surreal, frightening and – dare I say it? – wonderful! You'll have to read the whole book to get my drift.

Whether foul fish, or former foal, there's no doubt that our ancestors were wise to the mysteries of nutrient cycling, knowing that, with the soil, death and decay provides the best guarantee of future life, and hence of prosperity. In these more squeamish times, none of us are as keen on burying corpses in the garden. At least, not solely for the purposes of soil nourishment. But we *are* more keen than ever, as we've seen, on composting with vegetable remains. The principles are of course basically the same, whatever dead matter is used, as we'll see below.

We'll get to the principles in good time, but having started on what compost *isn't*, for now it would be useful to carry on in the same vein. Because as we've seen, just as there's more than one way to grope an elephant, there's obviously more than one way to make compost. Indeed, there are thousands of ways to do so, and few, if any, common gardening subjects have been so warped by passion and dimmed by mythology as this. The compost heap attracts more myths than it does fruit flies in summer, and I feel duty bound to explode some of the worst (myths, that is, rather than flies). So here's a muckraking exposé of "Compost Canards", presented below in all their hideous falsity, although in no particular order of demerit.

Don't put old carrots on the compost heap, they'll only attract rats

Why do so many people hate rats? It's a puzzle, since apparently we can't even catch the Black Death off them nowadays, because the plague or black rat (*Rattus rattus*), has been completely kicked out of these islands by the Hanoverian or brown rat (*R. norvegicus*). So thorough has been this takeover that reports of a Black Rat recently found under somebody's fridge in Cornwall should, I feel, be treated with the utmost scepticism. It was probably an escaped pet rather than a true wild animal, and just as one swallow maketh not a summer, surely one tame black rat maketh not a plague.

As for the brown rat, the popular legend has it that it first came to these shores stowed away aboard the ships of William of Orange's fleet in 1688, back in the days of The Glorious Revolution. For this reason the brown rat is still sometimes called the protestant rat, though enough said on that score, sectarianism of any sort being bad enough, without attempting to recruit elements of the animal kingdom to prop up either side. The real point being that this brown job, which is nowadays a widespread beast, if not ubiquitous, apparently has the wrong kind of fleas for transmitting the plague to human beings. Apparently.

So, given that we don't have to worry about bubonic plague any more, here's a plea for tolerance…

A family of rats has lived under my shed for several years. I very occasionally see one of them scuttling about, but like all good neighbours – those, I should say, who share almost nothing in common apart from proximity – we each behave as if the other doesn't exist. Ignorance is bliss in such cases, being my experience. So the rats do what they do. I do what I do. And quite unlike my human neighbours in my block of flats back down the hill, they've never given me any particular grief: e.g., they don't stay awake until past four in the morning, sexually arousing themselves by playing *ABBA's Greatest Hits* at full blast. Time after yelping *Waterloo* time. Neither do they curse me in the High Street when I refuse to give them money. Or drink or do drugs. And, as far as I know, they don't bray the bairns.

Do they scour the brock dumped on my compost heap for decaying carrots? Being omnivorous, they could well do, but I've really no idea. Though I imagine they'd prefer something with a bit more protein in it, like a dead horse, in the remote event that I should ever find one on a skip, and bother to drag it up the hill. Failing that, I guess I'd say, that if they can find some goodness in the stuff that I can't eat, peelings and the like, well, good luck to them. After all, as we've seen in a previous chapter, our own species started out as generalised scavengers, and in a curious way I'd like to think that some local creature is carrying on these old traditions which, by and large, we ourselves have forgotten. Yes, even if it is only rats.

Like any opinion, this isn't an impartial view, and if you're still concerned, here's a tip: if you want to avoid the possibility of creating a rat's nest when putting up your shed, either set it on a proper concrete base, or else raise it high enough on old bricks or paving slabs that a cat could walk under it without difficulty. If you do this, your prospective neighbourhood rats either can't nest under it, or won't – you'll avoid the whole issue to begin with – and then you can stick your wizened old carrots wherever you like…

You shouldn't put too much citrus fruit peel on the heap
The regularity with which this particular canard crops up, whether in conversation, or in the media, is a mystery that I've pondered for many a long hour. Which might otherwise have been wasted. Although I have to own up that I've never been able to unravel it. I wonder how many of you old allotment hands will have experienced some version of the following scenario? There you are, chilling with your brethren on the plots, indulging in some harmless and convivial compost chatter whilst waiting for the kettle to boil. When suddenly, one of the assemblage will inevitably blurt out, "Of course, you shouldn't put too much citrus fruit peel on the heap." Everyone nods in agreement, such being the ordinary mechanics of such convivial communication, and not one voice is ever raised in dissent.

Why, oh why?

My guess is that the citrus peel canard dates back to the 1920s and that its author was Nick Carraway, narrator of *The Great Gatsby*, F. Scott Fitzgerald's paean to that notoriously "roaring" decade. This is a novel of such howling snobbery that nowadays it's almost unbearable to read. Maybe it always was. But I'd have to say that it still contains a valuable lesson for our own times, insofar as it explains the origin of the citrus/compost canard.

As the story opens, the twenties are emphatically roaring, and the West Egg cocktail scene is at full summer blast. At the core of this social cyclone, the impossibly romantic James Gatsby, formerly Jay Gatz, is indulging in some especially conspicuous consumption, with party poured upon party, spilling out of his mansion into its extensive grounds, a drunken orgy of truly tedious length. From which, of course – in keeping with timeless moral principles – no participant ultimately derives any good. Here's Nick Carraway on just one detail of this seemingly endless overindulgence, namely citrus fruit:

> Every Friday five crates of oranges and lemons arrived from a fruiterer in New York – every Monday these same oranges and lemons left his back door in a pyramid of pulpless halves. There was a machine in the kitchen which could extract the juice of two hundred oranges in half an hour if a little button was pressed two hundred times by a butler's thumb.

Serious boozing, of the Gatsby sort, has a distinct social history. I'm thinking here of something related to me by my old Hampstead landlady, a person extremely well-connected in the realms of law and politics. In the late-eighties and the nineties, the period when I knew her, Lady B. was a wise old stick: and she'd lived long enough to witness both the beginning and end of the Binge Age, an era which, weirdly enough, matches in its duration almost exactly the period that historians are now calling "the short twentieth century":

> People started drinking cocktails, my dear, quite soon after the First War. Before then, nobody would have dreamt of brandy or gin or other spirits before dinner, since these would ruin the taste of the food. Although they would often have a small glass of champagne

or sherry before going in to table. But in the early twenties, as I remember, cocktails and large measures of spirits were quite suddenly all the rage. This remained the case until recently. Then just a few years ago, as you know, everyone started drinking fizzy mineral water – Perrier and so on. This fashion started somewhere in America, though it soon came over here, and now the virtues of a decent bottle of whisky appear to have been quite forgotten...

I'm often reminded of her words, particularly in the light of modern claptrap about the government's need to clamp down on a perceived overuse of strong drink. As if the mere fact that a nation's political elite decides it no longer wants to get regularly pissed, or at least pretends as much, entitles it to stop the rest of the citizenry from doing so.

And where, you'll no doubt be asking by now, does this leave our citrus peel? It's quite simple, because unless you're so badly old-fashioned that you still throw parties with the same frequency and on the same lavish scale as the fabulous Mr Gatz, I'm quite sure you can fling as much citrus peel on to your compost heap as you like. A decent bottle of whisky goes to the first reader who can write and tell me why this isn't the case.

You can recycle household dust by dumping the contents of your hoover on to the heap

"Hoover" is used here in its colloquial sense, meaning any vacuum cleaner.

The household dust canard is a singular example of what Professor Oliver Rackham, renowned father of landscape history, would call a *factoid*: "A factoid looks like a fact, is respected as a fact, and has all the properties of a fact except that it is not true."

Indeed, this particular canard reveals an essential factoid attribute, which is repetition. It's been recycled down the decades, time and again, from one too-hastily-written gardening book to another. This is a sizeable literary genre, the worst specimens of which genuinely strain the reader's credulity with the fat freight of vicarious information that they feel obliged to impart. In such unhelpful tomes, household dust usually sneaks in towards the end of one of those breathless, thoughtless "look-at-all-the-amazing-things-you-can-compost!" type of lists. If you do ever happen to encounter such a list in any gardening book, my advice is that you by no means alter your domestic cleaning regime. Keep slinging out the hoover contents along with the rest of your (unrecycleable) rubbish, as per usual, and – taking a chance on its inky chemicals – *compost the book*.

The reason I say this has to do with what kind of matter actually makes it into the hoover. And in exploring this intriguing line of enquiry, the first thing to mention is that I'm not going to enter into that old debate about 90% of domestic dust consisting of what's known in North America as "dander", i.e. exfoliated skin cells. Because, unless you're unlucky enough to inhabit a household in which one-and-all, including the cat and the goldfish, suffer from rampant psoriasis, this is yet another classic factoid. In the normal household, most dust comes from cloth and its derivatives – whether furnishing fabrics, curtains, clothing or bedding – or from carpets.

In those long-past times when all such necessaries were made out of natural stuff, mostly wool or cotton, the household dust canard may not in fact have qualified as such, since these materials are readily biodegradable. They also contain a significant proportion of nitrogen, one of the major plant nutrients and also essential to feed the bacteria that keep a decent compost heap ticking over. What's happened of course is that as technology has changed, so domestic furnishing materials have changed, closely followed by the constituent parts of household dust. But the original idea hasn't kept pace and, by such weird historical processes, are canards born. Take carpets, for instance…

Since it takes a considerable flock of naked sheep to make a few square metres of traditional Axminster, quality all-wool carpets were ever a luxury, monopolised throughout most of their history by the wealthy, whilst the rest of society made do with rushes or rag-rugs at best, or else rolled about uncomfortably on the bare floorboards or on the lino. As the old music hall joke goes: "Oh yes, my family are all dead posh. And right talented. Most evenings, mother performs for us on the linoleum…" Ah, the Good Old Days.

Nowadays, we're grateful to live in a "carpets-for-all" society, but most of these cosy floor coverings are made of artificial fibres, polypropylene, polyester and/or polyamide (formerly "nylon"). Maybe with a small proportion of high-status wool woven in, to big up the price.

Nothing wrong with that, I might say; quite the reverse. Who wants to roll around on bare boards or the *linoleum*, as their ancestors had to? Except when it comes to compost making, because all of those tiny fragments of polywhatever that get sucked up by the hoover are, in biological terms, practically inert. So it's like loading up the compost heap with bits of foam rubber or shreds of bubble wrap. At best, pointless.

But it gets worse. Especially, that is, if you give credit to the latest scientific investigations into pollutants in the modern home, an area scarcely yet researched, but the initial findings of which frequently show that household dust contains not simply a great deal that's *inert*, but some components that are positively *harmful*, such as:

- lead and other metals
- asbestos
- pesticide residues
- PCBs – polychlorinated biphenyls
- PAHs – polycyclic aromatic hydrocarbons
- PBDEs – ("sons of PCBs") – polybrominated diphenyl ethers

The presence of such matter being a logical consequence of our use, in domestic life, of a huge range of non-natural materials, most of which have never been properly tested for any harm they may do to human health. These are mainly found in plastics but also in dyes, in cleaning products, and in fire-retardant chemicals.

PBDEs are a good example of this last use, since they're widely employed to prevent upholstery from erupting into flames, and if constantly ingested through inhaling the dust of crumbling cushions and disembowelled sofas, etc., will accumulate in the body. Overdose levels can cause tumours and affect brain development in the young.

Not that you're ever likely, at home, to swallow a great deal of such stuff. But, as with a lot of these things, the point is that nobody can agree on what constitutes a "safe", low-level dosage. Also, there may be "cocktail" effects, where absorbing a number of chemicals in minute amounts is ultimately more damaging than absorbing a much larger dose of just one of them. A bit like drinking "snakebites", that potent combination of lager, cider and blackcurrant cordial. Those of you depraved enough ever to have drunk the stuff will know exactly what I mean.

All this sounds quite horrible, of course, though to be fair, it's worth saying there's no immediate need to panic. For example – and you can try this at home quite safely (as long as no-one sees you) – if you were to drop down on to your hands and knees and lick your carpet for a few minutes, or else spend an idle quarter-hour sniffing your sofa, you're not going to drop dead straight afterwards, as if you'd swallowed a cyanide pill.

But it's precisely these kinds of concerns, about our constant exposure to what are admittedly low levels of toxicity in the environment, that are leading more and more people to consider less poisoned ways of living. And these days, it's not only "health fanatics", whatever that quaint term might really mean, who are interested. I'm not myself an exemplar of healthy living, but like many people I do think that I have rights to name my own poisons, and not to be done damage to by ones that I scarcely know exist. Which means that amongst my other activities I grow as large a proportion as possible of my own food, using the simplest and healthiest methods available. So it becomes a considerable and totally unwanted irony if gardeners and plotholders like myself, in pursuit of such objectives, inadvertently end up turning their compost into a miniature toxic waste heap.

Unfortunate as it may seem, the twenty-first-century message has got to be: Get Your Factoids Straight... Dump the Dust... Don't recycle it.

Composting gets rid of weed seeds because the heap reaches such a high temperature that they're destroyed

This canard travels in distinguished company. A few words here from two of our best gardening writers of the past half century (but with my italics, *as they say*). Ben Easey's ground-breaking work, *Practical Organic Gardening*, was first published in 1955. Despite the title, this book really isn't about gardening at all, being devoted almost exclusively to how to make compost – almost 150 closely printed pages on the subject – such being the measure of the author's dedication to the said art and mystery. Ben Easey remarks that composting works as follows, by:

> ...speeding up the process of decomposition, by natural means, partly at high temperatures which reap incidental dividends in *weed seeds... cooked like grains of rice...*

And here's Lawrence D. Hills, legendary founder of the Henry Doubleday Research Association (HDRA), the leading organic gardening body, who noted a similar effect in his classic *Grow Your own Fruit and Vegetables*, from 1971:

> Composting garden and kitchen wastes is more than a matter of re-christening the rubbish heap, for a good compost heap is a bacterial bonfire, cooking weed seeds like grains of rice.

Oh dear... Shades of Household Dust...

On a cursory reading of these two quotations we might reasonably assume that both of their authors were demi-gods of the compost-making world. Well... either that or else one of them was, whilst the other one was being a bit naughty. Whichever is the more accurate, I'd make so bold as to say that they're both entirely wrong. Because I've never managed to make a single batch of compost, in over a decade of trying, that didn't sprout up copiously with weeds as soon as it was spread on to the soil.

So, neither author's view matches my own experience, which is that no composting method ever reaches rice-cooking temperatures throughout. Not even Easey's ultimate pile, the carefully layered "Modified Indore Heap". The precise construction details of which have, for the moment, curiously fled from my memory. The truth is that even if your heap heats up nicely in the middle, it won't do so around the edges.

Not that I'm bothered, personally – I enjoy weeding – but if you hate it, the answer is embarrassingly simple. Don't sling *any* weedy plant material on to the heap that's had time to set its seed.

Successful compost-making requires a compost bin

Zim bam boddle-oo… hoodle ah da waah da… as Gershwin wrote… *It ain't necessarily so…* Here are two very different approaches towards composting, presenting between them a total contrast both in method and, I daresay, in underlying attitude – whether to composting in particular, gardening in general or indeed, to life itself. The only remotely common factor linking the two is geography, as both are Fitzroy Park stories. First off:

The most efficient composting regime that I know of is that employed on the plots by Sally and Mike Gallagher. It doesn't require a receptacle of any sort, and comprises a fine example of the kind of best practice, adapted to local conditions, mentioned in the opening remarks to this chapter.

Mike and Sally's allotment is divided into eight rectangles, of equal size, with seven growing beds separated by narrow grass paths, plus, at the top end, one patch of lawn for flopping out on during the warmer months. This simple and unfussed layout, so I assume, facilitates Sally's use of an arcane crop rotation system learnt from her father when she was a youngster – a "maid", as they still say over there – growing up in the West Country.

Where weeds are concerned, Mike and Sally take the long view, one in which neatness, for its own sake, has no relevance. So that over the course of a season only the most rampant encroachments into their crops are weeded out, with the guilty weeds left to wilt on the surface of the ground where they are pulled. The rest get removed in late autumn, which is also the time for Sal and Mike's main composting effort, when all crop remains and other unwanted plants are scoured from the soil and raked downslope across the beds to the comfrey patch at the bottom. At which point the comfrey gets cut back, and rolled in with the rest of the brock, along with a fair quantity of manure, the whole forming a single long heap across the foot of the plot. (For more on comfrey, see the Comfrey Dumpty chapter.)

And that's it, until the next spring, when the compost gets rolled back up the beds and is lightly forked-in. In gardening terms, the cause of maximum return for minimum effort was never better served.

Curiously enough, Sally recently told me that back in the early 1980s during the course of a long holiday in Majorca, she had the job of whitewashing the Casa Luna.

Although she never got to meet the owner, as he was away at the time, I still can't quite explain why I should be so strangely unnerved at hearing this fact. Perhaps its enough to say that if Sally's whitewash was applied with the same efficiency that she brings to the art of compost making – well, by Crikey! – Robert Graves must have been very pleased indeed with the result.

Anyway, freakish digressions aside, time to consider the other end of the scale, bin-wise, and much-else-besides-wise, with the second of our Fitzroy composting examples, courtesy of Ricky and Jodie X. These aren't their real names, I hasten to add, just that they're amongst the few people I've spoken to up at the plots who asked not to be named in this book. Not that Jodie or Ricky are what you'd call shy, more what you'd call self-contained.

Much, in fact, like the top-quality compost bin that they built on their plot three or four years back. Ricky writes computer software – the kind of job that demands a mastery of detail as well as exemplary planning skills. Plus, he certainly knows, during moments of quality time, which end to hold a hammer. A winning combination on any allotment, as evinced by the tidy series of complex raised beds into which their plot is divided – artfully constructed from all-new timber and separated by bark-chip paths – as well as by the famous mega-bin itself, the most handsome that I've ever seen, or ever expect to see.

It was a stoutly built perfect cube, four feet each way, carvel-built out of planed and treated boards, screwed with countersunk heads to three-inch upright posts, each of which was set on a tile, to keep the damp from rising up through the wood. The front panel was demountable for purposes of ingress, and a hinged roof it had, of three-quarter ply, covered in roofing felt to resist the weather, and keep out the rain withal. It was also designed to keep out rats – Ricky and Jodie eschewing such a risk – being entirely covered on the outsides, as well as on its otherwise open base, with bright, narrow-gauge chicken wire mesh, tacked on tight with netting staples. The most magnificent detail was the insulated interior, opulently lined on all sides with three-inch thick polystyrene sheet, which was itself protected, being covered with some dark blue plastic stuff, cut from a tarpaulin. As yer old granny used to say, it looked as well in the dark as it did by daylight, it was that good!

That August night, when the bin caught fire, it went up like an old paint factory. During a firemen's strike. A parched summer, that year… very parched.

"What with all that insulation, all that wood preservative," as Ricky confirmed to me a day or two after the grim event, "the Towering-Bloody-Inferno…"

"The weird thing was," Jodie added, "it seems nobody even saw the flames – despite it being a complete burn-out. No witnesses!"

We were inspecting the scorched remains at the time. What little there was of them. The intensity of the heat had wrought an awful charry change, an ugly pyre of destruction. Leaving only a few pitiful burnt scraps of wood. A blackened and cracked tile at each corner. A central cube of shrunken, sooty compost. Surrounded by a drooping chicken wire frame, too large for itself, patchily pink, grey and black, its galvanised lustre lost for good. As for the rest – gone. All gone.

I was close to tears, with sympathetic shock, feeling the loss of such a treasure, so only God knows how the owners must have felt. "All my fault," said Ricky. "We had the barbecue going late, on Saturday, by the time we left for home it was practically dark, and the last thing I did was dump the ashes in there – I thought they were well out, but they must have been still alight. And we'd only had it a few months."

"Yes, I was up here quite late on Saturday myself," I said. "But I'm afraid to say I didn't see anything."

We stood about for a bit, gazing at the burnt mess, each wrapped in a silence, presumably rueful, with their own thoughts.

But the great thing about Ricky and Jodie is that they simply aren't the kind of people who dwell on things. They're experts in disaster recovery, which is a quality largely derived, I should guess, from the mutual support to be found in one another's company. This is a kind of strength which, as we all know, or should know, can be far greater than the sum of its component parts. And as we stood there, it was Ricky who first gathered his wits.

"Well sod it!" he said to Jodie. "We'll build a better one, won't we?"

"Of course we will," she soon replied, gathering her own. "Besides, we can still use the compost, can't we? Once I've scraped off all those burnt bits on the outside the middle stuff will be fine."

"Might even be better than fine!" he said. "For a start, you can bet there won't be any weed seeds left in it. With all that heat they must have all been cooked…"

"…*like grains of rice*…" I thought.

However, what with discretion being my middle name I made no further comment, except to make polite excuses, and wandered off, leaving them to retrieve their mutual optimism with future plans. And – very like the phoenix – in due course a new bin did rise up on their plot from the ashes of the old, not quite as magnificent as the one which had succumbed to the flames, and lacking, I noticed, the fateful, flammable insulation. Still, a good and workmanlike job done.

Hands up anyone who remembers The Oomygooley Bird? For those of you that do, no gold stars awarded to whoever can guess which out of Sally and Mike, and Ricky and Jodie, are "uppies", and which "downies"…

In reality, of course, there's not so much to choose between their widely divergent composting approaches, since, for practical purposes, the end result is indistinguishable. If I wanted to carp, which I don't, I might say that Ricky and Jodie's method erred a tad towards complete overkill, not to say hubris, whilst Sally and Mike's method takes up too much space. So, where compost bins are concerned, here's my tip, a rational "third way" between our pair of illustrative poles.

Starting in the late autumn or winter, get hold of a dozen or so straight(ish) sticks, about an inch-and-a-half in diameter at the thick end. With a handsaw, cut them all to the same length – about five feet or so – and then tap them about a foot into the ground at regular intervals to form a circle, four feet or thereabouts across. These are your uprights, or "zales", as a hurdle-maker would call them.

Next, gather a large quantity of "weavers" or "binders". Any pliable or whippy stuff will do, such as thin prunings from fruit trees, or any other handy trees, raspberry canes and the like, as long as they're still fairly green, not so dead as to be brittle. Blackberry stems are also quite good, though you'll have to take off the prickles, which is best achieved by wearing thick thorn-proof gloves and pulling the stems through your hands.

Weave any and all of this stuff in and out around your zales,

144

My cost-effective answer to the compost-bin conundrum. Such a rustic device can be knocked up for nothing out of any old bendy twigs you can find.

working around the circle, and after each half dozen or so circuits press the weave down with firm pressure from hands or feet.

If you're short of weavers, you can always wait until someone dumps more prunings or canes on the allotment tip, though if you prefer the deep rustic look, try to get hold of some willow or hazel. Those of the more urban persuasion will easily find some industrial-type bendy stuff in a skip, failing which, two-inch wide strips cut out of abandoned estate agents' boards will do the trick. In fact, these can produce quite an interesting pattern to the weave which many people, including some estate agents, find particularly attractive.

Work round and round until you've reached the top of your zales – if short of weavers, you can always trim off the uprights at the height at which you ran out.

I've made quite a number of compost bins like this, and they've each been stronger than you might think. The weaving, of course, binds the whole thing together, and the greater the tension built into it, the firmer the end result. Weaving a bin is a pleasure on a calm and mild winter's day, with the added benefit that it should cost you nothing in the way of materials. Don't even contemplate spending any money on such an item – if absolutely desperate for a bin, but lacking materials, either find some or else ring up the council for a subsidised "armless Dalek" instead.

The woven bin made out of twigs lasts two to three years. The main disadvantage to it is that it has no front to open, so any removing of compost has to be done from above, which is quite a chore unless you're agile enough to climb on top of or inside it. Or you can always leave it a bit longer and then kick it to bits, as to which, see the final paragraphs of this chapter.

Should this, or for that matter any other type of bin, have a lid on it? Such an addition might be handy to keep heat in, and excess water out. But in my own experience, lid or no lid, I've never noticed whether it makes a difference to the quality of the end product or not.

Compost is made by woodlice

I'm not sure if this counts as a true canard, since I've only heard it once. But it was told to me in all seriousness, and by a person appearing elsewhere in this book in the capacity of an expert, who you'd think would know better.

Disrespecting woodlice is nothing to be proud of, and I don't intend to start doing so here. They are in fact fascinating little animals, belonging to that vast secretive army of humble creatures that inhabit any allotment or garden, and known to the world of ecology as detritivores, i.e. they feed on dead stuff. In so doing they play a big part in nutrient cycling, principally – although not exclusively – in a physical capacity, by chewing up relatively large bits of grunge and excreting it in smaller packages. Detritivores include worms of all sorts, millipedes, springtails and mites, as well as woodlice. Without them, our world would be as diminished as it would be without whales in it. Possibly more so.

But – always a but! – however marvellous woodlice might be, they've only bit parts to play on the compost heap stage. The big players here are bacteria and fungi. These do the essential task of breaking down the proteins in your brock into amino acids and then ammonia, and also breaking down its carbohydrates – into sugars, acids and carbon dioxide – warming up the heap in the process. Reduced to its one key essential, the composting process is about lowering carbon content and increasing the amount of nitrogen in the heap, technically known as the C:N ratio. Reasonable compost will have a ratio of about 20:1, i.e. 20 parts carbon to every one of nitrogen. Really good stuff will have even less carbon. When compost is dug into the soil, it's this extra nitrogen from which your crop plants will gain the most immediate benefit.

In order to work at their best, our composting bacteria and fungi require a nitrogen source to kick the process off, plenty of oxygen, and moderately alkaline conditions. Suddenly, I find the details of Ben Easey's "Modified Indore Heap" returning to the foreground in my brain. The recipe is: an initial thick layer of brock supplies the raw material – most waste organic matter will do, but nothing too twiggy and nothing so wet or prone to compaction that it'll keep the air out – then a thin layer of well-rotted manure supplies the extra nitrogen; then a dusting of lime corrects the heap's tendency towards acidity. Repeat the three layers as necessary: Matter – Activator – Neutraliser. MAN, no less, as I've only just noticed.

Anyway, that's how it works. If you've got masses of woodlice in the heap, all this means is that you've accidentally hit on their ideal ambient humidity, one which is somewhat on the dry side for the essential fungi and bacteria, which make your actual compost.

That's the end of the Compost Canards

I'm well aware that for at least the first two-thirds of this chapter, I've veered wildly away from any practical goings-on at the Fitzroy Park plots, into realms that are more abstract, not to say theoretical. I don't know if it'll make up for it much, but for what it's worth, these final paragraphs mostly set out how I myself make compost.

I gave up trying to be a sophisticated compost-maker several years ago, having decided to keep the whole process as straightforward as possible. Each year in spring I slap together a woven bin of the type already described. I look out for brock throughout the year, though the source varies with the seasons. Firstly, once the soil warms up and grasses and weeds begin to grow in earnest, I scour the plots all over for any useable stuff, mostly by collecting from paths and odd corners or by begging suitable material from other plotholders who've fallen seriously behind with their weeding, or else have too much lawn to keep trimmed. I chop down all this fresh stuff with a sickle, then rake it up into any handy receptacle to carry away to my own plot, to that year's new bin. If there's a lot of grass I let it shrivel for a few days on the ground after cutting, and/or mix it with a few bramble prunings in the heap, to stop it getting too wet and compacted.

This initial gleaning tails off from June when many of these weeds and grasses etc. start to set seed, though there's always a bit of something or other to be had, comfrey or nettles or the like. And, of course, there's always plenty of weed seeds which manage to sneak into the heap unannounced, where they remain, as noted above, *entirely raw*.

As this springtime weed procurement tails off through the summer, so crop residues from the plot start to become available, and this second brock collection phase continues over the next few months, until I put the plot to bed with the following winter. The next phase involves scouring the allotment tip over the dead months – once again, scrounging other people's weeds – even on the allotments there's a deluded minority who aren't too fond of composting and dump bags and bags of weeds on the tip – crazy people. An example of just how mad this is, is explored in the next chapter.

All three brock gatherings go into the same bin, joined the year round by any opportunistic additions, by kitchen peelings, wizened carrots and so on, and (though I rarely have any) any overly fresh manure. And when I remember, a rare dusting of lime, for which I use crushed-up chalk. This is available in lump form, for free, in any abandoned quarry on The Downs when you're out of town rambling for a day. I don't ever urinate on the heap, a disgusting habit. So the many woodlice who live in it tell me. Neither do I turn and/or remix it, though it would probably benefit from this – can't be arsed, basically.

Each bin gets "closed-off" when a new one is built the following winter or spring – after that the "old" heap gets left for the next six to eight months, to rot down further, until the next autumn when I knock it to bits and sling the compost roughly about, mostly as a top dressing. That's all there is to it. I don't put any more time into it than necessary. And don't spend too much time thinking about it. Not very exciting really, and as mentioned at the start of this chapter, many of you – I suspect, a majority – will already have worked out your own methods for achieving much the same result.

The only real problem with compost, so I've found, is that there's never enough of it. Nine-tenths of the brock that I use – at least in terms of bulk (all that spring grass!) – comes from sources outside of my own plot. But in spite of this, I can't ever seem to make enough compost, in any single year, at roughly a barrowful per square yard, to cover more than about a sixth to a quarter of the growing space that needs it. Anyone with a garden bigger than your average rug must surely have found the same. I suspect this is one reason that I'm not more interested in the stuff than I might be. Quality issues, so it seems to me, count for very little besides the paramount issue of a lack of quantity. No matter how much brock you can find, it shrinks and shrinks, to not very much end-product. Which is not something that's very often stressed in the literature.

The best I can say is that composting, more than most other gardening activities, demands in large measure the employment of our native talent for improvisation. That grand tradition which over the ages has produced, *inter alia*, the British Empire, Piltdown Man, the Sinclair C5, the Docklands Light Railway,

Ricky and Jodie's mega-bin, and the Wobbly Bridge.

To any newcomer to the art: don't be too fussed with it. You'll soon find your own way to grope the mythical elephant, and the Compost Canards say the rest:

(a) if you want to, you can use a bin, with a lid or without, at your own discretion;
(b) whether your heap ends up binned or binless, lidded or lidless, you can put onto it whatever brock you like, or that you can get, but avoid:
    (i) hoover dust;
    (ii) dead horses;
    (iii) fish; and possibly
    (iv) seedy stuff, if you abhor weeding; and
(c) use alcohol responsibly.

That's about it. Whatever or however you do it, you won't ever have enough.

In view of this last fact, the subsequent chapter looks at soil fertility alternatives to the scanty home-made heap, such as manure, seaweed, leafmould, etc. Given the somewhat abstracted state of this chapter-just-gone, you might perhaps be glad to hear that I've attempted to pick up the pace a bit, and that we'll be very much back on the ground at Fitzroy, in the next.

CHAPTER SEVEN

Black Gold

black gold (colloq., chiefly N. Amer.) oil.

L ook after your soil and the plants will look after themselves. This is a view that's common currency amongst allotment gardeners, you might suppose, though as we shall see, not one that's accepted everywhere. And as ever, reality is a touch more complex than the theory. On the plots at Fitzroy Park, one of the most fearsome aspects of this reality often descends in the shape of wood pigeons (*Columba palumbus*), swooping down off Hampstead Heath. Here we have many generations of birds whose courage has never been tested by the bark of a shotgun. The flocks are considerable and the journey's no distance; the birds could walk it.

Some plotholders swear that in fact the birds *do* walk it. Far too fat to fly. These are hefty birds, their fatness a marvel. So it takes no great leap of the imagination to picture them massing for another attack, waddling and huffing through the grass. Here they come! The very earth trembles under the stamp of untold pairs of their gnarly claws, as they squeeze and pop between the iron railings that separate the allotments from the Heath. Like some tribe of grisly dodos resurrected from the avian Valhalla, with revenge in their hearts – yes, it's payback time! Starting with the murder and pillage of *your* cabbages! Whether you've planted these in rank clay, or in the richest soil imaginable, the end result is always the same. The total biomass of the local pigeon population takes yet another fat leap forward, leaving your once-beautiful brassicas pared down to a few bits of stump and bony ribs. It's always an ugly sight, one you never get inured to.

Further courses in this thieves' banquet inevitably follow: soft fruit, hard fruit, ripe or unripe... it hardly matters. Also salad stuff, broad beans, peas... It's all a great big outdoor hypermarket here in Paradise Pigeonland, where you never have to queue at a checkout, because it's all free... In fact, just about the only thing that these pigeons don't seem partial to is tomatoes, so apart from the odd experimental peck here and there – which inevitably means the punctured specimen is lost to mould – you should be safe from pigeon mayhem with that particular crop.

So much for pigeons, though leaving such nightmares aside, you can't be too hard on them. For all that pigeons know we really are growing this stuff on their behalf. And when it comes to the pigeons' shopping list, in terms of nutrition they basically need much the same food that we do. Plants are different of course. They eat sunlight, devour dirt! Which is our general subject here: soil fertility, and how to achieve it in the absence of lashings of compost, as described in the last chapter.

Soil is the strangest thing. It's hard to think of anything that's more taken for granted, even regarded with contempt, as in soil/soiled, dirt/dirty and so on. But without it, life outside the oceans wouldn't have evolved – *we* wouldn't be here. And if soil didn't exist, you certainly couldn't make it up. Couldn't dream of it. You can't produce it in a factory, or replicate it up in the lab, because what goes on beneath the sod is so complex that nobody has ever been able to work it all out, with a huge mix of physical, chemical and biological processes all jumbled fantastically together. As the boffins customarily describe it: S = CORPT. Soil equals Climate plus Organisms plus Relief plus Parent material plus Time. In other words, soil is comprised of the weathering rocks or whatever else lies beneath it, combined with whatever lives or grows or dies in it which is affected by how high it sits above sea level and whatever the local weather might be over however long it takes to make it what it is. An equation so loose it's almost gibberish, though it does give you a rough idea of what's involved.

So far as a good growing soil goes, it's *alive*. Teeming with strange biology, much of it microscopic, with a hectare of fertile soil containing 800 kilogrammes of bacteria, over 3,000 kilogrammes of fungi, about 300 each of protozoa and algae, and at least 1,000 kilogrammes of worms and insects. In chemical terms, soil can contain over 90 different elements. Our average horticultural plant can take up 50 or 60 of these through its roots, if they're available; an indiscriminate process. It's only once they're contained in the plant's tissues that it sorts them out into good, bad or indifferent. Here's a basic list of the goodies, our average plant's soil nutrient requirements:

Major nutrients	*Minor nutrients*
Calcium	Boron
Potassium	Copper
Magnesium	Chlorine
Nitrogen	Manganese
Sulphur	Molybdenum
Phosphorus	Nickel
	Zinc
	Iron

There may well be others that science hasn't discovered yet. Without them the plant can't live out its straightforward natural fate, which is to grow, flower and set seed. What all this actually means to the gardener is always the same, however, which is (1) that growing top-quality vegetables always needs a soil to match, and (2) that whatever the condition of the soil you started out with, there's no escaping the fact that substantial stores of plant nutrients will be removed from it each year in the harvest.

Where number two is concerned, as it were, unless you're strangely determined about earth closets, not very much of what you grow and eat returns to the soil from whence it came, but finishes up wafting through various pipes, in various stages of bacterial decay, to the sea. Thus providing an eventual boon to the fishing fleets of the world with the extra phosphates, nitrates and the like supplying the single-celled plants at the foot of the major marine food chains. It's strange to think that your allotment's fate is to turn into fish food. Such is the weird world of nutrient cycling.

So, as a first resort, we vegetable growers rely on manure from animals other than ourselves to keep a soil fertile. But for those of us shallow creatures with pockets to match, and no driving licence, there's never enough manure to be had. The catch between the devil and the deep blue sea, for us particular subset of landlubbers, is either that we can't afford to get manure delivered in sufficient quantity, or else we don't have the means of transport to collect it, whenever or wherever it can be picked up for nothing. Which in London is usually from the capital's city farms, or else from suburban stables. City farms in particular are often great dung depositaries. They can't get the stuff off the premises fast enough. At my nearest city farm in Kentish Town the accumulated weight of crap once demolished a fence along the main railway line to the north and spilled down the cutting onto the track. Services between Euston and Edinburgh had to be suspended for 24 hours.

In fact, if you look hard enough it can be quite a surprise, in our thoroughly motorised age, just how many places there are in and around London or any other big city that can still yield a dole of dung. On a picnic at Hampton Court once, I gleaned a whole sackful of fewmet, better known as deer droppings, from beside the banks of The Long Water. Fallow deer, going by the shape and texture. Prompting a slight bemusement from my girlfriend of that time. Nothing too serious, but I guess she felt that I'd actually forgotten what the day was supposed to be about. "What amazed me most, Mick," said Pamela, "was your sense of anticipation – you actually had the forethought to bring along that dirty sack!" Deer-oh-dear.

I'll admit, deer manure's a tad exotic, most of it's horse (of course). Some time ago I was employed down in The City of London, and one day after work took the chance to check out the mounted police stables in Wood Street, EC2. This is an area you'd think is about as thoroughly urban as you could find, but yes – there was plenty of manure to be had – so I was informed by the sergeant who looked after the nags. I don't know if he was amused by the novelty of my request but if so, he was far too polite to show it, and straightaway loaded up a binliner with the real fresh stuff before ushering me politely-but-firmly out of the stable door.

So I set out for home very pleased with myself. The feeling didn't last, because in less than a minute I realised I was heading for grief. The bag weighed *a ton*. It *dripped*. It *reeked* of horse. It *stretched*, and started to *fall apart*, even before I'd made the short walk from Wood Street to Moorgate tube.

In those days I was much more determined than I am now. As several years have gone past since that foul journey, I feel I can safely boast about it, having proved – beyond doubt – that physically it's possible to negotiate the evening rush hour on the Northern Line with a bursting binliner of fresh shite. BUT. It's not something I'd do twice. By the way, it's a worthwhile tip to pass on to anyone who's new to the manure-moving caper. Whatever you shove the stuff into, don't use ordinary binliners, they're just not designed for the weight.

Similar problems of acquisition, in terms of quantity at least, if not transportation, apply to the gardener's second main soil-improving resort, which is compost making. For those of you who have suffered total memory loss since the last chapter, my main conclusion therein was that you can snatch up every bit of suitable brock, down to the last wisp of grass. It is never enough. Ever.

A third fertility option is seaweed. Fabulous stuff – instant compost, you can use it as a mulch or dig it straight into your soil, and it's particularly rich in trace elements, the minor nutrients shown in the list above. When I first read about its horticultural benefits I hadn't actually had my allotment all that long, but was straightaway enthused. At the time, Pamela was driving around in a clapped-out Nissan Sunny, and catching my enthusiasm she volunteered, with a casual recklessness, to drive us down to the sea shore. We set off from her flat in Surbiton, KT6, just after the morning rush hour, destination Littlehampton, on the Sussex coast. I'd volunteered to read the map, but on getting into the vehicle found there wasn't one. Using a map to find our way, I should have known, would represent to Pamela the kind of spiritless and nitpicking attitude to life she always finds repugnant. Instead, she waved a hand toward the dashboard, where a compass set in a clear plastic bubble was stuck with a rubber sucker next to the glove compartment. "Half-price in Halfords," she said. "just keep that sucker pointing south and we'll hit the beach in no time."

It didn't quite work that way, but after some interesting diversions around the roadworks of the South Circular and various rural byways, some of which the highway authorities hadn't even got round to covering with tarmacadam, we rolled into Littlehampton in the late afternoon of the very same day. And it wasn't long before we'd filled my dirty sack collection with enough seaweed to load up the boot. Also, this being a typical English Channel beach, with the various plastic bobs and flotsam and other junk mixed up in it: condoms, syringes, tar balls, squash balls, and countless cigarette lighters, sculpted into fascinating shapes by the ceaseless action of the waves.

Time was now of the essence, so after sharing a quick punnet of winkles in the seclusion of the dunes, we pointed the dashboard compass north, arriving back in Surbiton around midnight. The next day took us the last lap from Surbiton to Highgate. This time, a mean-spirited pedantry prevailed, as I insisted on using my *A to Z* to get us there. What an adventure! By the time the seaweed-filled boot was emptied and its contents strewn about the plot, we agreed that we were both exhausted. Not to mention the huge amount of petrol used up. Ten years later, the seaweed has obviously long since decayed and added-its-value to the soil, but when digging I still occasionally turn up one of those sea-dredged fag lighters, and whenever I do I'm reminded that so far as living in London is concerned, seaweed mulches are best left to those who live no more than a hundred feet from the coast.

Given such difficulties, it's not surprising that the slippery slope of soil nutrient depletion can get badly out of hand, at its worst taking on forms that would really be laughable if they weren't so downright tragic.

Take if you will, or if you *can*, the bizarre gardening habits of my near-neighbour on the plots, Dave Mundy. Dave is one of the calmest and most understanding men I've ever met. Amazingly so. Which he needs to be, having kept his head above water for years in the thuggish world of second-hand book dealing. So placid is this man's demeanour that it may well hide a sense of humour of the finest astringency. Or indicate its complete absence. I've never worked out which. Sometimes I do wonder, though, such as the time he asked me what was the name of a certain unknown species growing on his plot: "I don't think it's something I planted," he said "so I guess it could possibly be some kind of weed." On hearing my reply that the plants were plantains (*Plantago major*), he started to express hopes for a crop of wild bananas. That's wiiiillld bananas! Another unique facet of his character lies in not being able to grasp what a molehill is. Every time he trips over one he says "You know, I'm not entirely sure it's moles... probably rabbits, in fact almost certainly rabbits..."

...or mutant muntjacs, the ones the size of guinea pigs reported tunnelling their way south from High Barnet, with little miners' picks and little miners' lamps on their heads. So I wetly think.

Dave hates manure. Wouldn't touch the stuff. In fact, it's one of those very few things, the contemplation of which can make him somewhat perturbed. The strength of this perturbation dates back to the time he collected a load of heavy horse from up at College Farm, just off the North Circular. This being on a day before his weekly stall at Winchester Mews market at Swiss Cottage, NW3. By the time he'd driven back and unloaded his shiten van it was far too late in the evening to clean out afterwards. Market traders are of course early risers, but this lapse in vehicular hygiene was clearly a mistake, because shifting dog-eared copies of Camus to the fastidious folk of Swiss Cottage is no joke at the best of times, but both dog-eared *and* smeared with horseshit, well it's a total non-starter, as Dave rightly pointed out.

As for compost making, I'm sorry to have to say so but Dave belongs to that surprisingly large number on the plots – persons I've alluded to previously – in whom the compost-making gene isn't exactly dominant. Weeds get piled in a corner of his plot year after year, a tall and narrow hump that's become an allotment landmark, known as "The Grass Man". When The Grass Man gets so tall that he threatens to topple over, that's it, he staggers off to the allotment tip, and within a month or so a new man starts to rise up in place of the old. The current Grass Man is eight feet tall with a bad stoop. Surely his Time is coming soon. Which equals a lot of weeds, which obviously equals a lot of organic matter and a lot of soil nutrients heading off the plot. Together with the removal of Dave's poor food crops, yearly more feeble, disaster looms.

With the departure of each Grass Man the soil itself is vanishing. Over the years, the drop in soil level, technically known as a "negative lynchet", that began in the top corner has crept all around the edges of Dave's plot, which is starting to resemble a sunken pool, particularly in winter when this London clay is notoriously slow to drain. Ever more cold, more sticky, more hungry, the outlook for this particular patch of ground is bleak, fit only for soft rush (*Juncus*) and similar lank rubbish. The Poor Horseradishes of The Apocalypse, hanging on in there along one edge of his plot, might prove to be the last of his (remotely) edible inhabitants, before they too keel over and die of starvation.

Well, they might be if it weren't for the current fashion for American Blueberries. The most forgiving of plants. In the State of Maine – so I'm told – these will grow straight up and plentifully in hopeless soils, even out of solid rock. Dave has confirmed this fact on his terrible wasting ground, and each year he sticks in a few more examples of the season's most popular *Vaccinium* (on offer in Woolworth's this spring, £4.79 for two). So far they're doing fine. So far, Dave is a happy man. To echo Fats Domino, you might say that Dave has indeed found his thrill. In Blueberry Hole. But any joy that might be had from such tropes is immediately overwhelmed on remembering the dismal context from which they've sprung. Such is the reality, at least, in the deadly serious world of soil degradation. We cannot live on blueberries alone. I'm sure that not even in the bleakest corner of Maine has anybody seriously tried.

When it comes to maintaining soil fertility, what's still true today on the small scale was at one time true on the large. Out of necessity, the old pre-industrial farmers would hoard their stocks of manure like silver coin. If they ever sold any, rumours were said to fly of looming bankruptcy. Mixed farming was kept up not only because there were local markets for meat and milk, but because without the animals there'd be no manure, no manure meant no arable and so, no bread. And with horses or oxen to plough and pull wagons, farming operated on a closed fuel circuit, with no external energy inputs to subsidise the everyday work. Food production may ever have been precarious, but was sustainable, in the simplest sense of that nowadays overused word.

Giant plough horses have of course long been cleared from the wider agricultural scene, and the pastures that sustained them turned over to other uses. The few remaining Shires and

Clydesdales are these days confined to odd corners of the countryside, in Museums of Rural Life and other Heritage sink-holes, or else maintained in small herds by an even smaller band of enthusiasts, and there are even websites devoted to their decline and fall. Meanwhile, down on today's farm, energy is brought in from far away in the form of diesel and other fuel. Farming processes are thoroughly scientific and industrial, and as a result, yields are fabulous compared with ye goode olde times. This effort is kept up, of course, with inputs of chemical fertiliser, the point being that as with the rest of our present civilisation, the whole edifice rests on oil, those stores of fermented plankton, cached long ago beneath the surface of the earth. Oil reserves may still be vast, but they won't be forever. Then what the hell happens?

A late spring or two ago, I was up at the plots one morning much earlier than usual. Soil depletion and soil quality were far from my thoughts, as I was wrestling to make a pigeon scarer out of a long stick, an old bicycle wheel and six dead CDs. What I was after was a fearsome contraption that would see off the waddling brutes as soon as the slightest breath of wind spun it round. No doubt it wouldn't work, like the previous umpteenth efforts. I was puzzling over the mess of bent spokes when the sight of Tomasz Milewski, appearing from behind a curtain of runner beans in the near distance, distracted my attention.

He'd been telling me a few weeks before about his days fighting in Operation Market Garden in the Second World War, one of the noblest Allied failures of that now distant conflict – "10,000 went out and 2,000 came back". As you might just suspect from his name, Tomasz served in the Polish paratroops, and after many grim adventures found that he was one of those 2,000 fortunate survivors. If "fortunate" isn't too insipid a word to associate with the horrible experience that all of them went through.

So, as a young man, Tomasz Milewski did more than his bit to save us from Adolf and his jackbooted posse. These days, he's an equally heroic gardener. He's not been at Fitzroy Park for all that long, but arrived with much previous horticultural experience, and in the fairly short time since taking on his plot he's got it well in hand. I remember his patch under the previous tenant, in very poor shape, with more Japanese knotweed and more horsetail than the whole of the rest of the plots put together, with sometimes a few choked spuds in one corner, struggling to survive. This being, in fact, the notorious Plot 36, one of the sites which Theresa and I had initially rejected, back in the winter of 1992/3, as mentioned in the Cold Feet chapter.

Once Tomasz turned up the days of the knotweed and other pernicious stuff were short. The next step was putting up a cage over his entire plot, a solid structure made out of two-by-two posts and covered in good-quality mesh. No pigeon nightmares there. In fact the whole plot came together with a speed almost magical, and the effort involved must have been considerable, especially if you recall that Tomasz is by now well into his 80s. Putting to shame many a far younger plotholder in the vicinity.

I think it's worth stating at this point that by no means am I a jealous person – on alternate Wednesdays in a leap year – and I really don't want to say too much about the abundant produce that now springs up each season on Tomasz's plot. But I must mention those onions, almost the size of footballs. Like Something From The North. In fact I've never seen anything so magnificent in the onion line since the last time I was up at Unthank, at the Stanhope Show in Weardale, Co. Durham, during a lightning tour of the horticulture tent, after a far longer spell in the one next door, which sells beer. I used to sneak up to Tomasz's plot after he'd gone home and gaze through the cage, and wonder "How in earth does he do it?"

So there I found myself, on that same early summer's morning, clutching my useless pigeon scarer with not an inkling that I might soon find out.

I was more struck for the moment by Tomasz's odd behaviour. He had a short scaffold board stuck under one arm and a bundle of empty carrier bags under the other, and was walking fast downslope to the stream at the western boundary of the plots. Looking neither to the right nor to the left. Eyes front. Once at the stream he dropped the plank over it as a makeshift bridge then strode across and jumped up the low block wall that forms the far bank, then twisted down through a small hole in the chain link wire fence over the wall, dragging his bags behind and vanishing into the smokescreen of ivy that covers the wire. All with the deliberate speed and fluency of a well-practised manoeuvre. Having not noticed that hole in the fence before, I wondered if it was all Tomasz's own work? Or did he have accomplices? But more to the point, what was he doing trespassing in Rosewood? You can get shot for that!

I've no idea who built Rosewood House, but it certainly wasn't put up by George Peabody for the benefit of the deserving poor. It's a mansion built on the grand scale, and is nowadays owned by an Arabian Royal Family, grown vastly rich on the proceeds of fermented plankton. Common knowledge and common sense concur that you don't mess with such people, because superwealth needs super-security: alarms, laser beams, hidden cameras, men with guns and rottweilers. To put it mildly, you just don't go breaking holes in their fence.

It's supposed by most people hereabouts that the Rosewood owners keep similar grand houses around the globe, on the irrelevant evidence that for almost all of the year the place isn't lived in, but is kept ticking over and ready for immediate occupation by an efficient security and maintenance team, in case the Family jet in to sample the local delights. Maybe they suddenly decide that the cappuccino served up in the local Café Rouge on Pond Square, N6, has no equal anywhere (which is in fact true, on certain days). Alternatively, it might be Curry Club Nite at The Gatehouse, on the corner of Hampstead Lane and Highgate High Street (likewise, N6).

✦ JD's Curry Club ✦
Thursday 5–10pm

Choose from our fantastic range of curries, all served with rice, naan bread, mango chutney, poppadums and a drink – £3.99

Few could possibly resist at that price. I never miss it.

The actual "house" part of Rosewood is itself a stately pile, a classical exterior of immaculate whiteness, fronted with the elegant Ionic, on the large side. As for the interior there's nothing to report, as of course no-one of inconsequence has ever been invited in. Though I'm happy to pass on the non-information supplied by Doctor Philip (who we met in the opening chapter, Off the Plot). He was on a call-out there once, after a rare lapse by catering staff at The Gatehouse left one of the Family groaning and yakking-up half the night. A fine house with many rooms, was the Doctor's spare diagnosis, "*domus bella multas mansiones habens*". From which I guess GPs nowadays have to swear oaths about not discussing the details of their patients' tastes in interior design, as well as their other symptoms.

The House sits on the false crest of Highgate Hill. From the rear, there are views to the west over Hampstead Heath that would have been even more open and magnificent in the times when geezers were men, and (with fuel then always short), heathland trees were pollards. Within the curtilage of this fine property the lawn clippers are permanently set at Low. No weed pocks the wonderfully smooth texture of the grass, from which arise well-ordered specimen trees in spare, graceful groupings, including noble pines. The grounds tail away downslope in the direction of the setting sun, forming on the map the exact outline of the back half of a Dover Sole. In the centre of this tailpiece arises one of the headwaters of the River Fleet, which is among several local springs that surface at the interface between the Bagshot Sand of the hilltops and the less permeable Claygate Beds which lie beneath.

This particular spring has been sensitively excavated and landscaped into a large and impressive pond, with imported rocks around its shores, a charming feature enhancing the beauty of the whole.

Whilst the stream that tinkles out of this cunning pool has never been known to fail, in late summer its flow is often meagre as it runs out of the grounds, first marking their boundary with the allotments (where Tomasz had flung his scaffold plank bridge), then through an egg-shaped brick culvert under the railings and a footpath onto the Heath, and so on down to our popular bathing ponds. Where in the warmer months the paltry aquatic discharge is supplemented by the waters of thousands of pissing bathers enjoying a fetid dip. After which it disappears gratefully into a sewer. And so on, joined by sundry other drains, down to Old Father Thames and out of our story.

Not that I knew or was concerned with very much of this, on that particular early summer morning, when the first of Tomasz Milewski's no-longer-empty carrier bags came flying back over the fence. Tied-up and doubled-up carriers if you want to be fussy about it. Which don't lose their contents or burst on landing. For all I know, a homespun adaptation of some trick originally learnt in the paratroops. Over they flew, one after another, plopping down into a handy nettlebed, which cushioned their landing.

I didn't count the bags, in spite of normally being the sort of mathematical twerp who can't step on the cracks between paving slabs without a vague feeling of guilt. What instincts held me back I'm not sure. There were at least a couple of dozen. Bags, that is, not instincts! So I played indifferent and half turned away, feigning attention to my own business, the dud pigeon scary thing. It pays to be a bit canny-like on the plots, I thought. Barefaced enthusiasm is often a source of embarrassment amongst gardeners, like dropping your trousers when you ought to be shaking hands. After a time the rain of flying bags ceased. Shortly thereafter, Tomasz emerged back through the fence and picked them up, making a number of repeat journeys to cart them all up to his plot. On the last trip he picked up the plank. And that was the end of that…

Not. I realised that I had to find out more, and that to do so would involve committing a heinous crime. What was in the flying bags? To find out I'd have to open one, thus breaking a cardinal allotment rule, the one that says never, but never, touch something on someone else's plot without their prior permission. Such knowledge being common, or "customary" as you might call it, so it doesn't get recorded in any official document. But it follows that breaking such a rule, one that isn't written down, is far worse than breaking any of the ones that are. Which means, whatever you do, don't get caught. Such was the depth of my curiosity, I was ready to take that risk.

Not without first taking precautions, of course. My bulk being too well known hereabouts I realised that any superficial disguise would be seen through straight away, and besides, I don't normally keep a collection of different hats and false beards in the shed. So I played the waiting game. A long wait, with most of the day still unexpired and the longish evenings at that time of year. I fiddled with the pigeon scarer thingammy. It was no good. I flung it down. Picked it up and took another look. Flung it down again. Made coffee. Did other stuff. Maybe even some gardening. Ended up skulking in the shed, where I rearranged the small display of religious medals that live over the door. Hang back, hang back, I told myself. Tomasz had long since gone, being a morning type, but there were still plenty of other plotholders about.

The long wait I now recall as a personal epic, a depthless struggle between emotional extremes. Caution. Curiosity. The latter finally prevailed at about that time of an evening when, with the sun having quietly slipped beneath the horizon, colours creep to shades of grey in its wake. At last, I welcomed with relief the failing light, and though I couldn't quite be sure because there's usually some insane latecomer who's forgotten to water their dahlias, I finally guessed that I must be the last person on the allotment. And so I emerged from the shed and sidled carefully towards Tomasz's plot. Like a stalking cat. Except for a couple of heavy falls – most of the paths up that side are badly maintained, and are not suited to crepuscular movement.

Picking myself up for the second time I made it to Tomasz's plot, and leaned for a moment against his cage, waiting for my breath to even out. I looked through the mesh and there were the bulging carrier bags, stacked well inside beyond the football-sized onions, many more by far than the 26 he'd buzzed over the fence that morning, long ago. There must have been a couple of hundred. I didn't count them. Honest. By now I was feeling – whatever you might call it I'm not sure – several states of emotion beyond curious. So I crept around the cage, to the door on the far side, and throwing all trepidation to the gathering night, made to go inside.

It was padlocked.

A bright new padlock. Hasped. I was flabbergasted – had the pigeons learnt to *open doors*? Had they *turned locksmith*? I couldn't believe it. Then the thought occurred that Tomasz must have guessed I was on my sneaky way. Having seen me watching him earlier he must have nipped down unseen to Cavour's hardware shop at Parliament Hill Fields, NW5, while I was lurking in my shed, and rushed back with some enhanced security. For a few moments I surfed in guilt, close to the paranoid shore. Thankfully, this condition lasted only seconds, but whatever the reason for the padlock, I was stumped.

A padlock?! No problem there for the genuine villain, who'd simply cut the netting to step inside. Slit and go in – you can always sew it up afterwards.

I'm ashamed to admit that I may actually have been reaching for my penknife before arresting the mad moment. Cutting just wasn't an option. Not only a question of sinning against the customary allotment code, but vandalism, violation. A psychic insult. This much I knew: to cut someone's net – for any lesser reason than to save a life – is to do evil. Like cutting another person's string. So forget it.

So, whilst somewhat overwrought, I gracefully accepted defeat, and toddled off back to my own plot, packed up and made my way slowly home.

A veritable lie. I ran gibbering up to The Gatehouse for last orders! I can't remember getting there, my head was replaying over and again the last scenes from *The Man Who Shot Liberty Vallance*. I was Tom Doniphon just after he'd gunned down the notorious bandit. What cared he, who got the credit for destroying this evil? Because in doing so he'd committed an atrocity far worse, which was that he'd destroyed a part of himself. Beer didn't help matters, as my weak grip on reality was further diminished by a couple of The Gatehouse's splendid real ales, though I can't remember what brand. I may even have caught the tail end of a Curry Club Nite. Don't remember that either. What does come back to me is that not long following the last bell at the bar I staggered out of the place, and after sobbing quietly alone at the bus stop for a while, caught the 214 back down West Hill and this time really did go home.

Subterfuge was clearly no good, so on the next occasion I saw that Tomasz was at his plot, I made my way over in broad daylight. A frontal attack. "Hi Tomasz, how's it going?" He paused. "Oh, slowly, slowly," he said, his normal reply, especially strange in such a fast mover. "What's in those bags Tomasz? There must be hundreds of them!" I was trying to sound casual, but the strangulated note in my voice mocked the attempt. Whether Tomasz noticed this or not I couldn't say, but without speaking he picked up one of his double carriers, opened the pairs of knots and tipped the contents onto the ground. Finally, "Leafmould!" he announced. And there it was, on that rich earth, a richer earth revealed. A dark, peaty morass of well-decayed leaf fragments – Black Gold.

What followed from Tomasz was indeed a revelation. I didn't exactly have the time to rush out and buy a Dictafone, but what follows is more-or-less what he told me, the longest speech I'd heard him make since he'd spoken about Operation Market Garden Mark I.

Leafmould! It's good for the soil. Nothing is better! When I first came here there was nothing but horsetails, knotweeds and all sorts of bleddy crap. I saw it, bad drainage. Too much taken out of the ground, not enough put back. The leafmould puts the ground in good shape – it gives you a start. Comes from Rosewood – they've got plenty – a mountain! I talked to the head gardener through the fence, he said, we don't know what to do with it. He said, it's rubbish! I said I know what you can do with it, you can bleddy well give some of it to me! So he made the hole for me in the wire. Now I can go through, no problem, dig a little bit in every time I come here. The gardener is Jerry. The other guy, the security guy, is Chas. I'll get you the phone number. And look at this soil now – look at it! It is beautiful soil!

He crumbled some handfuls and let them fall. I could see right away how good it was – you wouldn't get that crumbly texture with just plain clay. We both had a crumble, and it was that good I even felt like eating some of it, like the bloke in *Jean de Florette*. Although I didn't, as I didn't want Tomasz thinking that I was pretentious.

What about this quality of crumbliness which Tomasz and I were then both enjoying? Gardeners often speak of the ideal soil as being a "loam" or as having a "loamy texture". To qualify, a good loam soil is made up of different-sized mineral particles in roughly the following proportions:

Particle type	Proportion of all particles (%)	Particle size (diameter in millimetres)
Sand	60	2 down to 0.02
Silt	20	0.02 down to 0.002
Clay	20	0.002 and below

What we have in the London region, compared with this horticultural ideal, is basically that the proportions of sand and clay are reversed. So unless you happen to live in one of the few iso-

lated true loam areas such as Crews Hill, up under the northern
stretch of the M25, where – no coincidence – there's a strong market gardening tradition, you're likely to be dealing with a clay
soil. The bedrock isn't solid stone, but a yellowish clay, which, if
you could dig down far enough, turns a blue-grey colour, at levels no oxygen can reach. The weathering of this clay strata below
the topsoil provides it with a preponderance of particles below
the 0.002mm threshold.

A clay-based topsoil has advantages. With a large proportion
of much smaller particles, within such a soil there's a hugely
greater proportion of surface area per given unit of soil mass,
compared with other soil types made of bigger stuff, so that clays
can hold a higher proportion of water and dissolved nutrients
than loamy or sandy soils. But there are also disadvantages, for
instance if, as we've seen, overcropping and other malpractices
significantly reduce the amount of organic material mixed in with
the mineral component. One result, exacerbated by working on
them in wet weather, is that these starved clays are very easily
compacted, with the pore spaces between particles squashed out,
resulting in an airless, sticky soil which provides poor physical
conditions for the growth of crop plants, as well as leaving them
short of nutrients.

Not a problem, as we've seen, for blueberries. But for just
about everything else, the proportion of organic matter in the soil
has to be built up, using whatever suitable stuff you can get hold
of. Leafmould is particularly beneficial. There's a balancing act
involved here, because although a good quality leafmould will
already be well down the road to decay, at the same time it contains natural chemical compounds, called *lignins*, which slow
down the decay process, meaning that it lasts longer in the soil
than most other organic material. The decaying organic matter
binds together with the clay particles and with water to form larger particles, or "aggregates", creating in the soil a much more
open structure, with a big increase in nutrient storage capability,
which in turn provides excellent conditions for plant root pene-

tration and growth. If you take this far enough, you are in fact creating an "artificial" loam, one that's full of energy to be taken up by your growing plants. An effect which Tomasz had achieved, in spades. In doubled-up carrier bags.

I came away from this meeting with Tomasz Milewski with quite a lot to think about. His finding a huge, hidden cache of free leafmould within spitting distance, albeit a spit that needed to pass through an obstacle course, seemed to me to be his greatest coup. One that no-one else on the plots had discovered before, or for all I knew, maybe had discovered but hadn't bothered to exploit. Then having got hold of it, regular leafmould applications to restore the soil – sound tactics indeed.

Tomasz's words came back to me later: "The leafmould puts the ground in good shape – it gives you a start." Clearly, he had a few more tricks. But, truth to tell, I wasn't about to ask, and if it took me a while to match his football-sized onions, then so be it. Tomasz's generosity over the leafmould supply was more than enough to be going on with, an excellent kick-off, and I'm still in his debt for revealing it.

As an aside, I realised that it sometimes does pay on the plots to forget being canny, and take the direct approach, a realisation honed in the light of my initial furtive investigation, which had produced nothing but a spell of guilt-fuelled derangement. And as for why Tomasz actually had a padlock on his cage – as it says in the joke about the catatonic fawn with impaired vision – I've still no bloody idea.

Soon afterwards, I made a foray down between the plots to the stream, opposite the Rosewood House fence. I'd noticed that the arrival of the Rosewood gardeners, at this tail-end of their grounds, was always heralded by the approaching chug of their small tractor. They could be heard long before chugging into sight, which was to my advantage. So I felt secure enough, particularly as I wasn't actually meaning to breach the fence, merely to tidy it up a bit on the allotment side.

I found myself a convenient spot a dozen yards downstream

from Tomasz's entry point. Here, sitting on its foundation wall, the fence towered above me to the height of nine or ten feet at least. I tore away at its obfuscating coat of ivy, which was a bit of a stretch over the stream, but it was less than an arm's length wide just here, and not exactly a raging torrent. In under a minute of ivy bashing I was gazing at the perpendicular flank of Leafmould Mountain. The fence was the only thing holding the stuff back from engulfing the stream, and it reached a level well over my head!

I rushed away for the ladder that's kept at the top of plot 18. This ladder being the property of a gentleman, who, by prior arrangement, had agreed that he'd never stoop so low as to chain it to a tree when another plotholder might need it. Security be damned. So, back down with the ladder to my convenient spot, I hoisted it up against the fence and scuttled to the top like a lizard up an adobe wall. And there I was over the fence on the summit of Mount Leafmould, an extensive plateau ranging 20 feet or more to my front and at least double that across, with a sheer eight foot drop behind me, down the retaining fence, to the stream. Tomasz was right – they'd got plenty.

In due course, he supplied the Rosewood number, so last winter I called up, spoke to Jerry first, the head gardener, who ran my request by Chas, head of security. I was invited over. Sure enough there were cameras about, tucked away, but none of the armed guards or rottweilers of our somewhat formulaic local gossip. In fact, the staff could not have been more friendly. I was given a tour of the grounds – immaculate, with scarce an autumn leaf remaining on the lawns or a single pine needle. All swept carefully up and carted down to Mount Leafmould with the miniature tractor. Here we ended up. Jerry admitted disposal was an issue. "Take as much as you want," he said, "Probably you'll hardly make a dent in it. And if you're wondering – no chemicals. We don't use them." All this was The Music o' the Mountain to my ears.

Well, several trips around our rough allotment paths and up the ladder later, my whole plot's now covered with a two or three-inch thick mulch of this excellent leafmouldy matter, a happy situation I hope to maintain, as long as I've got enough energy to negotiate the obstacle course required to get it. If Tomasz Milewski can do it, at half his age I've got no excuse. A further notable development is that other plotholders have started to express a shy interest. Even my neighbour Dave, would you believe? The dog-eared book trade's flat, but this stuff doesn't cost a penny, and it doesn't take a van to collect. There's yards and yards and yards of it left, and each passing autumn adds to the pile.

With soil fertility now sorted, all I have to do is fend off the pigeons, though I'm not quite yet ready to cage the whole plot, as per Tomasz. Hijacking one of his bright ideas is bad enough, hijacking two of them might run me into a row over intellectual property rights.

There is of course a final irony, which you may well have spotted, that the salaries of the gardeners who made Leafmould Mountain, like so many of our wages and everything else besides, are paid for out of oil money. What to make of that?

Sheikh Yamani, Saudi Arabia's Minister for Oil between 1962 and 1986, and a former OPEC leader, once memorably said that since the Stone Age didn't end because people ran out of stones, no more will our Oil Age end because the world runs out of oil. A lapidary statement indeed. Not to say seriously optimistic. The implication is that there'll be some kind of product replacement, a visionary technical development that will make oil obsolete. But for now we just can't see it. Can we? And we're not all about to dump our cars and jump on pushbikes, any more than our farmers are about to trade in their tractors for Shire horses.

Renewable energy sources are fine by me, though try telling that to any village that's about to have its local beauty spot studded with giant wind turbines. But whatever your personal take on renewables, they'll never be enough to meet our current, let alone projected, energy needs. Nuclear fusion seems about the only possibility at the moment that offers us an oil-free energy future, without incurring the excessive environmental costs we're experiencing at present. The International Thermonuclear Experimental Reactor (ITER), the world's first serious fusion reactor, is soon to be constructed by a consortium of industrial nations at Cadarache, in the Provence region of southern France. Obviously, it'll take more than a year to build, but over the next decade or so it's set to become the world's biggest terrestrial science and engineering project. Commercial fusion reactors could be a possibility in 30 or 40 years or so. This would free us from our dependence on oil, solve global warming, etc. etc.

Of course, we've heard all this before. It's the exact same pie-in-the-sky-when-you-die that was promised by the champions of the previous nuclear marvel of the 1950s and 1960s. And look what a bollocks *that* turned out. The best we can say is we're stuck with what's left of the planet's oil for the next 30 years at least, with no quick fixes to be had in the meanwhile.

Given this context, how should people respond? Most of course won't, or can't. Not interested, not informed, too busy or too poor – whatever. The minority who do take an interest often talk about "sustainability". This word is something of a cliché these days, but it only got to be one because it represents a truth, holding out in its very many versions as many responses to the environmental threats that we face. All sincerely meant, though in my view, varying greatly in their value. My own take on sustainability, which I've been pursuing with a great deal of serious fun for the last 12 years, is to dig. Dig or die! This hasn't furnished some magic blueprint to Save The Planet. Far from it. But at the same time, it's meant more than simply fresh fruit and veg, not least because I've learnt which is the true Black Gold, and which is the false.

This was put most succinctly back in the seventeenth century by Gerrard Winstanley, spokesman for the Diggers at St George's Hill, Surrey. "The one true religion and undefiled is that each person hath land to manure."

CHAPTER EIGHT

Comfrey Dumpty

*H*alf *a league, half a league onward...* and after the high jinks and tomfoolery of Black Gold, I'm fearful that this next chapter might seem a bit of a postscript. But nevertheless... *Was there a man dismayed?...* A few chapters back, in Blue Murder, I mentioned our need to judge each matter on its merits. This chapter gives an example.

Whatever else can be said about compost, manure or leaf-mould, and I've just said plenty, the one sure thing about them is that they're heavy. No, I don't mean depressing – far from it – but they do weigh a lot. Wouldn't it be a fine thing, then, if there was some other stuff you could use to improve your soil fertility that was just as impeccably organic but was also relatively light and didn't involve humping sacks of dead weight around?

Well, as many of you will already have been informed, there is.

Russian comfrey – *Symphytum* x *uplandicum* – instant manure, herbal medicine, and all-round-miracle plant – Come On Dooooowwwn...

Comfrey is much promoted as the organic gardener's best friend, in particular by the Henry Doubleday Research Association (HDRA), Europe's largest organic horticultural association, of which I have long been a supporter. The HDRA is one of those admirable organisations built from the ground upwards, now having over 30,000 members, and enjoying the patronage of Royalty. For all its success, it retains much of its founder's idiosyncrasy, not least its peculiar name. (The spellchecker on my computer – which admittedly is one of the older gas-powered models – wanted "hydra" for "HDRA", entirely appropriate where comfrey is concerned, since as soon as you chop of its "head", it grows a new one.) Like any such organisation, its chief asset is the enthusiasm and commitment of its staff, who are unfailingly helpful with your "agony plant" problems.

You can't sneeze at the HDRA. In most countries it just wouldn't have happened, or if it did, wouldn't last. It helps, no doubt, that the association has an agenda as clear as it's concise:

> ...our aims are to carry out scientific research into sustainable organic horticulture, to give advice on organic gardening and related topics and to promote organic gardening, farming and food.

It also helps that it produces an excellent seed and gardening sundries catalogue, one to drool over all winter, offering members a generous 10% discount on all purchases, as well as other benefits.

HDRA's original focus was somewhat narrower than that stated above: a case of comfrey, comfrey and *all* comfrey. It's fair to say that Lawrence D. Hills was obsessed by the plant, in particular its use as a fodder crop for livestock. In 1954, he founded the association with the aim of exploring comfrey's potential, agricultural or horticultural, in particular, by classifying the various comfrey hybrids in order to identify those with the highest yield. And he also wrote a number of books on the subject, including his magnum opus of 1976, *Comfrey Past, Present & Future*.

In pursuing these researches, Hills – as he ever was – remained completely committed to growing in the organic way, one of those rare and courageous voices prepared to cry "foul" at the excesses of the Age of Chemicals, during the second half of the twentieth century.

The eponymous Henry Doubleday was more a man of the nineteenth century, and was one of Hills's heroes, a Quaker businessman, full of ideas though far too dreamy, by Hills's own account, to ever make much of a fortune for himself. It was Doubleday who first introduced the high-yielding comfrey hybrids into the UK, having imported a consignment of them from the gardens of Catherine the Great's palace in St Petersburg, back in 1871. Doubleday's particular philosopher's stone was to use the mucose root secretions of the plant to manufacture an adhesive for the back of postage stamps, and whilst he ultimately failed to lick this problem, by the time his comfrey-root glue experiments were exhausted, "Russian comfrey" had been added to the nation's extensive naturalised flora.

It was Russian comfrey, in variant forms, that particularly interested Hills, chiefly because of its sheer productivity. It grows faster than just about anything else and produces masses of foliage in a short space of time. That the leaves have medicinal properties was an added advantage, one that it shares with its smaller and less vigorous native cousin, *Symphytum officinale*, long known to herbalists such as John Gerard. The 1633 edition of his *Historie of Plants* recommends its powers as follows:

> The slimie substance of the root made in a posset of ale and given to drinke against the pain in the backe, gotten by any violent motion, as wrestling, or overmuch use of women.

Whether comfrey really does glue wrestlers and other athletes back together more firmly than it could be made to stick stamps on envelopes, is somewhat outside the scope of my own interest in it, which is entirely horticultural. Here's a list of such uses, as recommended in the HDRA's most recent useful short book, *Comfrey for Gardeners*:

    (a) as a liquid feed;
    (b) in potting mixes;
    (c) as a mulch between plants;
    (d) to activate the compost heap; and
    (e) in potato trenches.

Apart from mere bulk, with a well-established plant providing up to 10 kilogrammes of useable leaf per annum, chief amongst comfrey's advantages is that it contains a great deal of potassium, as well as good quantities of nitrogen, calcium and phosphorus. These being four of the six major plant nutrients, as listed in the previous chapter, which it draws up from deep in the soil, beyond the reach of more shallow-rooted plants, which includes almost anything of food value, except (possibly) for large fruit trees.

Also, comfrey's carbon-to-nitrogen or C:N ratio is as low as 10:1, half that of ordinary garden compost, as seen in the Compost Canards chapter. This means that comfrey can be dug directly into the soil in its fresh state, without the risk of "nitrogen robbery", the process whereby, to start their work, decomposer bacteria get first dibs on the available nitrogen, leaving too little available for growing plants.

So, Russian comfrey. A miracle indeed. Let's have a practical peek, as far as my experience allows, at each of its uses given in the above list:

(a) **As a liquid feed.** Making this isn't rocket science. Put some comfrey leaves in a bucket or similar receptacle. Top up with water, and leave four to five weeks. As the leaves decay, they produce a blackish liquor that can be further diluted, if need be, and fed directly to your plants. It's that simple – an instant fertiliser fix.

The HDRA booklet is honest enough to admit the downside, that comfrey liquid is "very smelly". This is a consequence of the breakdown of leaf proteins under anoxic (no oxygen) conditions. It's also an understatement. In fact it's hard to exaggerate the stench. Rotten eggs don't come near it. If you can imagine an *ad hoc* olfactory scale of 1 to 10, with 1 being mildly offensive to the nose, and 10 being guaranteed to induce vomiting on a single whiff, comfrey water rates as follows:

comfrey water

1	5	10
mildly offensive	genuine pong	vomit inducing

i.e., an easy 9. Try stuffing a raw mackerel down the back of a radiator. Then shut all your windows. Wait a fortnight. On second thoughts, just don't bother, and take my word for it.

In my early days on the allotment, when I was fresh with that kung-fu bungee-jumping exuberance, there was no way such a trivial thing as a gagging stink was going to stop me. Comfrey plants are dotted all over the place at the Fitzroy plots, and the *idea* of lashings of fertile comfrey water was something too good to turn my hooter up at. I made gallons and gallons of the stuff in a big blue plastic barrel.

The problem wasn't my own nose, forewarned of the stink, but the noses of my allotment neighbours, which weren't. These were soon well and truly turned up in disgust, as – breathing solely by mouth – I began to water some of the contents of the blue barrel around my plants. Dave Mundy, my bookselling next-door plotholder, was first to react:

"You must have noticed it, Mick, but something around here has died. Maybe one of those rabbits over there" he told me, gesturing towards some nearby molehills. "I've been looking for the corpse, to give it a decent funeral, but can't find it anywhere. Which is weird, because the stink is actually unbearable."

"Really? I don't think I can spell anythig," I lied, "Deb Rabbib? Baby, bubb by doze is bugged-up. I god a code."

Pleading the old bunged-up nose trick earned me no more than a quizzical look, but did leave me feeling guilty. In fact, as this was one of Dave's historically busier periods on the plots, I hardly dared touch the contents of the barrel for the next few weeks.

The next person to notice was Sally, the expert roller of compost. Unlike Dave, not much gets past her, and she was straightaway wise to the fact that I was the perpetrator of the reek of phantom dead rabbit.

"I see you're making comfrey water," she said. "*Smell* you are too. Mings a bit, for sure, I don't bother with it myself – but have you noticed those weird maggots in it? – it's fairly seething with them."

Of course, I hadn't noticed, so we both went over to the blue barrel and held our collective breath, while I gingerly stirred the contents with a stick. Weird maggots a-plenty. From amongst the gack and sludge of overripe, decaying comfrey I dredged up more than a few, though for obvious reasons, didn't attempt to count them. My natural curiosity overcame extremely high levels of both stupefied amazement and hovering nausea, as I fished out a sample maggot into a polystyrene cup, to give us a close-up look. Where, once out of its stinking element, it wriggled around, most energetically. Neither of us had seen anything like it before.

"Yuk" said Sally. "Double yuk. A tampon larva."

And lo, it did look very much like a miniature tampon. Though more animated. A fat, blunt maggot – muscular, glossy, off-white – about two centimetres long, dragging behind it a three-centimetre stringy tail, as it circled the bottom of the cup.

It was some time before I tracked down the biological pedigree of this beast, which wasn't new to science at all, as I'd at first suspected. Quite the opposite, so I discovered. It's quite a common species, with a name less charming than the one Sally had given it: the "rat-tailed maggot", the juvenile stage in the chequered life of the drone fly (*Eristalis tenax*).

The adult Drone Fly uses mimicry to escape from predators. It resembles a bee. No such tactic is required of the larva, which doesn't need to mimic anything at all since its abode is stagnant water, an environment so unsanitary that there's no other creature prepared to dive in and chase it. The "tail" is no such thing; it's actually a snorkel. Even the rat-tailed maggot needs oxygen, and this breathing tube pokes up just above the water-line, whilst the remainder of the larva sucks safely on the decaying vegetable matter beneath the surface.

An awareness of such details of the drone fly's life cycle, genuinely fascinating as they are, did nothing at all, I'm sorry to say, to dispel my feelings of deep repugnance for its maggoty youthful form. Nor did the fact that my comfrey water comprised its idea of paradise, albeit an overcrowded one, do much to cheer me up.

What we have here is one of those classic contrasts between *ideal* and *real*, with nature pleased to furnish all manner of examples, including some instances even on the humble scale of the allotment. So you don't have to travel as far as the upper reaches of the Nile, by hovercraft, to watch cute antelopes being chewed to collops by crocodiles, to get the general idea. That nature's autonomy is complete, its workings unconnected with our own preferences except by chance. Or by our own meddlesome compulsion. And even in situations such as that of the garden, where we think we've got the upper hand, we can still sometimes feel horror and disgust. To say the least, it takes a special kind of person to love a tampon larva, and I'm not such a one. *Ideally*, comfrey water is a nutritious tonic for your plants. But it's also, *really*, stinking maggot soup. If you were a French intellectual you'd probably call this sort of thing "mediology".

In between the stench, which soon attracted further complaints from other plotholders, and the maggots, I'd no idea what to actually do with my vile water, and for months, gave the blue barrel a wide berth. Then, the next winter, on a chilly afternoon when I was feeling somewhat more daring than usual, I fetched it a hefty kick, in the last gloom before complete darkness. Then ran like hell in the opposite direction as it toppled over and its yet-purulent contents gushed out and drained into the cold ground. And that was the end of that.

Incidentally, if you spend over £10 in the current HDRA catalogue they'll send you a bottle of concentrated seaweed extract for a mere £1.25. As a liquid feed, this does just as good a job as comfrey-water – probably better – and comparatively speaking is odourless. In the light of this excellent offer, quite why the HDRA is still plugging the obnoxious concoction of water and comfrey leaves is a mystery.

(**b**) **In potting mixes.** This is one for the more dedicated gardener. According to the HDRA booklet, proceed as follows: put alternate layers of well-rotted and sieved leafmould, and then chopped comfrey leaves, into a bin bag or a dustbin. This initial mixture should be on the dryish side of damp (or the dampish side of dry), and kept that way for the two to five months it'll take for the comfrey to break down. During this time, whatever in the way of plant nutrients the leafmould on its own may lack, will be made up for by the potassium and other useful stuff in the comfrey. Thus forming a good general-purpose potting medium. Genuine enthusiasts might consider adding other ingredients to the mix – sand, lime, etc.

Apart from the simple enjoyment of making up such mixes, if such be your wont, the reason for doing so is to avoid using the peat on which most commercial potting mixes are based. As the booklet points out, "it is not ecologically acceptable to use peat in the garden".

Not that I'd recommend chucking bales of peat around, but so far as small quantities for potting purposes are concerned, well, I'm not so convinced. There are untold stores of peat in the world, especially in the far north, as tundra, and the like. And there's still plenty nearer home where – its undoubtedly true – local extraction for use in commercial composts can cause much *local* environmental damage. In these cases, planning laws need to be invoked to put a stop to the destruction, and nowadays, if there's an outcry, they usually are.

Historically, the drainage of peatlands for farming has laid far, far more to waste. Until recent times, for example, much of central-eastern England was a biologically rich quagmire, with peat-based soils dozens of feet thick. Once these fen soils were drained they proved excellent for growing wheat, but with this "improvement" of the land the peat began to dry out, shrink, and blow away. About a million acres' worth. Which is one reason why, when the tide is up, huge areas of Norfolk and surrounding counties now lie below sea level. As the land surface continues to sink, the famous Norfolk windmills – which were once adequate to lift the surplus water from ditches and rivers up to the level of the ocean – have had to be replaced with diesel-powered pumps.

Amongst the many other consequences of these changes, great flocks of migrant birds which once used the fens no longer exist, and most of our country's wetland archaeology has been destroyed. Without wishing to go too far down this dusty path, it seems to me that peat extraction purely for potting compost purposes can't hold a candle to such extensive depredations, and on its own, might even be positively beneficial. After all, you don't hear many people complaining about the ecological nullity and ugliness of the Norfolk Broads, which are of course of manmade origin, being old peat diggings.

Well, it's far too late for our fenland – except for a few fragments, its gone. And we need the wheat that its disappearing soils still support. On the wider scale, the human activity that will emphatically put paid to *the world's* peat isn't either mining or ploughing, or both put together, but global warming. Peat forms wherever dead plant matter is preserved under cold, waterlogged conditions, and when it warms and dries out it soon vanishes, by much the same natural processes of oxidisation and weathering as if it were artificially drained and put under the plough. So you don't even have to go within a thousand miles of it. Just heat up the planet a few more degrees and it will start to disappear, big time, of its own accord. Releasing yet more millions of tonnes of carbon into the air to cause yet more global warming. A "positive feedback loop" of scary hugeness.

In considering such issues, particularly in terms of their relative scale, I can't help but think that anyone who seeks to minimise their personal environmental impact by making ecologically sound, peat-free potting compost, yet is happy to travel by jet aircraft or to own a motor car, has got things totally arse about face. Thus, for me, the whole peat-versus-leafmould/comfrey argument is a true cock's egg. A "cocken-ei" as it used to be known. I use this expression in its broadest archaic sense, meaning a thing that's too small to count, is malformed, and unlikely.

Perhaps this is unfair. If you can be bothered to make your own potting compost: good. The London "cocken-ei" has an apt expression: "if you ain't tried it, don't knock it". Since I ain't, I won't. But if I change my mind about this in the future it'll be for reasons other than Saving the Planet.

(c) **As a mulch between plants.** Welcome news at last – this one definitely works. A decent layer of comfrey leaves strewn onto the soil in summer will do much to reduce moisture loss through evaporation, and will gradually break down, releasing nutrients, until by the time the growing season is finished, your mulch will be mostly decayed away.

Nevertheless, a word of caution. Until this decay process is complete, your comfrey mulch provides ample daytime hiding space for as large a population of slugs and snails as your adjacent crop plants can support. Not caring to repeat the horrors we've witnessed in the Blue Murder chapter, the only place I use comfrey mulch is around fruit trees and bushes. My local slugs don't climb trees. Yet. Though no doubt they're working on it.

(d) **To activate the compost heap.** Lots of things will do this. Something with some spare nitrogen in it. Stinging nettles are just as good as comfrey, and aren't exactly rare. If you haven't already got a comfrey plant it's hardly worth planting one for this purpose alone. Plant a spud instead. If all else fails, and if you've been too well brought-up to do so yourself, ask your best friends over for some *bière de limace*, then invite them to *faire a pisser* on your *compote*. If they're as hopeless at French as I am you might just get away with it.

(e) **In potato trenches.** Now we're getting down to the serious stuff. When I mentioned at the start of this chapter that its purpose was to give an example of the importance of our judging matters on their merits, this potato trope was what I particularly had in mind. Because, as far as I know – which admittedly isn't all that far – I'm the only person to have recently tested Lawrence D. Hills's claims for comfrey as a potato manure. Properly. Using experiment. Science and what not.

To explain how this came about entails a brief return to biography, so I hope you'll forgive the following intrusion into the course of our narrative:

A couple of years or so on the plot meant that I had a much better diet than ever before, and my growing fascination with how best to secure its ingredients prompted a broader interest in matters of quality, especially that of the soil, air and water on which my plants relied. Whilst I'd long had a vague interest in environmental issues, the actual practice of horticulture gave such concerns a fresh focus.

Meanwhile, although my old landlady expressed great pleasure at my occasional gifts of surplus produce, she remained shrewd enough not to accept broccoli or raspberries in lieu of rent. So, in the early summer of 1995, I was still proofreading, but had recently given up the uncertainties of the freelancer's life and taken on a six-month contract plying my trade down in the City, working an evening shift. The regular cash did much to ameliorate my usual status as an individual of very low net worth, and in subsequent years I ended up working several such contracts: evenings, days and nights, in turn. This particular evening shift was seven working hours between four and midnight with an hour's break (unpaid) between eight and nine o'clock.

During one such break I was sitting on a bench with a pair of my colleagues, both young chaps in their early twenties, Nick Rackstraw and Mart Lostwithiel. The bench was one of several set in the garden at Love Lane, EC2, next to the mounted police stables. (These same stables were later to become the source of the bursting bag of horseshit episode, as already described.)

The garden itself is a gem. In a particularly bleak stretch of the City's concrete jungle, it's a tiny oasis with formal box and yew hedges, and much planting of herbs within a neat parterre, parked in a desert of pavement and utilitarian office buildings of no architectural merit whatsoever. The site was actually a gift to the nation from the Nazi air force, with the garden being planted on the site of the former church of St Mary Aldermanbury, bombed flat in 1940 along with most of the rest of the neighbourhood.

For some curious reason, the garden boasts a bust of William Shakespeare, whose bronze egg head has provided a perch for many a weary townie pigeon. One of the gardeners' jobs used to be swabbing the crap off it with a mop, every time they made their rounds. They may still do, for all I know, though nowadays might leave it up to specialists. All in all, if you're unfortunate enough to be stuck down in that part of the world, a lovely spot to pass an idle hour on a warm evening.

I've never really liked the expression "country bumpkin", since it's derogatory. However, working with Nick and Mart did give me an inkling as to why the phrase was coined. They were both improbably rural, physically dissimilar – one short, one tall – but as alike in outlook as two peas in a pod, and bonded since childhood, having grown up together in the same small market town in the far west country. This was a place where – if you lent any credence at all to their tales of rustic boyhood – the goats that frolicked and fornicated over its rude cobblestones were far more numerous in the town than motor vehicles. And where at night, the black moors which loomed above and beyond the walls sparkled with the camp fires of marauding bands of cannibals.

The story of how they'd arrived in London in the first place was revealing. "We decided to travel and see the world," said Nick. "So we caught the coach for Launceston. Or thought we did. But that cloth-eared bugger there didn't hear the announcement properly and as it was non-stop we ended up here instead."

On that particular evening during our break in the garden, they were sharing a bottle of cider, an infamous brand known as White

Reaper, not to my taste one of Somerset's finer vintage scrumpies, so I'd declined their generous offer to stretch it three ways. From the horned animals and anthropophagi back home, their conversation turned to wider matters, namely, global pollution.

"I've been reading today's *Evening Standard*, I have" said Mart, portentously. "Terrible what's happening. They say that all the smoke from our power stations gets blown to over Germany, where it makes their rainfall more acid, they say, than the juice of lemons. Which is destroying all their lovely pine forests."

("Ha! Late revenge for the Luftwaffe making this here garden," I thought, but as usual on such occasions, held my own peace.)

"Acid rain? Bollocks, that is," said Nick. "Just only last month *The Standard* was saying about all the filth your precious Germans pour into the Rhine river. Which comes out in the North Sea, where it's making all the fish so radioactive they're unfit to eat."

"You want radioactive, what about that frigging Chernobyl?" Mart fiercely replied. "And that was caused by your communistical Russians, not the German race. There's still reindeer up there in Lapland so radioactive they glow in the bloody dark!"

"You talk like that, and 'Cher-nob-yl' drop off, and all!" came Nick's reply...

...and so it went on, between swigs of White Reaper, with frequent invocations of the authority to be found within the pages of London's favourite evening paper. They finished up wrestling on the lawn for the dregs of the cider bottle. Such playfulness meant we were five minutes late back on shift, with the two of them stuck with grass mowings. This combination of circumstances didn't earn us any brownie points from the shift supervisor, whose name was Hermione, and a bit of a stickler so far as professional conduct was concerned.

Anyway, I realised that if I was serious about my new-found interest in environmental issues, I was going to have to dig a bit deeper than the ordinary newspaper scare stories. I told Nick and Mart as much. "I'm going to sign up for a degree course in environmental science," I told them the next evening.

"Well, the best of British luck to you, you sad bastard," they both replied.

It wasn't many weeks later before the two of them, presumably having saved up a sufficient few quid, promptly disappeared. Some years later, I heard that after various adventures in the cities of the Midlands, they'd given up on their world tour and returned to their birthplace, where they married twin sisters, acquired an HGV licence apiece and made a small fortune in the haulage business. From which information, if remotely true, I suspect that their old home town didn't occupy quite the crazed Arcadian time warp that they liked to pretend.

As for me, I didn't even get as far as the Midlands. The next autumn found me queuing up at the University of North London, Holloway Road, N7, to sign the relevant application forms. At that time, UNL had an excellent geography department, built up over decades, the life's work of many of its professors.

Once I'd started my studies I soon caught the gist of how environmental science fitted in with the wider geographical – and historical – picture. Geographers, biologists, botanists and allied professions had long been used to fieldwork in beautiful parts of the globe. Then, from the late 1950s, they'd started to wake up to a frightening trend. That the largely pristine natural environments in which they worked were being altered, degraded, worn out. In some instances, were vanishing altogether.

Such processes of change and degradation, so I learnt, might involve any number of interactions: from a newly introduced species quietly supplanting a less aggressive one (brown rat/black rat), all the way up to obvious whole-ecosystem devastation, with the forests of entire nations cut down and burnt; encroaching deserts; shrinking seas.

Environmental science is about understanding these natural systems, identifying change and what causes it, and in the worst instances trying to do something about the damage. The common denominator in such environmental change, as you might well suspect, is that most successful of species – *Homo sapiens*. The brainy, handy ape, the only life form ever to have popped out of its original ecological niche, on purpose, somewhere back in far antiquity amongst those African savannahs. Starting out from there, so we've continued to appropriate almost all the rest, from the frigid Arctic to the most remote Pacific atoll, anywhere on the planet with sufficient resources to sustain a human population. Not in itself exactly a new process, but one that in our times has accelerated out of all proportion, compared with the speed of the damage gone before.

In reading about such phenomena, it struck me that location itself could provide a minor footnote or two, since the UNL campus occupied an entirely urban setting. If it was botany you were after, for instance, you'd not find much to look at beyond the chickweed (*Stellaria media*) and pineappleweed (*Matricaria matricarioides*) poking up between the paving slabs. There was also a trio of lonely looking trees fronting the site on the Holloway Road side, but even these, I recently noticed, had been felled to make way for Daniel Libeskind's dramatic new foyer building, all shiny sheet metal, zany curves and mad angles.

So, for the student of the natural as opposed to the human environment, one of the main treats of the UNL course was provided by the various field trips, offering the chance to escape from Holloway Road to places that still had plenty of nature left. Which was great fun – drilling small holes in Welsh hilltops to see how the soil and vegetation were related, and so on. As a part-time student, I managed to stretch such pleasures out over five years.

All too good to last. UNL's splendid geography department began to be dismantled even before I was halfway through the course, as the university's administration decided to concentrate their cash – which was admittedly always short – on the task of imparting legal and commercial knowledge to inner-city youth. The message seemed to be: "Nature is a long way from Holloway Road – let's make sure we keep it that way."

I could rant and rave at this outrageous error at some length, but as its relevance here is – arguably – remote, I will only indulge in a single-sentence conclusion. Which is that if the weasel-worded bureaucrats who destroyed geography at UNL were to be carted off to the guillotine to pay for their myopic and patronising crimes, I would rush down to Holloway at once, and cheer myself hoarse as the tumbrels rolled them to their doom.

Anyway, back to the point. The main highlight of the course was that each student should demonstrate their ability to run a proper scientific experiment, and write up the results in the form of a dissertation. Within reason, we were told, we each got to choose our own subject. After some indecision on my part, involving various schemes to return to the small holes in Welsh hilltops, I decided to play to whatever few strengths I already possessed, and to set up a project at Fitzroy Park. Inevitably, this was to be a horticultural experiment, the question it posed being as follows: "Can desiccated comfrey (*Symphytum* x *uplandicum*) be used as a manure to increase the yield of a crop of potatoes (*Solanum tuberosum*)?"

Not, I have to admit, quite the most exciting dissertation proposal ever received by my tutors, who initially demurred. Despite all having formidable scientific credentials they were a romantic bunch at heart, and much preferred their undergraduate students to be camped out on some remote glacier for dissertation purposes, or at least, flailing around in deep estuarine ooze in pursuit of rare shellfish. But in the end I managed to convince them that my idea was valid, and got their doubtful blessing.

First, I needed a site on which to plant my spuds, an area of nine by six metres, which would give six equal-sized, three-metre squares. Since my own allotment was divided up by miscellaneous structures and bisected by (too many) paths, I couldn't fit the test site anywhere onto it. So I approached a friend of mine, Fiona MacKie, on Plot 6. I happened to know that Fiona was planning to spend most of 1999, my planned potato-growing year, in India.

"Can I borrow your plot next year for a spud experiment?" I asked, somewhat brazenly. "You're very welcome" came Fiona's immediate response, "as long as you don't disturb the parterre," she said, without obvious irony, waving an elegant hand over a low mound of nettle-grown rubble. Not quite as good as the one at Love Lane, but maybe she was practising something for the Orient. Anyway, there was plenty of spare space alongside the parterre. I was in business.

Theirs not to make reply, Theirs not to reason why… Here's the post-postscript. I won't risk sending you into a coma by quoting chunks of my actual dissertation, but will attempt to summarise the experiment – and my conclusions – in what I hope is fairly plain English, as follows:

Lawrence Hills's own results, as recorded in *Comfrey Past, Present & Future*, showed that potatoes grown with leaves of the organic gardener's best friend produced on average 26% more yield, or weight of spud, than those grown without.

For the sake of slinging some comfrey around this seems marvellous, and I sneakily hoped for a similar outcome from my own experiment. Since access to growing space had been solved by Fiona's generosity, the next problem was actually getting hold of the comfrey in time for planting the potatoes.

Whilst immune to short periods of slight frost, over the course of the winter comfrey's foliage is generally destroyed by repeated frost attack, leaving little above ground but some few blackened remnants. Where using the stuff with potatoes is concerned, a time lag occurs between when seed potatoes are normally planted and seasonal regeneration of the comfrey, which normally only gathers pace several weeks after the spuds go in.

In his own experiments, Hill's favoured method was to delay planting seed potatoes for a month, until mid-May, by which time sufficient comfrey leaf would be available. The main problem with this is that the growing season of the potatoes is thereby extended into the autumn, for much the same period of time as the initial delay, thereby severely increasing the chances of blight attack. And given my earnest appeals to all, in a previous chapter, about the importance of avoiding this most fatal of diseases by planting earlier rather than later, it is not something I'd risk.

The answer I came up with was to save comfrey from the previous year, when there was still plenty about. Hence the word "desiccated" in my experimental question. Over the summer of 1998 I cut swathes of it, which were dried off, then tied in bundles and stuffed in the shed. It hardly weighed a thing by this stage, which was something to be said for it.

It took me forever to dig Fiona's plot, most of which was in no better shape than her parterre, being smothered in rough grass and other weeds. But all was cleared by April 1999, when I planted out a gross of seed potatoes, a variety called Stroma, in alternate blocks – 72 with comfrey at 100 grammes ration per plant, and 72 without. For the "withs", the dried comfrey leaves and stems were broken up, weighed out, and buried around each single seed potato, to break down and release their nutrients into the soil in proximity to the growing roots. The "withouts", of course, got nothing extra at all. Five months later they'd all finished growing and I dug them up again to see what subterranean magic had been worked. That's the great thing about spuds, digging them up is like finding buried treasure. What I found was:

Yield per plant with comfrey = 2.122 kilogrammes
Yield per plant without comfrey = 2.139 kilogrammes

Not quite Hills's 26% increase. In fact, the plants *without* had done fractionally better than those *with*, by 0.79%. No matter what statistical tests I ran with the spreadsheet, there was no significance in this negative fraction of less than a single percentage point. Whilst I was glad of the mountain of spuds produced, from the scientific point of view the whole thing was a flop.

Next, I ran soil tests, the details of which I won't inflict on you here, though if anybody cares to contact me, I'll supply the whole works free of charge. These tests showed that the ground I'd grown the spuds in already had enough calcium, potassium and phosphorus in it, so whatever extra input of these nutrients the comfrey supplied was irrelevant. A bit like offering a cracker to someone who has just eaten a horse. And now it's time, you'll be relieved to hear, for the conclusion.

Does comfrey increase potato yields?

Nope. In my experience, it makes not a blind bit of difference.

You might well ask, why I've chosen to lay this comfrey egg? The reason is that using comfrey in potato trenches, to get more spuds, is a myth. A cocken-ei to beat them all.

I called up the HDRA, for discussion purposes. The member of staff that I spoke to was enthusiastic about my whole experiment, up to the point when I told her it had flopped, and that comfrey was *all a lie*. I experienced the odd sensation of hearing some other person's feet cool, by tens of degrees, over the telephone. But she was still gracious enough to offer to put a copy of my dissertation on the shelves of the HDRA library at Ryton-in-Dunsmore, Warwickshire. So I sent one off, where it still may languish, if they haven't burnt it for heresy.

Never underestimate the power of myth; it's what keeps us all afloat. This quality exists quite independently of whether the actual myth itself is a load of old cobblers or not.

Nowadays, whenever the virtues of Russian comfrey are being extolled, which they still frequently and fallaciously are, it's not *The Charge of the Light Brigade* that I hear, but a bowdlerised nursery rhyme:

> Comfrey Dumpty sat on a wall
> Comfrey Dumpty had a great fall
> All the King's horses and all the King's men
> Couldn't put Comfrey together again.

CHAPTER NINE

Design and the Broken Man

"*Wroooombs*," said my informant. "The key concept is *wroooombs…*"

"*Wroooombs*," I echoed. "Yes, I'm with you. *Wroooombs*."

Needless to say, I wasn't with him at all. For all I knew his key concept might be an onomatopoeic rendering of the sound that *Hippopotamus amphibius* makes when farting underwater: "*Wrrrrooooooooooommmbsssssssss*!" But I forbore to mention this idle thought, in anticipation of my imminent enlightenment, on the subject of garden design.

The problem being: this was a topic about which I knew nothing. Up to that very minute, you could have written everything I'd learnt in my life about actual design in the garden, or on the allotment in my case, on the back of a second-class stamp. Using a can of spray paint. All that was about to change, however, and "*wroooombs*" was the key that would unlock the door of the dark shed of ignorance in which I had – up to that moment – been incarcerated.

"…thus," he went on, "the designer will think in terms of various *wroooombs*: such as 'shady', 'secret', 'open'…"

Suddenly it clicked.

"Oh, you means *rooms*, as in a house!" I said. He'd been extending his vowels somewhat, was all the matter. And in an instant, the flatulent hippos vanished from my brain. *Rooms.*

"...yes," he replied. "Exactly. An example: you've been to Sissinghurst, haven't you? Down there in deepest Kent?"

"Indeed I have."

"Well, what Vita Sackville-West did at Sissinghurst was to create not a single garden but what in effect is ten or so separate gardens, planted over six acres, sited with exquisite care between whatever remained of the ancient Tudor brickwork of the semi-ruined house and its outbuildings. The weathered brick was further softened by climbers – honeysuckle, vines and so on – and the pre-existing spatial divisions provided by these old walls were cleverly enhanced by new hedges – rose, yew, hornbeam – to make a series of intimate, interlocked spaces, their sense of enclosure punctuated by a complex series of vistas between them, connecting one with another, and also with the rural surroundings beyond the grounds. Between the garden spaces the planting is wonderfully diverse in both type and scale. Small stuff in the Herb Garden, tall in the adjacent Nuttery; vibrant colours in the Cottage and Rose Gardens, contrasting with the cool greys and whites of the foliage and flowers of lavender, primroses, clematis and many others in the famous White Garden. The phrase you always hear is "outdoor rooms". Entirely apposite, if rather too brief a description of what is a beautifully sophisticated garden design."

"Good grief! And not a trumping *H. amphibius* to be seen," I thought (keeping it to myself once again).

It wasn't quite a falsehood to say I'd been to Sissinghurst. I had *been* there, many years previously. It's just that I hadn't exactly *been in*, since as soon as I'd arrived and found out the exorbitant entrance fee, I'd turned tail and fled. Later, I found out that this price was set specifically to discourage the more cheapskate visitor. So if I'd dug a bit deeper in my pocket at the time, and taken the tour, my intellectual nullity where garden design was concerned might have terminated a long time sooner. Though now, of course, it hardly mattered, because I had a handle on the subject – *rooms*, no less – and thus, a handle on the subject for this chapter, which considers various aspects to do with design, on the plot. And associated matters.

Because if your well-designed garden consists of a series of interconnected rooms, à la Sissinghurst, your typical allotment site is a block of flats. Rudely unstacked. Walls removed, and each floor laid out alongside the next. A crude grid. Private made public. With each component of this grid "designed" – if you can quite call it that – by a very different mind. Sophistication you don't get, but what *is* on offer is *raw variety*.

This is particularly the case because degrees of aptitude and of effort vary so greatly from one person to the next. And so, one of the greatest joys on any collection of plots is to wander around and have a good old nose at what your gardening neighbours are up to. Or not up to, which is just as intriguing.

I'm talking here, obviously, about functioning allotments. Abandoned sites, of which I've visited a few, are a different thing altogether, with an entirely different aesthetic. One in which human design or intervention has ceased, and wild nature has started to return, usually in the form of nettles and brambles, at first, soon followed by seedling trees. A more profoundly horrific landscape type, in my view, is scarcely to be imagined. So I won't mention it again.

The point being that I'm concerned with the functioning site, as busy and densely populated a space – albeit intermittently, in both respects – and one that expresses the richest diversity of garden-related endeavour and creativity, as our particular home-grown culture is able to devise.

A further word on this theme, before I move on. Who are these "gardening neighbours" I've just mentioned? A generation or so back, the answer would have been unequivocal. But these days things are much changed. At least, they are so far as the Fitzroy Park allotments are concerned.

I recall a conversation, now several years old, with one of our ancient and venerable plotholders, Lawrence Beecham, who with his wife, Moira, started gardening at Fitzroy in the early 1960s.

Whilst, after four decades, they've recently retired from the plots, Lawrence's words remain stuck in my head.

When we first came here, it was all very traditional. These allotments, like allotments all over, were for what you could call "the better sort of working-class man". Almost all the chaps here were of that stamp, and I suppose, if pressed on the matter, I'd include myself among them. And it *was* all chaps! No-one would ever bring their wife up here, not for all the tea in China, it was unheard of! A strict division of labour. The men would grow it, wash it, take it home, where their wives would cook it.

The difference with me and Moira is we've always done everything together. Except during the war of course, over in France, no way they'd have let her in my tank, though she'd have made a better driver than the fellow we had, who was a menace. He went mental towards the end, they had to sent him home.

Anyway, when we both showed up together at this place, most of the others thought it was shocking, a woman on the plots! They could scarcely believe their eyes, and we weathered some rough comments, I can tell you. But we stuck it out and the others had to get used to the idea. No way they'd put us off…

Things really started to change in the late sixties and early seventies. That's when you got the middle classers first turning up. A lot of the old boys were going, by then, and these new ones that started to come in were a very different kettle of fish. You had the picnic hampers, bottles of champagne, all that. Some of them were very nice people indeed – 'come and join us for a glass of bubbly!' – not that we usually did, me and Moira aren't what you'd call drinkers.

A lot of this new mob didn't last all that long, I'd have to say. Your middle class being professionals and office types, so as you might expect, they don't make the best of diggers. Manual work wouldn't be their strongest suit, to put it mildly. A few of them stuck with it though, and are still here today…

Nowadays? All sorts! In a quiet way we were pioneers ourselves,

196

with Moira being the first woman here, and now we're about the last of the old lot. Plus these days you've even got plenty of women doing it on their own. Best of luck to them! But it just shows how much it's changed over the years…

Lawrence's words – and the above captures their gist with what I hope is reasonable accuracy – certainly went to the heart of it, in anthropological terms. Without wanting to go too far down this obscure byway, it's a fact that you'd be very hard put to pin down today's local plotholders on the basis of any particular sex, age group or social class: joiners to journalists, librarians to labourers. I'll avoid a long list, just for once; suffice to say, we've got the lot.

Generally, the trend is *upmarket*, and is also switching fairly radically from men to women. There are more female plotholders at Fitzroy these days than male. And whilst I've not seen anyone quite rolling-up in the chauffeured Bentley, I have more than once seen people clambering out at the gates from the back door of a taxi, fork in one hand, fare in the other. Considered on economic grounds alone, such a mode of arrival is completely bonkers, since even a shortish London cab journey costs more than a small mountain of fruit and veg. Enough to feed the hungriest vegan for a week. Still, allotments are no longer simply about keeping the wolf from the door; there's a lot more to it than simply fending off the pangs of hunger.

May 2005, and I'm off on an informal Fitzroy tour of inspection. Starting with my immediate neighbour, Dave Mundy. I'm standing next to the tall and narrow hump of Dave's Grass Man, who we met earlier in the Black Gold chapter and who is well overdue for his final stagger up to the tip. Despite an embryonic interest in nutrient cycling, Dave still hasn't quite got his head around the concept. The tiny amounts of manure and compost he's recently taken to incorporating into the base of his sunken pool are nowhere near enough to restore the lost fertility. I predict a bad year. There's little edible in sight – a half row of stunted, yellow brassicas that even the winter pigeons didn't stoop to bite, plus some early apocalyptic horseradish sprouts, spindly and sick-looking. And the parsnip seeds he put in haven't come up, even after two months. The one cheering note is that Dave's blueberries are obviously loving it, in his hopeless soil.

A few plots up, and by way of contrast, Sally and Mike's plot is already looking lush and cheerful. Six weeks or so back, they unrolled their overwintered compost/comfrey/manure long heap back up the beds. Most visible right now is a riot of last year's rainbow chard, it's vivid orange and purple stems jostling for attention amongst the dusty grey-green of huge artichokes. OK, I know people always say "huge" where artichokes are concerned – but these *really are* – bushed-up to almost six feet tall. Then there's haphazard rows and rows of spuds and bunches of rampant rhubarb, next to onions, garlic, broad beans, peas, shovelfuls of burgeoning shallots. An oversupply of strawberry plants in flower, a couple of seedling melons hunkered under the cold frame, waiting for the real heat of summer.

The herb patch is particularly bright. Flowering thyme crawls with bees and hoverflies, alongside a swathe of purple sage and rounded clumps of pale yellowish oregano. Also fennel, rosemary, other more exotic stuff which I can't immediately identify. Their new fruit trees are in blossom, goosegogs are just starting on the bushes beneath, and nearby, asparagus spears rush up amongst self-seeded rocket.

A bit further on up, and I reach Fiona MacKie's. This year, Fiona is spending a long summer with some old buddies who run an organic farm in El Salvador. This devotion to tropical agriculture means that once again her temperate estate at Fitzroy is looking somewhat neglected. The lower portion of her plot – which in a previous year she kindly lent for that spud experiment described in the Comfrey Dumpty chapter (and also for one concerning wheat, as to which see the following chapter, Six of the Best) – has at least had a good dose of manure, which she laid down before setting off for more exotic climes. I've no idea where that manure was from or what weed seeds it might have carried, but by now it's sprouting a lusty monoculture of creeping buttercup (*Ranunculus repens*). This does look jolly but it isn't quite the most sought-after food plant around here, I'd have to admit.

On the upper half, the infamous parterre is a rich mess of brickbats and nettles. So, still a bit of development work to do there, I note to myself.

A further saunter and I reach Dr Philip's, which he works together with his indefatigable other half, Andrea Beetison. It's a well-ordered classic, designed for ease of use, and to maximise food production. One large bed, divided into four parts. Potatoes in one quarter – then peas and beans – then cabbages – then onions, squash, root vegetables, salad stuff. This being your basic four-part rotation system. Potatoes one year, peas and beans the next, cabbages the next – and so on, round and round.

This particular set-up has an efficient rationality of which I'm really quite envious. I know vaguely how it works, although I've never achieved such impeccable order on my own patch. Going by the evidence here it certainly does the trick. Everything is healthy and well set, and last year, for instance, their carrots were botanical specimens. Perfect. *Carotae perfectae*. He and Andrea even persuaded their three teenage sons to eat them. "Now *that* was a result!" as Andrea told me, some days after her famous victory over run-of-the-mill teenage tastes.

I went even further up then, round the edge of Tomasz Milewski's solid cage, which was as usual bursting at one end with tree-trunk onion stems, soon to be football-sized bulbs. And then to Ricky and Jodie X's all-new raised beds, planted out with total precision, and within which they won't suffer a single weed to live. And…

…so on. But as that's enough to give you an impromptu taste, I'll draw a line under the lengthy remainder of my informal tour, and leave hanging all the rest, to provide a merest whiff of the stupendous variety that's on offer here, like the tip of the proverbial iceberg lettuce.

Time to move on now, because amongst all this, it needs pointing out that there's a counter-current always running through the plots. *Variety* is balanced by certain ideas of what *will do*, and want *won't do*. Quite what the totality of this counterweight, this unifying aesthetic, is comprised of is beyond my powers to fully express, or even understand. However, here are a couple of pointers.

A note on clothing

What do people wear on the allotments? I think I've already made clear, early on, my views on the need for a decent pair of boots. For the rest of your gardening garb, you could do worse than think along the lines of Thomas Carlyle, "the Sage of Chelsea", writing here in *Sartor Resartus*:

> ...I – good Heaven! – have thatched myself over with the dead fleeces of sheep, the bark of vegetables, the entrails of worms, the hides of oxen or seals, the felt of furred beasts; and walk abroad a moving Rag-screen, overheaped with shreds and tatters raked from the Charnel-house of Nature, where they would have rotted, to rot on me more slowly!

Carlyle's mock-horror at his apparel here is obviously a total front. He's having a giraffe. What he's really saying is simple: wear your old clobber. The more faded, the more ragged, the better. After all, so far as the plots are concerned it's what everyone else wears. And don't worry if you look like a tattered twerp. No-one else will mind.

A quiet word of caution, though, aimed at visitors from some of the more progressive European nations. Naturism on British plots is out. Get all your kit off and you'll definitely cause a riot. A pity, but there it is.

A note on paints, etc.

Much the same applies to paint, etc., as to clothes. When it comes to sheds and other structures, light and/or bright colours and gloss finishes are best avoided. Clear or natural-coloured preservatives or dark green paints are much more sympathetic to the hues and mood of an allotment. Also, as far as paint is concerned, the best allotment colours are those *past* their best. Cracked and faded paints are much preferred over the shiny and new, particularly if you happen to have chosen an outrageous colour scheme to begin with. Although relying on the weather to effect such a transformation can be a chancy business.

I had a lesson in this not long after first arriving at Fitzroy Park, when, for a spell, there was a certain amount of plot-swapping afoot. Being the new kid, I couldn't quite understand the intricate reasons for all this shifting. Partly it was gardening, but mostly it was personal. Some of the characters involved didn't get on too well and hadn't, apparently, for quite some time. Thus, there were several near-neighbours who wanted to put more space between themselves.

To achieve this Byzantine end, delicate negotiations had dragged on behind the scenes for months. All above board, I was told, i.e. the Council was involved. Eventually, a number of separate peace treaties were signed, and once this had been accomplished, the official reshuffle started.

There was one ancient fellow – whose name I don't dare mention – who was a key figure in these various manoeuvres: "...a bad lot. A tea leaf, no loss as far as I'm concerned, be damned glad to see the back of him...". He'd been Lawrence Beecham's long-term, next-door plot neighbour, and this was Lawrence's relieved judgement on the reprobate's move – a brief summation which didn't entirely disguise the heavy emotional freight that lay beneath. You'd think the old villain was emigrating to Canada rather than moving just four plots away.

"Plus," said Lawrence, chuckling slightly to himself, "he'll have to move that blasted shed of his; it's been blocking my light for years." And there indeed was the offending shed, looming large across the narrow path from Lawrence's, and, it must be said, it was a bit of a sore thumb.

Anyway, the shed got moved, and after it had been, its owner decided he'd give it a lick of paint. I was actually back at Lawrence's at the time. We were sitting on the bench at the top of his plot – though Moira wasn't there; she was still recovering from her new hip – when the owner came along with his tin and brush, and got to work.

I thought nothing of it, but Lawrence's beady eye must has been following his former neighbour's every brushstroke, because after a while, as we sat there, he began to get more and more agitated, until at last he could sit no more and jumped to his feet. "Good God!" he raged, "what's he up to, the wicked devil? I can't believe it. No. Never!" With this he snatched up his walking stick. "SKY-BLOODY-BLUE!" he roared, and hared off in the direction of the half-licked shed at a kind of hobbling sprint, cursing like the ex-trooper which, of course, he was.

It wasn't just the shed that was turning blue – likewise the air. A ferocious shouting match kicked-off, with the two ancient foes spitting fire at one another at barely an arm's length, for a full fucking five minutes.

I was a trifle nonplussed, to say the least, realising that their mutual antipathy contained such dark deeps of bitterness that it was beyond my new boy's standing with either of them to play peacemaker. I kept clear.

At last they'd both spoken their minds, and Lawrence hobbled back to the bench. "Sky-bloody-blue!" he repeated, with residual vehemence. "That daft bugger must think he's flogging seafood on Southend Pier. He's making himself a whelk stall!"

This incident, eight or nine years old by now, has somehow

made it into the local folklore. Lawrence and his adversary have both since left, and two loud, charming and alternately pregnant sisters have taken over the tasteless villain's plot. They grow spuds, spuds, nothing but spuds – which I guess must be one of those odd pregnancy craving things. They've also taken over his shed, which still sports the last few peeling shreds of its coat of sky blue. And is still known, on the plots, as The Whelk Stall.

So there we have it. Choice of clothing and of coating both provide pointers in the direction of a common allotment style, an aesthetic that defies a thoroughgoing definition, at least by me.

What I will say is, it's not simply style we're looking at here, but also structure. By which I mean certain specific, consciously designed and executed objects which crop up all over the plots. Elsewhere in this book I've described one or two of the less usual constructions that I've tried or am trying out: for tomatoes, for onions. Here, however, I'm determined to concentrate on the three most popular items to be found on any British allotment. Namely, cold frame, fruit cage, and finally the mother of all structures, which is, it goes without saying, the shed.

At the same time as narrowing my focus in this way, I've further decided to concentrate on the home made. Obviously, all three of my chosen structures are easily obtainable in handy, factory-fresh forms – at nightmarishly high cost – as any glimpse in a gardening sundries catalogue or trip to a garden centre will make plain. So, if it's shop-bought that you're after, it's in those places you'll have to look.

You don't need to make something that's fit for display at the Chelsea Flower Show. The main consideration should always be: does it work? It's worth a reminder that you can easily get away with stuff on the plots that you wouldn't suffer for a moment in a smart back garden. With this thought in mind, the following is written for those who want to make their own, a far cheaper and more rewarding course of action, for anyone who isn't entirely cack-handed when it comes to DIY, than lashing out oodles of cash on the sort of overpriced and feeble junk that's commercially produced.

For those lacking confidence when it comes to trying out their practical skills, the trick is to start small, i.e. with the cold frame. But before I get around to describing my first cold frame, some thoughts on sources of materials – stuff you need to actually get making with…

The answer to the question – where to get materials from? – is blindingly straightforward.

Wherever you can.

But, with two provisos: (a) don't filch anything; and (b) don't spend money, except as a last resort. Even then, only assuming you've recently won a rollover on the National Lottery.

The reasons for these qualifications?

(a) Theft is inimical to allotment life, letter and spirit. The communal arrangement of space demands high levels of mutual trust. Let me put it like this. If everyone on the plots was habitually light-fingered, how soon would it be before the whole system collapsed? Imagine every person's patch surrounded by a seven-foot chainlink fence, topped with razor wire. Video cameras. Floodlights. Plotholders camped-out all night with sawn-off shotguns loaded, chewing amphetamines in an uninterrupted vigil. All to defend their radishes.

Pinching from *off* the plots to bring *on* is no different, encouraging bad habits, and bringing disrepute in its wake. However, reusing clearly dumped or unwanted stuff is entirely different. See, e.g., the stern admonitions regarding correct methods for the acquisition of *For Sale* boards that come later in this chapter.

(b) How much are those radishes really worth? Quite a bit, if you've just spent a ton on tanalised timber, to build raised beds to grow them in.

Given these self-imposed limitations, your materials will obviously have to be recycled.

Everyone knows: we have these days, in the UK as elsewhere, the luxury of living in a wondrously wasteful society. Historically, this is a new phenomenon, something that would have been seen as quite impossible in our pre-industrial past, when everyone, from monarch to churl, was required to "live off the land". I'm not going to trot out a bunch of mournful statistics in support of this fact; the simple truth is, our ancestors could all have lived as wealthily as their kings, on the contents of our modern dustbins.

So when it comes to scrounging around for your allotment-structure materials, there's plenty of stuff lying around in this country, and you shouldn't need to go too far to find what you want. Friends, family and neighbours are all prime sources of reusable bits and pieces. Once the word's gone out that you're a plotholder, and on the lookout, often they'll come to you, so you won't even have to ask.

Demolition and construction sites are worth a peep, so long as you make sure to talk to the wreckers or builders first, as they'll know full well what's surplus to requirements, and will often be glad to get rid of it.

Also, nowadays, in most urban areas you'll find some kind of recycling centre not too distant, managed by your local authority. A well-run such centre is a mythical cornucopia, one endlessly replenished by a stream of local chuck-outs.

However, amongst all these other excellent sources, the deeply-committed self-build allotment adept will usually exploit, at first instance, that moveable feast known as The Skip.

Rootling around therein is known – at least it is in my neighbourhood – as skip-skanking. Any serious scavenger needs to cultivate this noble, if not exactly ancient, Art. In so doing, the main barrier to be overcome, for many people, is mere embarrassment. It's uncool to pick over other people's dross. If such is your own initial and entirely forgivable reaction, remind yourself: you're a plotholder. So act like one. You know it makes sense. You're Saving the Earth, and even better, saving yourself the earth, by bringing back into circulation what others, in their sinful ignorance, have foolishly taken out.

Technically speaking, you should ask the householder's permission before removing stuff from their skip, as legally it belongs to them until the skip is removed, when it becomes the property of the skip owner. Quite why someone should still want to own something they have already thrown away beats me, unless it's to give a bit more retrieval time to careless politicians or celebrities who accidentally chuck out government secrets or embarassing photos, but if you're the sort of person who wouldn't dream of cocking a snook at even the most ridiculous of laws, then it's best to check before you skank. Either that or go quietly in the dead of night. It's really up to you.

I could waste a great deal of paper talking about the innumerable treasures that I've managed to glean out of skips over the years. Mindful of this, a single example will have to stand in for many others.

The best skips I've known were to be found in Hampstead, where I lived for nine years and where wealth (not that I actually had any myself, alas) has long been lightly worn. The kind of place where wasting good stuff is conducted on the epic scale. Out of all the hundreds of Hampstead skips I investigated, one of the best of the best was a real curiosity. Some kind of house clearance – a gargantuan disgorge of perfectly decent clothing, furniture, crocks, pots, cutlery and the like. Sitting on top of all of which was a Victorian steamer trunk, with a curved lid, like a pirate's chest.

I clambered up onto this household shipwreck for a glim inside the trunk, which even still had the original key in its lock, and when I opened the lid, could hardly credit the evidence of my senses.

Because it was full to bursting – with *pies*. Tinned pies, top-quality Fray Bentos puff-pastry steak-and-kidney. The round flat ones. Like a hoard of gigantic doubloons. Not even past their sell-by date. What bizarre domestic foundering, I briefly mused, had cast up this amazing jetsam onto the Hampstead shore?

Well, naturally I didn't hang around too long up there trying to figure out the unknowable. Taking possession of this buccaneer's stash of pies, in their splendid casket, I quickly jumped overboard from this fabulous hulk of a skip and dragged the trunkful back home. It even had miniature castors underneath to facilitate the voyage back to my flat.

Thereafter, I must have been a pie-a-day man for nearly two months. Probably overdid it, in fact, since I've never eaten another such since.

This episode has nothing to do with allotments, as you'll have noticed. So, well gone time for my three structural examples.

My first cold frame

I'd read about cold frames for quite a while before getting one. And since my first ever frame foray, have never been without. It's no exaggeration, indeed, to say that today I can scarcely imagine how I ever existed without this essential allotment device.

In making such a confession, I'm aware that plotholding readers with a greenhouse on their allotment will no doubt be snickering madly at such pathetic candour. But as I've said previously, greenhouses at Fitzroy *sind immer verboten*, thanks to some arcane peculiarity of our local plot regulations. In such a parlous situation, the cold frame comes into its own. Nothing matches it for bringing on those spring seedlings, protecting them from cutting winds, battering rain, even from half a degree of late frost, if you're lucky. And if your frame is large enough, after those carefully nurtured seedlings have gone out in April and May, you can use it to grow melons, okra and other sensitive plants under.

So. My first cold frame got made back in my Hampstead years, as follows. One occasion I was wandering down the lower end of Arkwright Road, past a big house which was undergoing big repairs. Plot devices were far from my mind as my eyes idly scanned over this building site and suddenly fell upon several redundant torn-out window frames, leaning together up against a worse-leaning garden wall.

Immediately a mental light-bulb pinged on, and in a thrice I marched up the garden path, and got garrulous with the first builder I met, a no-nonsense-looking Caribbean character who was laying some bricks.

Instantly overexcited, I began to extrapolate the urgency of my need, urge and longing for one of those old windows... how I *had* to make a cold frame... *must* protect my seedling plants... so how great a boon such a window would prove on the plot... a donation that would amount to a considerable act of charity...

(Knackered windows aren't actually all that rare, of course. No doubt, in my naivety, this speech was a tad too voluble.)

...therefore, what an *unexpectedly magnanimous* gesture it would be...

"You are talk too much," cut in the bricklayer, with a voice like gravel. "You are annoying me with your foolishness. But," he sighed, relenting suddenly, "Makk you appi, mon, you takk im... and *go away*!"

I was so overjoyed at this spontaneous generosity, I could almost have kissed him. However, as I wanted the window intact rather than busted over my head, I made a brief thank-you and immediately scuttled off, as requested, fenestration under one arm, back home two or three doors up the hill.

To make a cold frame, first find your window, because whatever size it is will determine the size of the box that goes beneath. In this particular instance, Cold Frame Mark I, it was a smallish piece of glass. Getting hold of the materials for the rest of the box was thus no great feat, a matter of less than a minute's skipwork, which yielded up sufficient wood offcuts for corner posts, and bits of plank, to finish the job. Rocket science, it ain't.

I've never looked back, since then, cold frame wise. The latest version is Mark VI, a curved-lid monster, not, in design, altogether unlike that Victorian steamer trunk full of pies.

Thus, as we learn, history repeats itself, first as treasury and later as forcing-house, essential to safeguard those vulnerable spring-sown seeds.

The Mark VI cold frame. Very handy for growing melons under later in the year, once all the other seedlings have been planted out.

The easy fruit cage

To the randy spinster, in the words of a perennial pick-of-the-pops favourite: "the world is full of married men". But for those whose hunger extends no further than a longing to protect their soft fruit, rather than have it ravaged, the world is full of discarded estate agents' boards.

The purpose of a fruit cage is to look after those plants that are commonly targeted by marauding birds, so it's useful as a protection not just for your currant and gooseberry bushes, but for things like brassicas and broad beans, as noted in the Black Gold chapter. To construct such a cage, estate agent's boards make the perfect frame.

Not the actual board, obviously. It's the stick it's attached to you're after. The dimensions of this are just right, roughly two-by-two inches in section, which is neither too thick nor too thin, and most commonly found in eight foot lengths. This is exactly right for the upright posts of your cage, with 18 inches buried in the soil, a deep enough fix for anything except severe hurricane conditions. Leaving six-and-a-half feet poking up above ground, plenty of head room for all but top basketball professionals. Not many of whom, I'd guess, take much of an interest in such things.

The posts need to go in, as a rough rule of thumb, six feet apart. The actual distance will vary depending on the area to be covered, which you can determine when measuring up, e.g. a 24-foot long cage will require five posts each side. Once you've done your measuring, not forgetting the top bars as well as the uprights, all you need to do is scour the neighbourhood for sufficient *For Sale* boards.

Any estate agent reading this will no doubt by now be pop-eyed with rage, reaching for the mobie to call their solicitor. So, a warning is in order. Never, but *never*, remove a board that's strapped, or nailed, in the vertical mode. Leave the tinsnips and claw hammer at home, and wait for some irate householder to tear it down for you.

In my part of the world, these boards tend to sprout up in clusters, like fungi, and most of them are snide, bunged up for purposes of free advertising in front of properties that aren't even on the books. So many people inform me. Be that as it may, exercise some patience until someone else lays them flat out. Then exercise some more, to see if they get collected, and if they don't, you're in business. Grab all you can, chuck away the sign and keep the stick. Unless you fancy a cage of many colours, bare wood is best.

Slap on two coats of your wood preservative of choice, and leave to dry. For the uprights, paint the lower two feet with two further coats of blackjack, i.e. bitumen paint. This is to keep water out of the buried end. Which will still be the first to rot, whatever you do, but blackjack will keep it going for far longer than it would otherwise.

Dig holes for the post ends, 18 inches deep, as mentioned, and

A netted cage is invaluable for protecting vegetables as well as fruit; in this case, for keeping the pigeons off overwintering broccoli. Note the cross-braces at the top, which make the whole structure far more rigid.

as narrow as you can get away with, to save labour. In goes each post, and as you backfill you'll certainly need to use a spirit level or a plumbline of some kind to ensure that they're straight. Once all your uprights are in, and truly are upright, cut the horizontal top pieces to fit.

As for actually attaching these, there's no single ideal method. What I use are salvaged metal angle brackets, screwed in place, also with a small 45° two-by-one wooden brace, to make the top far more rigid. You might also have a go at making a door, which if you do will definitely need cross-bracing. Either that, or a simple flap of netting will do.

It's this last item that costs, since I know of no source of free netting, and can barely even imagine one. Readers with uncles who are trawlermen on the cusp of retirement, or who are out for revenge on their local tennis or cricket club, may disagree. Everyone else will have to dig deep, and pay for the best they can afford. Such netting as you acquire is best attached to your frame, in my experience, using a staple gun. And don't forget, as a friend of mine on the plots once did, to cover the top as well as the sides.

Thoughts on the erection of a shed

In common with many people, I've a great fondness for old vernacular building – architecture that was very often small in scale and was home made (more or less) out of locally sourced materials.

Again, like many people, I've often wondered why on earth this is: where does this peculiar preference come from? Why do we readily warm to the poky pleasures of an antique fire-hazard, thatched-roof cottage, yet, if we were to be truly honest with ourselves, are left distinctly cool in contemplation of the vast grandeur of a Salisbury Cathedral – or its modern equivalent, a "randy gherkin" – or something of similar hugeness of construction conception?

Perhaps we've stepped here back into our "hard-wired" psychic territory, and possess in common an inbuilt realisation that for most of the human past, pretty much *all* architecture was vernacular. Ever since the Palaeolithic.

Imagine our typical Old Stone Age family, the Uggs, quaking with cold for more than half the year, under the unimproved geology of their natural rock shelter. With its non-existent insulation and impossible heating bills. Here they are, staring out glumly from under its mossy, drip-stone lid, over a landscape obscured by wave after wave of blustering, chilly sleet.

Finally, after aeons of such gormless gazing, our Uggs have had enough. When the good weather returns – if it does, and they're not caught out by another of those ghastly Ice Ages – they vow that they'll at last put up that second home they always dreamed about, right down there on the distant coast. A snug hovel of driftwood and pebbles, with a roof cover of washed-up whale hide. And yes, spend the summer lounging on the beach, snacking on samphire and limpets.

Of course, no sooner had the Uggs swung into action and built their summer home, than vernacular architecture was born. They'd set in motion a pattern, a theme of humble construction, that has dominated the built world almost ever since. In terms of providing shelter, particularly in our cool northerly latitudes, the story – notwithstanding the odd Salisbury Cathedral – has mainly been about scrabbling down in the nearest hole or hacking through the local woods to glean sufficient sticks, rocks, moss and mud to put up adequate walls and a roof.

Thus, matters stayed for millennia, right up until the Industrial Age and especially the building of a national network of railways. As every schoolchild knows. Materials could now be brought in from further and further afield at less and less cost.

For instance, vast quantities of our locally famous yellow bricks, known as "London Stocks", were in fact dug out from the sludge of the Medway estuary, down in Kent, pressed into moulds and fired there on a gigantic scale, before being shunted westward to build the Victorian capital. More famous contemporary travellers, still, were the Welsh and Cornish slates, transported by rail throughout the land, to roof millions of new buildings.

In the face of all this efficient competition, the local, the vernacular, didn't disappear. Far from it. It simply went downmarket, or to be more precise down the end of the garden, retreating from the main (industrial) house to its periphery, to be reborn in the form of a workshop, studio, chicken shack and/or shed. Likewise, of course, it retreated to the local allotments, where a highly-inventive built vernacular is still very much alive and kicking, in the shed form.

As the nearest woods and quarries gradually went off-limits, an even better source of local materials was found: salvaged or secondhand. The chief and most convenient repository for which these days is, as we've seen, your nearest skips.

So if your plot needs a shed, and you're not feeling flush, but you *are* capable of picking up a saw and hammer without causing grievous injury to yourself or others, there's a rich vein of useable stuff right there to be had, under your very nose. Get *skip-skanking*…

Here's how my own shed got built: bits from skips, bits that were gifts. But first, a cautionary note. There's lately been, to quote Mark Twain wildly out of context, a great deal of "hog-wash and soul butter" talked about sheds, especially when it comes to their association with the male sex. I'll bet you've come across as much, or more, of this kind of nonsense as I have: Men and their Sheds; Men *obsessed* with their Sheds. *Getting it up*, they're never happy: can't stop staring, can't stop *fiddling with it*, every 15 minutes… and suchlike rubbish.

To be honest, I've recently had about as much of this as I can stand. So it's my self-appointed task at this juncture to cut all the crap. Get rid of all the unfunny conjecture and smutty innuendo, and get back to basics.

The bare fact is, guys, *you need a big one*. No avoiding it – the bigger the better. Because as well as being a (relatively) safe repository for tools and materials, your shed is an essential multi-task carapace, a shelter not only for all your gear and for yourself, but also serving as a one-stop meeting point for your less well-endowed, shedless mates. A place to dole out the tea and Hobnobs whilst the rain falls outside, where you can shoot-the-breeze on the one subject that a bunch of blokes together on the plots always get around to talking about sooner or later:

"What's the best way to avoid clubroot?"

I shouldn't have to spell it out but there it is. A heated topic, and not one to be broached in close confines. So, strictly in shed terms, *size matters*. And this is something that's every bit as appreciated by women as by men.

Not long after Pamela and I first met, I was giving her a first quick tour around the plot. It was that kind of early summer's weather with a fine all-day drizzle. Creepingly drenching. Pamela took the whole issue of my gardening obsession in her stride, as I proudly displayed my almost-ripe broad beans, vigorous onions, thrusting asparagus and the like.

After this rapid tour, we retired to the comparatively dry confines of my shed, to enjoy the bacon and asparagus sandwiches we'd made earlier. At this point in time, I'd just acquired the basic shed structure, seven feet by five. Which was almost enough for all my essential gardening stuff as well as the two of us. With a bit of a squeeze. Standing room only.

We ate our sandwiches, sandwiched ourselves together awkwardly, in between tools such as: spades, hoes, rakes and mattocks, in stacks, in racks; also between seed box lamp box cool box food box nesting box, pulley blocks, rope and string, riddles and saws, watering cans, wheelbarrow, hose and sprinkler; amongst crates, slates, ten types of tape, fresh lettuce, flame gun, primus stove, netting bag, hessian sacks, billhook coat hooks grass hook, rice sickle, salvaged religious icons, duck-headed snake, countless tins and jars; besides buckets and several metal bins, a barbecue or two, kettle, cooking pots, cutlery, cruet set, tin plates and mugs, towels, trowels, books and old boots and a spare Belfast sink.

"Not much room in here, Mick, is there?" said Pamela, not entirely without good reason. Which didn't stop my eyebrows warily raising themselves.

"Really?" I cautiously replied.

"No, not much room at all! I can barely move. In fact it occurs to me Mick that *you haven't got a very big one, have you*? It *hardly does the job*. Now, my last boyfriend's over in Kilburn, NW6, was *massive*. A *real big boy, twenty feet long* at least. He used to repair his motorbikes in it. Couple of Goldwings, in bits. A Harley. Triumph Bonneville…" (for a moment she seemed lost in an epic memory) "…Oh my goodness! That Bonneville! What power! He used to give me a lift up to my Women's Self-Assertiveness Class at the top of Willesden Lane…"

"That would be the NW2 end," I croaked, in a vain effort to disguise my dismay at Pamela's sudden revelatory outburst. *Not big enough*. My jaw dropped, and my eyes flickered around our narrow and cluttered space like those of a hunted animal, cornered after an exhausting chase in its formerly happy lair, now become a hateful trap. But I obviously had to *stick up for myself*.

"As you know, Pamela," I said, "*It's not how big it is, it's what you do with it*. Don't you agree? I don't do motorbikes, I do gardening. So this size of shed is entirely adequate for the job. Don't you think?"

Pamela sniffed, shifting uncomfortably. Causing several tin cups and other small metal objects to clatter down noisily around our heads. "Up to a point, Lord Copper," she replied.

Well we all know what that really means, don't we, guys?

"Why don't you *put on an extension*?" she said.

Thus encouraged, I fairly soon did.

The original bijou seven by five had been a chuck-out supplied by another good friend of mine, who lived in Blackheath, SE3, where she had a garden flat. Having paid for the shed, and having had it put up at great expense, she straightaway found it blocked the view from her back bedroom window. This blockage effecting a thorough aesthetic estrangement between garden and flat which she soon found intolerable.

Obviously, it would have been churlish of me to dispute the matter, so she was overjoyed when I said that I'd help to get it sorted. So, I'd got the offending shed *gratis* and, at less than a year old, in very good shape. All I had to do was the dismantling, and then get it carted across London to Highgate, a transaction involving half-a-day's van and driver costing fifty quid. Still, a bargain.

A tip here concerning freebie sheds. This is one occasion when it seems to me fair enough to look a gift horse well in the mouth. Be sure to check out the offered structure personally, and also ask yourself: "What motive does this person have for getting shot of it?" – and if you can't think what the reason might be, don't be too bashful to ask.

Even top-quality off-the-peg sheds are flimsy things, and nine times out of ten, it's off-the-peg you'll be dealing with. Proper vernacular is more solid, and lasts for longer, therefore isn't normally what's on offer. The sad truth is that the previous owner's most likely reason for wanting rid of a shed, *any* shed, is that the thing's badly rotten. Offering it for free to whoever'll take it away is thus no more than a sly saving of labour and, possibly, skip hire.

Having participated in such a deconstruction exercise recently, with some old pals of mine, I can confirm that taking apart a half-gone shed without wrecking it is an extremely tricky business, worthy of the skills of a forensic archaeologist. Nails and any other iron fixings are rusted securely in place, and panels are correspondingly weak, so you can easily end up, as we did, with little more than a heap of bonfire wood. Which you have to carry off anyway, having already promised to do so, and then spend forever and a fortune in bodging repairs.

Anyway, by luck rather than judgement I'd avoided this particular pratfall with my basic seven by five, and for a nugatory half-hundred notes returned from Blackheath in modest triumph, reassembling my prize at the top of the plot, in the line of the old "uppies" and "downies" boundary hedge, which already boasted a number of other rude huts.

Then, of course, along came Pamela with her invidious comparisons, and I was obliged to think – *extension*. The Force must once again have been with me, because not long after Pamela's first tour of the plot, a matter of weeks only, I was sauntering back home down Frognal one fine evening when my eyes lit upon an answer to the amateur shed-bodger's wildest fantasy, in the form of an entire skipload of barely damaged *tongue-and-groove* board, nearly all of it *poking out in incredible ten foot lengths*.

Ah, those legendary skips of Hampstead… The seasoned skip-skanker will tell you it's a once-a-year event to find even two pieces of such board with all tongues and grooves intact, since demolition workers aren't paid primarily for the delicacy of their labours. Well, these particular home improvers must have had the forensic archaeologists in to rip out their old panelling. Here were dozens of practically unscathed boards. Too good to miss.

I spent a delightful couple of hours that same night shouldering the lot back round the corner down to my flat in Arkwright Road. The same skip also yielded-up a plenitude of two-by-one inch planed batten, again, hardly damaged, to make frames onto which to nail the excellent "T and G".

An instant seven by six foot extension, and all for the price of the couple of boxes of wire nails needed to hammer the whole thing together.

Almost, but not quite, in financial terms, since there was still the question of transport from the flat to the plot. I'd followed the standard off-the-peg pattern by making flatpack-type panels, i.e. a prefab. The same Blackheath-trip van and driver humped these for me around the Heath from Hampstead to Highgate, for the same £50 fee. Which I blanched at slightly since it was obviously a far shorter journey, but as he pointed out, "still half-a-day's job, mate!" – which I suppose was fair enough.

So, in no time at all I'd more than doubled my shed space. Into the new extension went all of the ludicrous quantity of handy gear that had caused Pamela such consternation – don't worry, I'm not so dull as to repeat the list – thus leaving plenty of elbow and knee room in the main seven by five, now lacking the constraint of its original back wall, for three or four folding chairs. More than enough (almost) for those rainy-day clubroot bull-sessions. Hobnobbing with the lads.

Also, with chairs stacked away, for Pamela's future visits. Meaning no more games of "mosquito arse" in the dark open. Our record was 17 bites, and Pamela was always amused to count them for me – she always did have a unique sense of humour. And no more stand-up-type scenarios inside. Quite some improvement as far as I was concerned, in both respects, though I must admit, I never did let on to Pamela where I got the air mattress from. You've guessed it – out of another skip, right across from the allotment gates when they were having a clear-out at the Study Centre.

And all that one cost me was the price of a puncture repair kit.

Oh, but the Gods must have been smiling on me, back then…

Eventually, Pamela redeployed herself to Sheffield, and these days our friendship is more a matter of telephones. But her insistence on sufficient shed space to ensure bodily comfort set me off on a pattern to which I've kept. Over the years, the shed has sprouted several more home-made additions. The extension itself has grown an extension, in the shape of a cupboard tacked on to the outside of it. For useful low-value bits which benefit from keeping dry – I'll confess right now to having a great fondness for hessian sacks, and have accumulated quite a collection.

Next, I made a wood store around the side, little more than a piece of curved plastic raised on sticks and a bit of floor beneath. The one thing that basically sound wood needs, to last a decent while, is to keep its head and feet dry.

Then, guttering and water barrel, the overflow from which feeds the oyster mushroom bed. See the following chapter for that story.

Last – but not at all least – this year just gone, I rigged up a panel of solar cells on the roof, at 30p a cell, a tenth of the usual price. These charge up a 12-volt battery, a "Portable Power Centre" from Woolworth's, which in turn lights up a miniature strip-light called a "cold cathode tube". It's by the light of this lamp that I'm writing these present lines.

Not that it's actually dark outside the shed yet. But what the heck – free electricity, a real luxury…

So, yes, the basic shed has evolved into the essential multi-task carapace I mentioned earlier – a *shed system* – many of the features of which are shown in the sketch on the following page. And, also yes, I'm well aware that my Thoughts on the Erection of a Shed do nod towards the "hogwash and soul butter" of recent shed lore. But having started this bit by quoting Mark Twain out of context, here's an even worse solecism, which I've pinched this time from Percy Wyndham Lewis, founder of the Vorticist Movement: an allotment without a shed is "a giant with the brain of a midge". Think about it.

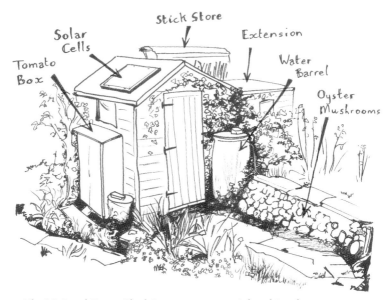

The M. Rand Patent Shed System – an essential multi-task carapace, equally useful for storage, shelter, social intercourse, etc.

A postscript: if you think my own shed history verges on lunacy, try for mental size the following Fitzroy tale, as told to me, in more-or-less identical words, by another of our long-serving plot-holders, Tony Ridges:

> This was before your time, Michael, another younger feller just like you, the go-ahead type, beg pardon and all that… his plot was right up the top of the slope there, high as you can get, and he put up this shed right at the back of it. Top of the top, you might say.
>
> He made a lovely job, you never saw a better. Not out of B&Q or Wickeses, not a bit of it, he did every piece himself, all out of scrap, what nowadays the Council mob have taken to call "recycled". And I watched him do it… I said I'll give you a hand with that young'un but he said "No, thank you, Tony, I want to do all this myself". So he did… a sight to see.

First went down his pavement slabs on the level ground he'd made... he was very careful making it level. Concrete slabs, stacked in twos... then some studding sat on them, bits of ex-roof joist or whatnot. Then the actual flooring, which was pukka, all of it scaffold planks the builders give him for nothing. You can't buy a shed with a floor that solid. Not now or ever could.

On that floor he put up a frame, more joists, old four-by-twos from somewhere. Then a couple of big old window frames with not a crack in the glass... one at the side, one along the front. And the walls he filled out with second-hand fencing board, all salvage but all posh stuff – I swear, every bit was oak, feather boards as they call it.

Then the roof, which was eight-by-four plywood sheets, heavy, three-quarter inch. And on that he had – not roofing felt, not a bit of it – but these big sheets of flat zinc. Last forever that would. How he made the joins in it I don't know, I couldn't see right on top.

But the best bit was, he made this veranda, out the front, to sit out and enjoy the view. You can see all the way over the Heath from up here, over to the Hampstead side. It was props from floor to roof, then proper railings... and none of it was old joists. No. it was real tree wood, round stuff. It looked great! Like Little House on the Prairie...

Anyway, a bit after he was finished, the Council got wind of it. So they come round for a butcher's. I was indoors that day but my wife, Jane, seen them. And they had a good look round, a pair of them, then they went away again, Jane told me.

Then a few weeks later they come back. Mob-handed this time. And this time both of us was there, me and Jane, and there was *seven* of them Council, I counted, ask Jane, she'll tell you. There was one from Conservation, one from Town Planning... half the bloody departments sent someone and we wouldn't have been surprised to see the Lady Mayor with her Gold Ball and Chain hanging round her neck – it was an invasion!

The young feller wasn't about, he must have made his self scarce. I was minding me own at the time but they still asked me: "D'you know him, Tony?" they said. "Nar, no call to get familiar, I pay me rates... it's Mr. Ridges to you. And I never clapped eyes on him," I said, "but you have to admit, he done a lovely job on that shed there, didn't he?" I had to put in a good word like.

"Well, that's what we want to talk to him about, that shed," says one of them. And so, off they went. Gourd help us I thought, if I had the young feller's phone number I'd have belled him up, and gave him a warning, what they was banging on about without a by-yer-leave, right there in front of me and Jane…

Course, they run him down in the end. And when they did, they said, "About your shed, we've had complaints from over the road. From the Big Place. You can't have it, it's too tall…" Too tall, I ask yer! "…being as how it's already right up the slope."

"But we ain't unreasonable people – we're glad to do a compromise – chop a foot off the top and make it lower and we'll say no more about it. Or else we'll have to bash the whole thing down and sling it on the shoot. *And* charge you for it!"

The young feller told me all this… they'd dragged him down in the Town Hall in Euston Road, you wouldn't believe the fuss they made, over a shed. And I can tell you, what a terrible thing it is to see a grown man cry. He was beside himself.

Anyway, me and Jane went off about then for our two weeks in the Peak District. Her sister run a guest house up there. Still does. And when we come back, what do you reckon?

He was gone. Lock, stock, barrel and Little House on the Prairie and all. The lot. Vanished. He even took up those pavement slabs; just as well, because if he'd left them behind I'd have had them away meself. They was quality, hardly even chipped.

I never clocked his name, and I ain't seen him around since, and that was 14 or 15 year ago, give or take. Someone else took over his plot, a right drooper he was. Then another lot. I didn't get on with any of them much and nor did Jane.

But I heard the young feller never quite recovered his proper mind. I mean, after what the Council done to him, and all over that lovely shed of his. Jane was as upset as me to think of it… we never seen a worst case. Making him take it down like that.

They say he was a broken man.

CHAPTER TEN

Six of the Best

A *re you sitting comfortably? Then I'll begin…*
Where do plants come from?

How do they work?

Why doesn't an oak tree look like a giant acorn?

And why is finding out answers to such questions useful to anyone who's ever attempted to grow their own food?

When I was in infants' school, the normal routine of lessons would be randomly enlivened in the following manner. We were marshalled into the freezing assembly hall, snot-nosed and shivering in groups of thirty or forty, to wait for an announcement from a crackling loudspeaker.

It seemed as if we had to wait for this announcement forever, enjoined to total silence and stillness, and growing colder by the minute. Then, with miraculous timing, seconds before we all fell into hysterics through boredom and exposure, the radio connected to the speaker would whine and spit into life. And from out of the ether, rising over a background clutter of noise that sounded to our young ears like frying bacon, but was in fact nothing more elaborate than clapped-out equipment and poor reception, would come a distant and patrician female voice, from the BBC.

This disembodied voice would proceed to urge us all to prance about to some nonsense that, I recall dimly, was known as *Music and Movement*. Reluctantly, everybody obeyed.

I'm not sure, to this day, what was the purpose of this desultory, unwanted activity, lacking as it did all excitement and spontaneity. The only advantage to be gained was that by joining in with it we did eventually warm up a bit. Meanwhile, most of our teachers would vanish into the staffroom, and put the kettle on. It seemed to me a mammoth injustice that not only were the grown-ups exempt from stupid prancing, but at the same time got tea and biscuits instead. So my participation in the exercises was even more half-hearted than that of most of my classmates.

I don't remember any of the *Music*, and not much of the *Movement*. But curious to note, the single one of the exercises that remains lodged in my mind was the one which pretended to run us through the life cycle of a plant. It had an especial horror, since we'd all have to start hunched up on the floor, with our clothes mopping up the fluff, wheezing and sniffling in the dust. Thus curled up, we were eventually told by the announcer that we were each, in fact, an acorn, waiting to grow up into a mighty oak. But it wasn't convincing, since no real acorn was ever made to lie so long in the dirt, before sprouting into life.

Then, with agonising, tremulous movement slow, we were encouraged gradually to uncurl, and to grow upward, inch by half inch from a crouching start, causing much pointless physical strain, particularly to our juvenile knees and ankles. God save the child, who out of this combined pain and tedium, tried to grow up too fast. He or she would always be shouted back down again by a mug-waving teacher, hovering near the staffroom door, in sinister league with the posh sadist at the far end of the airwaves.

By-and-by, we'd be permitted to straighten our legs and unwind ourselves in full, and after an age ended up on tiptoes, waving our arms in an unconvincing facsimile of branches blowing in the wind, whilst the wireless fizzed and popped louder than ever and the announcer yelped with a jollity that had nobody fooled but herself.

Even at age six, I knew the whole thing was ridiculous, not to say harmful, but there was no escaping it. The lifelong damage which some of us suffered in the lower limb joints was presumably compensated for by the insight we'd gained into the kingdom of vegetable life which we'd been temporarily forced to join.

Now then everyone pop crackle *that was such fun! Wasn't it? So much fun, let's run through it* hiss pop *all over again, shall we? ... Here we go again, scrunched up on that cold and filthy floor...*

A seed is a complete plant, in miniature, protected by a tough coat. With a water content of about 15%, it's dehydrated, compared with its parent, which is the main reason for its dormant state. Beneath the coat, a seed contains a nucleus, an embryonic plant consisting of two basic organs, root and shoot. Alongside of these, the bulk of the seed is made up of food storage tissues, which hold starch and various proteins – fats and oils. These food stores act as a kick-starter, once the seed germinates, by supplying an initial burst of nutrients to the embryo.

Dormancy is curtailed by external stimuli, chiefly by water in the surrounding soil, once the seed falls or is planted, and by a suitable temperature range, usually a moderate heat. The absorption of water into the seed at this initial stage of germination triggers the growth hormones giberellin and cytokinin, as well as the production of ethylene gas, which promotes the conversion of the stored fats, etc., into soluble sugar, enabling cell division and multiplication to start. So the nascent seed unfolds, and pokes through the coat its first root, the radicle, and first leaves, the plumule.

For a while, our emergent plant may still rely on the shrinking store of nutrients left in the seed, out of which it has recently emerged. But as soon as its able, when the plumule reaches daylight, our plant, just like any and every green plant that ever lived, begins to produce its own food. This process is photosynthesis, in which the plant uses the energy of light to combine carbon dioxide, captured from the air through the stomata, or pore cells, in its leaves, with water, drawn up to the leaves from its roots, to produce carbohydrates, i.e. starch and sugars.

The most useful wavelengths of light energy powering the process are blues and reds in the visible spectrum. What most plants can't use is green, hence wavelengths of this colour aren't absorbed but reflected back from the leaves. Strange to think, that the greater part of our own visual perception of the plant world is created by that part of the colour spectrum which the plant itself rejects.

As well as trapping carbon, the stomata serve two further key purposes. The first is to release excess water from the leaves. This creates suction, a liquid pressure gradient through the plant's tissues, with lower pressure in the leaves and higher in the roots. Which is the method, known as transpiration, by which water and its dissolved inorganic nutrients, obtained from the soil, overcome the force of gravity and are transported to all parts of the plant.

The second purpose of the stomata is to release oxygen, which from the plant's point of view is simply a waste gas, a by-product of its conversion of light into chemical energy. The oxygen in the air is all derived from plants.

… So here we are, once more, in our Music and Movement *of plants. We've done the uncurled bit and have reached the crouching point, all screaming knees and ankles, bursting to reach further upward and stand up straight …*

To work and to grow, a plant produces three different tissue types. Vascular tissues, which are elongated, hollow cells, joined end-to-end, transport water and various nutrients. Such tissues take one of two forms. First is xylem, which through transpiration carries the actual plant construction materials, those inorganic nutrients listed in an earlier chapter, lifted up from the roots. Secondly, phloem, which carries the organic nutrients that the plant has made from the inorganics, the sugars, etc., to wherever they're immediately required for growth, or to be stored for future use.

The storage tissue itself is called parenchyma, formed from large cells which comprise a kind of packing, but which also contain vacuoles, or spaces, for storing food materials. In many smaller plants, or small parts of larger ones, parenchyma is centrally located in the stem, as pith, with the vascular tissues arranged in bundles around the outside of it.

Meristem tissues are where new growth occurs. Apical meristem is formed by cell elongation, followed by division, and is most commonly – although not exclusively (see below, "monocots") – found at the tips of stems, buds and roots. It is common to all green plants. Many types of tree, including those species that we're most familiar with in the temperate regions of the world, also have cambium meristem, lying under their bark, forming a new growth ring each year. The tree gets fatter as it gets taller. Essential for stability, if nothing else. Meristem tissue exists in a permanently embryonic form, and in terms of plant morphology is the main reason, by the way, that an oak tree doesn't resemble a giant acorn.

My knowledge of science is clumsy enough. Nor I ain't no poet neither. Whatever language I scramble after in trying to describe these processes of plant growth is barely fit to capture their deep complexity, or convey the beautiful vision of natural unity and economy which they present, even with my partial understanding of them. For each and every one of us great human apes, as well as for the rest of animal creation – barring a few oddities – green plants are life, both food and breath. Unlike them, we can't create our own food within ourselves, so we need to eat either the plants themselves, or else other things which once ate them. The same applies whether you live exclusively on raw apples, or exclusively on fried bacon. Oddities aside, all food chains have plants at their base. Plus all we beasts breathe the same oxygen. We're only here because the greenery was here first.

So it's the same world for all animals, from the humblest and most thoughtless insect nibbling on a leaf, to the "inward eye" of a William Wordsworth, contemplating the higher aesthetic pleasures of dancing daffodils. Whatever the unfathomable differences in perception between any two such disparate creatures might be, photosynthesis is the link, the all-time biological wonder of the world, the mother and father of us all. Handily expressed in the following equation:

$$\text{Sunlight} + 6CO_2 + 6H_2O \longrightarrow C_6H_{12}O_6 + 6O_2$$

| | Carbon Dioxide | Water | Sugar | Oxygen |

... so, we've grown up at last, tall and straight, and can wave our arms about in a poor imitation of branches, and wiggle our fingers like shimmering leaves...hooray! HOORAY!

A basic knowledge of plant biology isn't obligatory for the gardener. Given any kind of a chance, whatever seeds you sow will do their thing regardless. But, to my mind, such knowledge can be enormously useful, by helping you to make your decisions about what to grow, and when and how to grow it, and most essential of all, *how fast* you can pick and eat it once it's ready.

Recently, I was listening to one of our growing breed of professional media gardeners, who was being interviewed on the radio. Her take on food plants was that she'd only bother with a small range of things which she knew were superior to their shop-bought equivalents. Unfortunately, this statement was simply an aside, so no examples were given or discussed. Which if anything left me even more bamboozled than I was already – I just couldn't fathom the sense of such an attitude at all. Our planet boasts upward of a quarter of a million species of flowering plants. Whilst some 3,000 species have at one time or another been used by human beings as sources of food, only 150 species are widely cultivated. Already we've narrowed our gastronomic choice down to just 0.06% of known plants, even before, in this temperate part of the world, we're obliged to discount all those staple food plants which won't grow outside of the heat of the tropics. Assuming that, say, half the world's main staples are tropical, we're down to 0.03%. Why on earth use "what's-in-the-shop" comparisons to cut this tiny percentage down even further?

My own choice is to grow as wide a range of edibles on the allotment as I can squeeze into its 16 by 8 yards. It occurs to me that I've never counted everything that I've stuck in the ground, over a single season, which would obviously have been a good idea. But it's probably about 30 species at the outside, not including varieties of the same species. And that's about as "wide" a range as I can manage with the space I have. Given more space, I'd go for more variety. An approach that I'd strongly recommend.

The reason I'd make such a recommendation is that every one of the things you grow, without exception, is far better than shop-bought. Because it's *fresh*. Even in the very best organic greengrocers, the food has been hanging around for a few days, at the least, between being picked and put on sale. But from the garden or plot you can cut this waiting time down to a few hours, and even, with a modicum of advance preparation, down to *seconds*.

The rest of this chapter presents my "Six of the Best" allotment plants, by which is meant six prime examples of the virtue of freshness in food, as well as other qualities, all of which there's no better way to achieve – as we shall see – than by growing them for yourself. Since my normal prolixity has achieved giant proportions in what follows, it might be better to regard each of the six sections as a mini-chapter in its own right. Up to you.

Asparagus *Asparagus officinalis* spp *officinalis*

This is a prince amongst food plants, a perennial, requiring little further work once its roots are established. Few serious vegetable growers can resist its aristocratic allure. Feminist readers may blanch here at my descriptive choice of gender, so its worth pointing out that asparagus, as well as being delicious, is dioecious, males and females being different plants, and that the ones most commonly sold and grown are all male. This is said to encourage a heavier crop, as no energy is lost in seed production towards the end of the season, but it remains instead stored in the rhizomic roots over winter, to enhance the next year's growth.

The ancestor of our cultivated varieties comprises, debatably, a distinct species in its own right. This being *A. prostratus*, a top ranker in Chinese herbal medicine, as the root of the plant is said to purify the lungs and promote well-being and wisdom, helping to overcome such sexual weaknesses as impotence and frigidity.

However, no matter how chained you might be feeling to the dross of experience, hacking and coughing your way through yet another lacklustre sexual performance, you'd be ill-advised to go searching, in post-coital angst, for a curative root or three in the UK countryside. Wild asparagus is vanishingly rare in the UK, being classified as "vulnerable" on the national species' lists, and has recently been given its own Biodiversity Action Plan, to help its few remaining numbers to recover. So, in the unlikely event you should ever see it in its natural habitat, leave it be.

In terms of location, this wild ancestor has somewhat in common with the mysterious ur-kale noted in a previous chapter, being confined to a handful of coastal sites, mostly to the west of the country, in open, well-lit situations, such as sand dunes or cliff ledges. Here, the wild asparagus hangs on – just – showered by salt spray from the ocean, with its stems lying flat to the ground in the face of the sea winds, and with its roots likewise running sideways, at the shallowest of depths beneath the soil surface. Unfortunately, such growth habits mean that it's extremely vulnerable to the scrabbling hands and boots of rock climbers and other tramplers, which is one reason why there's so little of it left.

The main purpose in mentioning these aspects of asparagus in the wild is that they furnish several intriguing clues as to our best treatment of its cultivated cousins. First, here's the kind of bog-standard information on how to grow domesticated asparagus out of one of those back-of-the-seed-packet-type of gardening books.

Whether you've grown from seed for a year, in pots, or have purchased those all-male, one-year old root "crowns", plant out as follows. In the early spring, excavate a foot-wide trench, four to six inches deep. Set the crowns in the bottom of this, 18 inches apart, backfill and gently firm down. Don't eat any of it in this

Asparagus: shortly after the end of cutting, these surviving spears are shooting skywards, prior to bursting into leaves which will feed the plant for the following year, by building up a "crown" of fat roots.

first year. Let it grow up, and apply liquid feed each month. In the autumn, once the foliage has yellowed, cut it down, remove it, and spread two inches of manure as a top dressing. Repeat this top dressing each year.

Nothing intrinsically wrong with such practical advice, although in my view, there's a number of ways – if we choose to recall the growth habits and requirements of the wild ancestor – in which it can be *finessed*. Chief amongst these finer points is that planting out at four to six inches deep, with a further two inches of mulch added every year, means your root crowns can easily end up far too deep down in the soil for the best results. My "all-males" were buried at six inches deep, long before I'd given the matter any independent thought, and grow well enough. But the two most improbably magnificent asparagus plants on my own plot, exactly like their wild relations, lie *shallow*.

At this point, feminist readers can breathe a sigh of relief, because neither of these two plants are the (imputed) "more vigorous" males. This is a pair of females. And since they're both self-sown, neither one owes their success to any skill of mine, having grown of their own accord from chance-fallen seed. In both instances, a careful brushing away of less than an inch of soil, in March or April, reveals a mass of dozens of healthy growing tips; and both plants are, indeed – from their shallow start – fantastically productive. Far more so than any of my deep-planted males. Contrary to my early expectations of their chances of survival, in spite of their lack of protective depth neither appears affected either by winter frost or summer drought. Fingers crossed. So there's a lesson from the wild – plant asparagus as shallow as you dare.

A second point about *A. prostratus* concerns the tendency of its stems to lie down, so as to escape a battering from strong sea breezes. This is, I guess, a useful survival tactic, balancing a need for protection against a contrary need for access to light.

Cultivated asparagus is quite different in its growth habit. In fact, it isn't at all prostrate, having lost the ability to grow sideways altogether. Its growing stems poke straight up to the light, and as they mature, develop a dense mass of foliage which presents a big target to any passing storm. Which means that whole bunches can be knocked over together, in a kind of "domino effect", particularly later in the year when the stems have hardened and become somewhat brittle at the base.

Not that this will necessarily prove fatal to the plant, but since we're talking about finer points here, it's better to anticipate wind damage than to lament its depredations once it's occurred. I always support the stems, once they're fully grown, using pea sticks, though a sensible arrangement of stakes and string will do almost as good a job. Then, let the storm winds howl their worst, they won't keep me awake at night, worrying about snapped-off stems.

Next, there's the whole business of salt, which presents something of a puzzle – given the present state of my own experience – between whether asparagus merely tolerates a high level of salt in its environment, or positively relishes it. This issue does creep in to the gardening books from time to time, such as my sixty-year-old Waverley's *Complete Guide to Home Gardening*.

> It is worth remembering, when asparagus is cultivated, that it grows wild only in districts where the soil is more or less saturated with salt. Salt can be used as a dressing over the beds, and will improve the quality of the crop.

Well… it's an intriguing point. Having been given a free sack of road salt some time ago, for the past two seasons, in early spring, I've sprinked a small handful per square yard onto the asparagus bed. Although to be honest, I'm not sure if it makes a difference or not. "Would merit further exploration", is all I can conclude.

The last two points are fairly minor, but nonetheless worth a mention. The penultimate is linked with our previous one, concerning salt, since salt spray is inimical to the growth of nearly all types of tree. Your apical meristem, which never stops growing, can be sensitive stuff.

Hence those lopsided trees which you may have noticed near to the seashore, with their branches reaching inland as if straining to escape from an unpleasant proximity to the ocean. Such trees are not so much sculpted by the sea breeze, as by the saline mist that it often bears, which stunts or destroys those buds on the seaward side of the tree, leaving only those on the landward side to flourish.

Obviously, if there's enough salt flying around in the air, for long enough, trees won't grow at all. This, I'm readily persuaded, being a crucial reason why *A. prostratus* is only to be found near to the unsheltered shore. With its love, or tolerance, of salt, it can escape from the inland "tree zone", out into the open.

No less so for cultivated asparagus, which simply cannot abide shade. Back on the plot, for example, one corner of my asparagus bed lay for several years in the thin shade of a clump of brambles, which my neighbour had trained up on posts, to form a crude screen. Those two or three crowns I'd planted alongside this screen remained relatively small and spindly affairs. Until, that is, my neighbour retired from the allotments. The day immediately following our fond farewells, I had down the "blasphemous vine", and dug out its poxy root. And ever since, this formerly shady nook has bounced strongly back.

Lastly, a further reason for the rarity of wild asparagus on our shores, apart from the heedless footwear of rock climbers, is that it's regularly assailed by those self-same colourful beetles mentioned in a previous chapter. So this is a reminder that if you do get asparagus beetles on your plants, squash and squash again, without raising your pulse rate, and avoid chemical treatments.

I've banged on at some length in comparing wild with cultivated asparagus, because there are few better examples where making such a comparison is useful for the dedicated vegetable grower. Time now to move to a swift conclusion.

As mentioned, let your asparagus grow up the first year after planting out the crowns, without eating any. In the second spring after planting you might risk eating the odd few spears. In the third year you can enjoy a full crop, from when the spears first appear, which in my part of the world is in the month of May. Keep cutting for about five weeks, and after such time, however reluctantly, give it up and let the following spears grow on. NB: remember that the spears you eat are *spares* – the plant has only a limited number in reserve; carry on for long enough and you'll eat the whole thing to death.

Most crop plants are picked once they've reached maturity, but in the case of asparagus, a large part of its excellence is that it's harvested during the initial stage of growth, being ready within a few days after it first peeps above ground. This happens during that part of the year when there's often little else to eat.

So you may find, like me, that you've reached the dismal stage of rubbing shoots from the last of last year's wrinkly spuds. And find yourself wondering whether you really do relish the wizened remainder of the previous season's stored carrots, or else should chuck them out on the compost. All fairly uninspiring. Then, up pokes the first noble spear, then another and within a week a rush of them. There's nothing, in my experience, that provides a richer promise in the annual round, to boost the gardener's morale.

Asparagus benefits especially from being eaten fresh after cutting, and quite a few of the plotholders up at Fitzroy will pick and eat it straightaway, in its raw state, a practice which I find a touch primitive. Instead, I always cook some up at the plot using the barbecue as a stove, and an old enamel saucepan.

Melt plentiful butter in your old pan with a tablespoon or so of water, maybe a bit of crushed garlic and some dashes of soy sauce. As this warms, quickly pick your spears and rush them into the pan without a second's delay. Steam for a few minutes until the water is driven off and the butter starts to sizzle. Invite anyone you can find over for a taste, which is a true bit of allotment swank, if properly handled from the social perspective.

Asparagus cooked this fresh has the best flavour you can find. Bar none. Shop-bought stuff, with nine-tenths of its sweetness and character lost in the time taken up by road transport and storage, is an insipid echo of your unbeatable home-grown stuff.

Sweetcorn *Zea mays*

A compulsory plant for any vegetable grower interested in the quality of freshness in their own produce. This being a class of gardener which should, of course, include any and all of us who've ever had the audacity to attempt to feed ourselves, rather than relying on third parties. In recent decades, new hybrid seed types have been developed which can bear up well in the erratic heat and sunshine of an average UK summer. But in many respects, in our relatively cool, damp climate – northerly and maritime – so far as sweetcorn is concerned, we're still pushing it somewhat.

No surprise, if you consider that the corn plant, also known as the maize plant, was first domesticated, from about 1500 BC, in the seasonally scorching hot and arid plains of what is now Mexico. The ancient inhabitants of those regions must have been a canny breed, not to say, I should think, quite desperate for a

The speed at which sweetcorn grows is a marvel. At six weeks from seed germination these young plants are already over 18 inches tall.

useable food crop. The wild ancestor of the modern cultivars is *teosinte*, a multi-stemmed, scraggy perennial grass, which puts practically all of its energy into vegetative growth, producing tiny and rock-hard "cobs" less than an inch in length. Making it an unlikely candidate for domestication in the first place.

But, as ever, persistence paid off. After 3,000 years or so, selective breeding had produced something resembling the modern plant, with a "massive" four-inch long cob, the cultivation of which had gradually spread amongst those New World tribes or nations who showed any interest in agriculture, all the way from Hudson's Bay in Canada, down to the southernmost parts of the southern part of the continent.

Sweetcorn itself was eaten by the Iroquois, and a few other native groups, but out of 300 varieties that had been developed before the arrival of Christopher Columbus et al., almost none were "sweet" but were *grain* corn, used much as the Europeans used wheat, barley, etc., i.e. they were principally valued for their starch rather than for their sugar content.

The new European Americans weren't slow to pick up on maize cultivation. Once, that is, they could actually make it grow to begin with. At first, straight off the boat, they tried chucking it about, "broadcasting" the kernels that the natives had supplied, as they were used to doing with more familiar grains. This proved a failure, so they went back to the friendly tribes, who showed them how to plant it properly, with each individual maize seed carefully buried, preferably with a small dead fish placed above it to fertilise the young plants with extra nutrients.

Thus, anyway, was more than one colony of founding fathers spared starvation during the winter months. And whilst corn plants have been improving ever since, modern varieties all still fit into one of the five basic corn categories that have long existed:

Dent   Mostly used for cattle feed. Since the kernels shrink on the cob, each has a *dint* in the top, hence the name.

Flint   The hard stuff. Used for polenta (corn meal) and also for processed-beyond-all-recognition breakfast cereals, such as cornflakes, etc.

Flour   High starch content. For cornflour.

The above three comprise the principle types of grain corn. Then there are:

Pop   The closest to the wild *teosinte*, with strong side shoots or "tillers", producing a dozen or more small cobs. When immature these are eaten whole, as "baby corn", a more immediately splendid Chinese innovation than chomping on wild asparagus roots. The mature kernels are each said to have a small pocket of air trapped inside. This apparently expands when heated, bursting the seed open, the well-known *pop* effect.

Sweet   Least widespread amongst the native farmers, but gaining greatly in popularity and nowadays bred for soft kernels, with a high water and sugar content.

With the exception of the last on this list, none of these will do brilliantly well in the present UK climate, although there are, apparently, certain dent varieties which are just able to make mature seed if grown in the comparatively warm weather along the English and Irish southern coastal belts.

I'm sure we'll stick happily enough with the excellent sweetcorn. It's a dashing plant, fast and furious. This dominant characteristic of its growth must be put down to the influence on its evolution of the seasonally arid environments where its forbears occurred. The whole process of germination, growth, flowering and setting seed might well proceed in a more leisurely way in areas where rainfall tends to be constant throughout the year. But this would not have been so in the plant's desert homelands, alternately either wet (for a short part of the year) or bone dry (for most of it). The kind of place where many plants had to learn – unless they were cacti, which can store water – to complete their lifecycle quickly, in the context of a fixed and finite rainfall season.

Modern corn varieties are bred for a wider range of climates, not just deserts, and many nowadays do best in areas where rainfall is more spread out over the months. Such developments haven't slowed down the plant very much, and the same ancestral environments are the reason, no doubt, for corn's extremely long and powerful roots, which positively rush through the soil after nutrients and moisture. Whilst, to a greater or lesser degree, it's always battling against our sluggish UK weather, if we get a good hot summer sweetcorn can be ready in a little over three months. Which is quite something for such a big *annual* plant.

On the allotment, the kernels are best sown under glass, in deepish pots, in early April if it's been mild, or late April or into May if not. You might also try storing your small bag of potting compost under the same glass for a few weeks before sowing, in the hope of warming it up. This is because corn seed will emphatically *not* germinate in a cold medium, but will soon rot. So if the first green tips don't shoot within a fortnight at most, after sowing, you have to start over again.

Plant out once the young shoots are about three inches high, as three-inch corn will already have at least one six-inch root, or longer, zooming around the base of the pot in search of an escape. If you leave the young plants longer than this, they can get pot bound, which if not fatal will certainly halt them in their tracks.

I invariably sow under the cold frame, as I've never had a result sowing directly into the soil, not even in late May. Though whether this has been entirely due to cold ground or also to some foraging mouse, I've not determined. Mice certainly can learn to love the ripening cobs, as to which, see further below.

Your soil should be open, well drained and manured. As you might expect, sweetcorn hates cold clay and the least amount of waterlogging. If you suffer such horrible soil problems, you'd be better off with something else entirely, a real dogged plodder, like parsnips, until you can knock your ground into fertile shape.

All types of corn are monoecious (contrast asparagus, above), having both male and female flowers on the one plant. The male flower is a spiky and stick-like arrangement, emerging from the top, with the female flowers that form the cob, or cobs, depending on the variety, located at or near leaf nodes further down the stem. Since the plant is primarily air-pollinated, this neat dispersal of parts takes full advantage of the prevailing force of gravity.

Air or wind pollination is the reason we're ever being advised to plant sweetcorn in blocks, 15 to 18 inches apart in each direction, rather than in single rows. As the airborne sperm, the pollen, usually wafts to all points of the compass, I doubt if this really matters. However, as I've only ever planted in blocks, I have no evidence to challenge the probity of such an oft-repeated claim.

Sweetcorn is ready when the cobs look fat enough. This usually coincides with the tassels, which flop out of the top of them, beginning to dry out and turn brown, although this isn't an infallible sign and needs to be confirmed by carefully peeling back the layers of husk, starting from the tassel end. If this reveals plump, yellow kernels running almost to the top of the cob, you're in business. Drop everything else, and spark up the barbecue at once.

Before I move on to cooking, a further word about those pesky mice. In each of the past three seasons, my sweetcorn has come in for attack, as the wee, not-so-timorous beasties have somehow learned to scuttle up the stem for a square go at the cobs.

Mouse damage isn't difficult to detect, as the husk and kernels are gnawed away methodically, in ever-increasing patches, usually starting at the top of the cob, i.e. it's not a question of a bite here and a bite there. It has to be said that mice do a fairly neat and thorough job of destruction. At Fitzroy Park this is a new(ish) problem, so no-one's worked out a solution to it yet. Some of the plotholders I've spoken to mutter grimly about the recent appearance of a veritable plague of mice, which they link to the concomitant *dis*appearance of some of the larger and more aggressive cats that used to stalk the plots. Strawberries and gooseberries are also vanishing fast, mostly before they're even ripe.

Last year I tried wrapping some of the cobs in plastic netting. Hopeless. This coming year, I'm working on a double wrapping of hessian with a mothball between the two layers, as mice are said to flee in disgust from the reek of naphthalene. I've even considered building a cathouse and scrounging a feral cat from the RSPCA, although I've no idea whether it would care to hang around any longer than, say, a three-legged hedgehog. Could be a lot of effort for nothing. Not that this has ever put me off in the past.

Anyway, assuming your cobs have escaped the mice, and are ready to eat, here's how to cook them, and it couldn't be more simple. Forget boiling, and likewise forget using silver foil. Once your barbecue is well alight, break off as many cobs as required, husk and all, and sling onto the coals. Turn frequently for about ten minutes, or for as long as it takes for the outer layers of husk to get thoroughly scorched. By this point, the corn will have been steamed to perfection in its own skin, and you don't need to do anything else except tear off the husk, and tuck in.

All plants are expert converters of sugar to starch, and back again. Sugar being readily water-soluble, it's how nutrients get moved from one part of the plant to another. Starch is basically insoluble, and has more to do with nutrient storage in plant tissues than with transport. There's no more dramatic edible example of this than there is with sweetcorn. As soon as the cob is detached from its parent, its vascular system is broken, and in response, the sugar in it begins to turn automatically into starch.

So in terms of getting the sweetest sweetcorn, timing is the key. Our record at Fitzroy, which involved a chucker at the corn patch, a catcher over at the coals and a timekeeper standing by, is $2^{1}/_{2}$ seconds from off the plant to on the barbecue. A speed and economy of movement beyond the maddest dreams of the most efficient commercial distributor on the planet. Which is why, in fact, money just can't buy the quality of the sweetcorn you've grown for yourself. Its full sweetness and flavour are unsurpassable, and are a revelation. Worth more than gold. In comparison, what's in the shops is hardly worth the cost of the petrol or bus fare needed to go and collect it.

Broad Bean *Vicia fava*

My old bramble-binding neighbour on the plots, at least when I knew him, was a man as short in speech as he was long in years. Even a "good morning" seemed to cost him a deal of energy which he'd rather save for something better. Not that I was ever privy to his opinions but I suspect, if anything, he regarded me as a *parvenu*. Certainly, it was expecting too much of him to reply to my upstart questions, concerning best horticultural practice, on quite the same level of naïve enthusiasm as they were pitched, and I soon realised that he'd rather not answer them at all. Thus I learned to keep quiet and leave him in peace.

He did, however, once prove unexpectedly loquacious on the subject of broad beans. "I'm very partial to a broad bean," he said; adding, enigmatically, "but then, so's everything else..."

I was caught off guard by this garrulous verbal rush and had no time to respond before he wandered off, string in hand, back to his brambles. The first part of his speech was clear enough, expressing a fondness I shared myself, ever since I was knee-high to a grasshopper. One of the reasons I'd always liked broad beans was that they were easier to shell, for a clumsy kid, than peas. So when it came to divvying up the pint-sized household chores, my sister with her more nimble digits always got to pod the peas, and I was allowed the broad beans. Neither of us, of course, ever got the runners, since their preparation required a level of manual dexterity that could cope without mishap with a sharp knife.

Nevertheless, I was quite happy with my broad beans. Peeling the pods apart never failed to fascinate, not the least because they were *lined with fur*, a bizarre luxury that no mere titchy pea pod of my sister's could possibly match. This furry quality seemed to hint at something vaguely animalistic about the beans themselves, once exposed, lying in their snug cushions in rows, a little bit like miniature fat piglets alongside an imaginary mother pig.

Talk to most people nowadays about shelling peas and they'll look at you as if you're describing some embarrassing practice that should have been stamped out in the time of the Druids. Such is the progress we've made in the way of pre-prepared and frozen food. If progress it may be called, not to have a child develop the least practical or tactile sense of where its food comes from.

Anyway, on one subject at least I could agree with my taciturn neighbour. We were both partial to a broad bean. It was the second part of his uncharacteristically overlong speech, about "so's everything else", that had me puzzled, at least for a while. I was still, at the time, johnny-come-lately to the plots, but it didn't take me too long to work it out. My first ever planting of overwintering beans, sown directly into the soil the next November, all germinated and were showing strongly. But having reached an inch or two of growth they were dug up, each with its own tiny excavation, and snipped off in batches until, after about a fortnight, not a single one out of the original 40 that I'd sown was left.

As noted at the start of this chapter, a seed is mostly food storage tissue, intended to feed the emerging plant. Broad bean plants have particularly big seeds, probably the largest you'll ever plant on the average UK allotment (not counting "seed" potatoes, which aren't "seeds" at all), and they are high in protein. What had happened was that by the very act of sticking up through the soil, the shoots had each flagged-up a valuable protein larder buried just beneath. A signal not lost on those pesky pillaging mice, who'd not taken too long to snaffle the lot. They weren't interested in the actual plants, but knew the value of a fat seed.

Any child who has ever been overzealous with their broad bean shelling duties, and out of curiosity has gone on from pods to pick apart a bean or two, to see what they're like inside, will have noticed that under the skin the bean falls lengthways into two matching halves. These are the primary, energy-storing seed leaves known as cotyledons, which kick-start the plant into life before it grows any of its "true" leaves. In terms of the classification of plants, such an inquisitive child has chanced upon the start of a trail which leads to the fundamental distinction of plant types, between monocotyledons (monocots) and dicotyledons

Ripening broad beans can need a lot of protection from marauding birds. Here, the heavy plastic mesh has been drawn back to give a glimpse of these beautifully bulging pods.

(dicots). All flowering plants belong to either one of these two groups, which are morphologically quite distinct.

Monocots have a single leaf as well as a single cotyledon contained within the seed, fibrous root systems which lack a main or tap root, and parallel-veined leaves, which tend to be long and narrow. In terms of human nourishment, the most important monocot family is the Poaceae, or grasses, containing the world's major food grains.

An intriguing feature of grasses and of some of the other monocots is that they grow from the leaf base, where their apical meristem is located, rather than the leaf tip. Some evolutionary biologists have speculated that this development first occurred in response to grazing, since the bitten-off leaf, particularly where grasses are concerned, usually retains its meristem tissue and so can keep on growing, despite being chewed down time and again. Hence, *en passant*, lawns and lawnmowers, football and cricket pitches, golf courses, etc., which would hardly otherwise exist.

This basal-growth feature is shared with our next main monocot group with edible potential, the lily family, Liliaceae, which includes all things of the onion ilk. Then there are many tropical monocot specialities, such as palms, bananas, yams and pineapples. Last but by no means least our asparagus is a monocot.

Dicots differ in their basic morphology with pairs of cotyledons and leaves inside the seed, branched root systems, usually with a tap root, and leaves with branching as opposed to parallel veins, which allows for a much broader leaf shape. Chief in terms of food are our peas and beans, the Fabaceae, or legumes, which are famous for their ability to fix nitrogen from the soil, with the aid of nodules which they build on to their roots to house certain species of bacteria.

As nitrogen is essential for building proteins, this symbiosis means that legumes can live in nitrogen-poor soils, with little loss of protein value when it's time to set their seed. This is one reason why, in subsistence agriculture, many legumes such as soybean and chick pea are valued as grain plants. They provide a storable source of protein in a diet which has very little meat or fish in it.

The Solanaceae is another major dicot family with important food members, such as tomatoes, aubergines and peppers, as well as our ubiquitous spud. Then there's Brassicaceae, cabbages and the like; Rosaceae (the rose family), containing our main temperate tree crops such as apples and pears, plums, cherries, strawberries, etc.; Umbelliferae (carrots); Cucurbitaceae (cucumbers); Chenopodiaceae (beets); and Compositae, the daisy family, with, amongst others, lettuce, Jerusalem artichoke and sunflower.

Back at ground level, or slightly below it, it's notable that our pillaging mouse makes no such fine distinctions. The best way to save your newly sown beans, peas and any other seeds that mice find toothsome, is some adaptation or other of the bottomless plastic bottle that we've seen in an earlier chapter, used to try to keep off slugs. In fact, if you leave the top of the bottle intact, and just remove the lid, besides cutting off the base, there is in spring an added bonus – the "mini-cloche" effect – protecting your new plant from the wind and late frost. But you'll need to watch out for overheating on cloudless days from late March.

Non-gardeners are sometimes curious as to why those daft idiots on the allotments have planted rows of plastic bottles – "as if they're growing bottle trees!". To those of us who know that these self-same bottles are one of the greatest allotment gardening aids since the invention of the fork, all I can say is, should you ever encounter such a reaction, try to be patient in dealing with it. Explain carefully to your scoffing non-gardener exactly what the bottles are used for. Don't be tempted to call them names.

Particularly not "dickhead", "slag heap" or "gut-bucket". These are childish, as well as politically incorrect. And bear in mind that even a simple "bampot", which may sound cute to more southerly ears, can cause offence north of The Cheviots.

"Your Dad's a squatter and your Mum goes like scratchcards out of an East End corner shop" is definitely not the way to go.

Although you might try "quincunx".

Not, I hasten to add, as a term of abuse, but as a planting pattern. A seed at each corner of a square with one in the middle, like the number five on a dice, is the traditional way to set out broad beans, with about nine to twelve inches between the seeds. As they grow, almost all varieties will benefit from support against the wind, and this pattern lends itself quite readily to an arrangement of stakes and string set close around the whole row. If you know how tall your plants are likely to grow, use stakes which will stick up about a foot higher than this, since as well as being assailed at the start of their lifecycle, broad beans are also vulnerable towards the end of it, this time, being ripped apart by birds.

This is such a common occurrence at the Fitzroy Park plots that woe betide anyone who forgets to net their beans. I've seen entire rows shredded in this way, birds being no less crazy for protein than mice. Arguments rage as to whether it's our old pals the wood pigeons and/or jays and/or some other species doing the damage, since no-one has ever got up early enough in the morning to witness it, although my money's on the gut-bucket pigeons. The point being that if you make your support stakes higher than the plants, this facilitates dropping a net over the entire row.

Broad beans are at their best eaten at a fairly young stage, before they get old and leathery-skinned, and the only way to really tell when this is, is by a bit of prudent dismantling of one or two pods. You can also eat the pods whole, as you would runner beans, whilst they're immature. Though why anyone would want to do this, and so miss out on a proper bean feast, I can't fathom.

Thus far I've said nothing on the domestication of the broad bean, and its probably best not to say too much, since it was a very early candidate for cultivation and its wild ancestry is buried deep, back at the dawn of agriculture. Sub-Saharan Africa was probably the home of the ur-broad bean, since "primitive" types are still to be found there. But the plant was highly valued, and had reached from north-western Europe to China, two thousand years and more past.

Where cooking is concerned, most people will steam the beans, to eat as a side dish, or put them in a salad. My own favourite recipe is an ill-remembered version of one cooked by Keith Floyd on TV, years ago, a Spanish dish involving white wine, shallots and *morcilla*, or black pudding. Not one for the faint-hearted.

Like fresh unpodded peas, fresh broad beans in the shops are an afterthought of the nation's frozen food industry. As such, they become available for a ludicrously short season, and are also left to grow too tough. Thus increasing bulk yield for the farmer, but doing nothing to enhance their popularity amongst the eating public. Unlike sweetcorn, I wouldn't say that they aren't worth eating at all. But if you grow and enjoy your own broad beans, whatever might be briefly available in the shops is an irrelevance.

Tomato *Lycopersicon* species

Italy's love affair with the tomato is well known, and its ubiquity in the cuisine of that country has often led to the question being asked: What did the Italians eat before they had tomatoes?

Since the tomato first arrived in Europe in the 1520s and Italian unification didn't take place until the 1860s, the answer is obvious. Italians have *always* eaten tomatoes.

But what about before the Italians? As with corn, so with tomatoes. We have – in the first instance – those same canny ancient Mexicans to thank for this most beautiful of fruits. They'd been cultivating the *xitomatl* for many centuries before the arrival of Don Hernan Cortez and his conquistadores, in 1521, which soon brought a gory end to their civilisation, though not to their tomato, which was dragged back across the Atlantic amongst other minor booty and apparently made its first appearance in European history in 1544, as the Italian "pomi d'oro", the "gold apple". Quite some irony if you consider what Cortez and his gang of cutthroats had gone to Mexico for in the first place, and the rich harvest of death that their gold fever caused amongst the natives. "Pomodoro" is the modern Italian name.

The rest of Europe wasn't quite so quick to catch on, tomato-wise. Indeed, the dour inhabitants of those northerly countries beyond the reach of the more genial Mediterranean zone regarded the plant (including its fruits) as a dangerous poison, chiefly due to its supposed morphological resemblance to *Atropa belladonna*, or deadly nightshade. Can't quite make this out myself, judging by the visual appearance of modern tomato types, although the two plants are related, both being in the family Solanaceae.

In Germany, amongst the scattered villages of its vast and scarce-trod tracts of wild forest, folklore had long regarded the swallowing of nightshade and its equally sinister relatives as an aid to the conjuring forth of werewolves. The poor tomato became guilty, principally by association, although some colourful connection with blood was doubtless also being made. Hence the original German name of "Wolfspfirsich", or "wolf peach". Modern German settles for the more neutral "tomate". Just as well really, because the idea that consuming a tomato would have you growing your own fur coat, and baying at the moon in some remote forest glade, should surely have long ago been consigned to the wheeliebin of history. *Nicht wahr?*

In the eighteenth century, no less a hero than the father of binomial nomenclature, Carl von Linné himself, had a hand in diluting this werewolf myth, by acknowledging in a backhanded fashion that the tomato wasn't poisonous after all. He did so by devising the Latin name *Lycopersicon esculentum*, which translates as "edible wolf peach". It's probably moronic to spell this out completely but here it is:

wolf	–	peach	edible
Lyco	–	*persicon*	*esculentum*

Surely one of the strangest official titles ever bestowed on a plant, and still in use, although many biologists nowadays prefer *L. lycopersicum* for the ordinary tomato and *L. pimpinellifolium* for the cherry type. Why this should be I couldn't say, since I much prefer the Linnean version and haven't bothered to find out the reason for the change.

Werewolves have never gone much in English folklore, perhaps because it's been a long time since we had a patch of forest large enough to hide any of them in. The last *real* English wolf, so I'm informed, was put up by the hounds and shot dead with a crossbow bolt in a field on the outskirts of Runcorn, Cheshire, as far back as 1601. And since, no less than nature itself, mythology requires some physical abode – not so much as a real but as a mental habitat, i.e. a stage on which to play out its various thrills and fears – the small, tamed and coppiced woodlands of medieval England can hardly have comprised convincing werewolf country.

The average peasant who worked in such familiar places, for a dole of firewood or lump of timber to repair the family hovel, could never have been soberly convinced that their local wood was the normal after-hours resort of fabulous, slavering beasts. So – unlike in Germany – the tomato/werewolf connection would have made little sense in this country. In fact, the chances that our average English peasant had an awareness of either fruit or fiend, let alone both, must have been slim.

Thus, as in so many other things, the earliest recorded English views on tomatoes tended to be more snobbish than fierce. "These 'love apples' are eaten abroad", one commentator reportedly wrote, in 1596, "but they are of a rank and stinking savour."

"Love Apples?" Well, since I seem to be able to do no better hereabouts than reinforce the crudest of national stereotypes, it'll come as no shock that this particular name for the tomato was dreamed up by the French. It may have been simply following the sound of the Italian, although the "pomme d'amour" did apparently have an early reputation in France as an aphrodisiac. This must have had more to do with its exotic and less with any genuinely erotic qualities, as tomatoes may be safely eaten with no greater increase in concupiscence than in hirsuteness, as we are all nowadays aware. But such was the tomato's initial strangeness, to the European frame of mind, that it was fairly plastered with such bizarre associations for three centuries or more following its first appearance over here.

In gradually familiarising themselves with this strange new fruit, the Europeans also set about changing its design, through selective breeding. The original American tomatoes were small and rough-skinned, and these initial Old World breeding efforts concentrated on producing a much larger, smoother result. However, other natural traits would also be selected for from time to time, if thought worth pursuing, and eventually a great diversity in cultivars was achieved. So that nowadays all kinds of shapes and colours exist, for our delectation, not only rounded but plum, egg, pear, pepper (as in capsicum) and baroque forms; in shades of chocolate, purple, black, orange, yellow and green, as well as red; plain, striped or mottled; ranging in size from smaller than a cherry to mighty beefsteak bruisers that can weigh over a kilogramme. Flavour and texture are likewise deliciously diverse. Somewhat less so than actual form, according to my crude sense of taste, though I have heard people argue the reverse.

How much of this fantastic diversity – the achievement of many generations' investment of human skill and curiosity – is available "over the counter"? The answer is so obvious as to render the question rhetorical, but I'll give it anyway:

None.

In our shops, tomatoes are standardised things, generically round and red, with the only common nods towards variation being either cherry types or else ordinary types, packed-up whilst still on the truss. In this latter case – pretentiously left "On The Vine" – such tomatoes are sold at an inflated price which has nothing to do with their imputed superiority and everything to do with a fallacy promulgated by professional marketing strategists, and successfully pulled off under the gullible noses of Josie and Joe Public. Not that I'm suggesting for a moment that anyone should get mad over such doleful and snobbish trickery. But the reality is, if you do wish to explore the diverse and delightful world of the tomato, not even the biggest supermarket can possibly meet your needs. The only way to do so is to grow your own.

This is a clear fact, and if you are not already a vegetable grower, you need do no more than flick through one or two catalogues of the leading seed suppliers to see the evidence. For instance, this year Chase Organics has some 50 varieties, from old favourites like Gardener's Delight and Ailsa Craig; exotics such as Purple Calabash, Budai Torpe and Andine Cornue; to real giants like Black Russian (also known as Black Krim) and Potiron Ecarlate. They are all beauties. Simpson's Seeds, which is the principal UK tomato specialist, has available, at the time of writing, a mind-boggling 88 different cultivars, including American favourites such as Amish Paste and the giant Mortgage Lifter; famous standards of the likes of City of Bath, Costoluto Fiorentino and Joie de la Table; as well as many yellows and golds including Jeune Flamme and St Petersburg's Plum Lemon... and so on...

This is just a taste of the choice that's readily – and *only* – available to the home or allotment grower. The point to underline is that each and every tomato in these and similar seed catalogues is acknowledged to have its own distinctive *character*, and so has its own *name*.

This means nothing whatever to a food retailer. So that even the most assiduous consumer, scanning the shelves for something a bit different in the tomato line, can't get far. Try going into the largest food shop in your neighbourhood and asking for a kilo of Black Krim, or of Costoluto Fiorentino. The staff will probably think you've lost your marbles, but whether they do or not, they certainly won't be able to fulfil your requirements. Some anonymous thing, not yet ripped off "The Vine" (until you've paid for it) will probably be the best they can offer. As with many other vegetable types, the true "freedom of choice" lies not in the hands of our giant retail conglomerates, but in the quality of your own patch of earth.

As far as the successful cultivation of tomatoes is concerned, I have of course already outlined my own techniques in a previous chapter, Blue Murder. No need to repeat the same. Except to emphasise once more that growers in the UK will enjoy considerable advantages if they can get the use of a greenhouse, as the hotter conditions therein, compared with out in the open, will help boost plant growth and early ripening, as well as forming a first line of defence against the horrors of blight. Plus, obviously, have as rich a soil as you can possibly make it – as black as your trousers, to use the vulgar phrase.

My last word on cultivation concerns the idea, currently gaining in popularity, that you should sow your tomato seeds by the light of the full moon. This is because there's said to be some mysterious positive correlation between the strength of moonshine at the start of planting and the subsequent strength of your growing plants. In my view it's exactly that. Moooooooonshine.

Each new tomato grower will eventually find out their own favourites. A handful of mine are as follows:

Gardener's Delight. Well named. A bush type, prolifically fruitful. Grows well, matures early in UK climate. Small and sweet, a real bite-the-head-off-jelly-baby type.

Andine Cornue. Pepper-shaped. Dense-fleshed. Mildly sweet. Wastes little on seed production. Hence, excellent for bottling and for sauces, for drying, etc. As to which, see below.

Marmande. Big. Baroque. As it matures, becomes deeply striated between apex and base, as if straining to burst skin. Bulges at seams like fat person in skinny person's clothes. Firm flesh and lively flavour for such an overweight slob.

Ferline. Anyone lusting hungrily for tomato flesh could do worse than get their paws on a ravishing beauty such as this. Succulent. Intense flavour and colour. Juicy, and sweetly suckable. Also said to offer minimal blight resistance. Which is a debateable point.

Black Russian/Black Krim. A big softie – soft and plump. Matures to chocolate. Very thin and tender skin. Piquant flesh, induces slobbering. Gnaw on a whole family of these until fully sated.

OK, it would be fair to say that I can sometimes become overexcited, especially when recalling the flavoursome pleasures which the allotment has provided over seasons past. And it must be further admitted – though I'm not really looking to excuse the above-mentioned feeding frenzy – that tomatoes are just the thing to get overexcited about.

No doubt the scientists at Calgene, the US biotechnology company, would have concurred on this point back in 1991, as they prepared to launch their Flavr Savr tomato upon the world. In a previous chapter, Blue Murder, I mentioned that I didn't care to say too much about genetic modification (GM) of crop plants, and to be honest, I still don't. But the Flavr Savr saga is too good to pass over in silence, because telling its tale casts a light into the perceptual chasm that yawns between tomato-as-home-grown-delight and tomato-as-tool-of-world-domination.

As with many other fruits, ripening in tomatoes is stimulated by their production of ethylene gas, tripping certain enzymes into action which are crucial to attaining maturity. This being the same gas, as we've seen, that kicks off seed germination in the first place.

Turning out tomatoes on the commercial scale involves a number of significant physical problems (irrelevant to the small-scale grower) when it comes to the harvest. These are to do with picking, packing, storage and transport. Ideally, the food industry needs a tough product that can take a great deal of bashing about on conveyor belts, in trucks, etc. without suffering damage. Properly ripe tomatoes aren't such a product. So apart from breeding a tomato type with a skin as tough as a condom – which may not exactly charm the consumer expected to chew on it – the normal way that big commercial producers get around rough-handling problems is to pick and package the fruit at its unripe, green stage before it has time to soften. And then, at an opportune moment during storage, to gas it artificially with ethylene, which kicks off the final reddening, ripening stage.

This works on a practical level, of that there's no doubt, but it can leave the average shop-bought tomato "with the same flavour as a brass doorknob", as more than one foodie has described it. Quite an apposite simile, I should think, although we're left to wonder at the slapstick antics required to educate the palate in making such a comparison.

What the bright guys at Calgene did was to sidestep the whole hard-to-soft component of the ripening issue, by putting a stop to the ethylene-triggered, soft-making gene, the enzyme known as polygalacturonase. They achieved this by identifying the enzyme's genetic make-up and then engineering a gene sequence which expressed its opposite. Introduce this into the plant's DNA and the two parts match and bind, blocking whatever function the natural half serves. Basically, you've thrown a genetic spanner into your plant's natural works, a process which is known in GM jargon by the sublimely appropriate expression, "antisense". If you can succeed in this particular aspect of antisense, not all the ethylene there's ever been can turn your tomato soft. Ripe – yes. Red – yes. Soft – never.

It worked a treat. Calgene's new rock-hard tomato got around all the usual handling issues, and the company set out to conquer the retail world with it. Not short on ambition, its first target was a quick quarter share of the US ripe tomato market. A slice of the action worth, at the time, a cool billion dollars per annum.

The marketing rationale went as follows: not only would growers jump at the chance to switch to a tomato which at one GM stroke got around all their normal problems of logistics and timing but – it was also thought – consumers would likewise snap-up such an ever-crisp product, which they could bring back from the shops and keep chilled in the back of the fridge, unchanged, until the final clap of the bells on Judgement Day. A minor dream of the immortal, in the humble shape of tomatoes.

Not everyone was quite as convinced. In fact, The Flavr Savr became the original "Frankenstein Food" or "Frankenfood", in the campaigns of those who lobbied against its introduction. But what, in the end, sunk the new supertom wasn't so much any action of its enemies as the inaction of its creators. The Calgene boffins had paid far too little attention to all those other factors in the growing of a tomato besides factory handling and shelf life.

In areas that received too much sun, their plants were frazzled. Or in regions with high rainfall they were bashed down and swamped. And/or they keeled over through disease. Seed supplies to the growers they'd lined up were delayed. Above all, yields were pathetic compared with existing non-GM varieties, and both size and quality of the individual fruits were well below par for the ordinary commercial course. The gangs of pickers that the firm employed must have sensed something was wrong. On one infamous occasion they were taken suddenly drunk, and out came their trusty knives. Serious argy-bargy ensued, with teams divided along the usual ethnic fault lines.

Taken together, all of these factors guaranteed that the Flavr Savr was a cast-iron flop.

What lesson might this bizarre parable have to teach, about the good Calgene doctors who first breathed life into their GM beast? Like so many Captains Ahab, they sailed forth to conquer nature, armed with the most dastardly of technical means, but wound up instead lashed to the hump of the very monster that their most profound wish was to possess. And so, were dragged down by it to the nullity of the deeps. Until – make no mistake – Wall Street can once more be persuaded to advance sufficient tens of millions of dollars to fund a new nightmare voyage.

Thus, you might successfully prove that it's possible, by using the most cutting-edge science available, to pervert a tomato plant's attributes at the molecular level. But the real test is, and will always remain, can you get it to grow?

A final topic, apropos *Lycopersicon*, concerns its uses. As diverse and versatile in growing, so in eating it.

Speed onto your plate isn't quite such a priority as it is with things like asparagus and sweetcorn, as tomatoes are excellent at keeping their flavour, whether raw or cooked. And assuming you've picked them off the plant when fully ripe, you'll always have the satisfaction of knowing that what you're eating is authentically ripened "On The Vine", and not simply kept there-on in a green state, before being gassed to maturity in the pur-pose-built chamber of some giant warehouse, in all likelihood located on the far side of the planet.

The Roman salad is always good: tomatoes, red onions and basil, with a plain dressing, generous with the olive oil, and fru-gal with the vinegar which should preferably be on the mild side, not the robust stuff used for drowning fish and chips.

As we've gone back to Italy, I can't not mention *sugo*, the all-purpose tomato sauce to which some Italians I've known were completely addicted. Some time back, I used to stay with a Scottish Italian family who lived in Oban, Argyll. There were four sisters and one brother, all rubbing along quite harmoniously in the same small house, but the one thing none of them could agree on was the perfect *sugo*. There was a big old stove in the living room, like a primitive Aga, which due to their various differences of opinion often had five different tomato pots quietly bubbling away on it. One with an added mite of celery. Another with none, but with mushrooms instead. With garlic. Or else with basil. And so on. The brother's one was the version never to be stirred, since he was convinced that the least such disturbance would ruin it.

I once suggested they try adding some carrot, which produced an effect amongst them not unlike the response expressed in the old Bateman cartoon, when the new man passed the crack-pipe the wrong way around the table. "Aghast" can barely begin to describe it, and for a few minutes I thought I'd be spending the rest of my trip sleeping on the beach. No joke in Oban, at any time of year.

So, once bitten and all that, here's a basic *sugo* recipe, and it could hardly be simpler to make:

Basic *sugo*
Ingredients (Serves several)
3 lb of tomatoes, skinned and chopped
1 chopped onion

¼ tsp of salt
¼ tsp pepper
1 tbsp basil
2 bay leaves
¼ tsp sugar
4 oz mushrooms, sliced

Method
Sauté the chopped onion in olive oil. Put the remaining ingredients into a large pan, and add the sautéed onion. Cover and simmer for 2 hours, stirring occasionally. Serve with just about everything.

A disclaimer addressed to any proper Italian person who might read this recipe and be outraged by it: *Se tu pensi che questa ricetta sia un travestimento di quella autentica del sugo data a te dalle tua venerabile bisnonna, tiene a mente che quella che ho fatto é stato semplicemente copiarta e te lo passo con nessun commento riguardo la sua qualita. Non rompermi le palle.*

When it comes to simply preserving tomatoes, I feel somewhat on safer ground, having worked out over the years a number of basic methods which mean that I can extend an autumn crop to all the year round.

Drying A dense tomato is required; and as mentioned, Andine Cornue suits the purpose as well as any you can grow outdoors in this country. Slice lengthways once or twice and scoop out the seeds and accompanying jelly. Save this to sling into the juice pot.

Place your sliced lengths onto a wire rack – something with a mesh size of a centimetre or two is ideal – and put this into the oven. Don't use a baking tray as the tomatoes will either stick to it or retain too much water, and if you put them straight onto the oven shelves they'll just drop through as they shrink.

Dry the slices in the oven, set to its lowest setting, with the door propped open half an inch. NB: it's quite difficult to *dry* as opposed to *cook* tomatoes treated in this fashion. Keep the oven at its lowest and if necessary dry your fruit in several stages, turning the oven off in between to let it cool down. Watch out for burning towards the last: the dried tomatoes are done when still just bendy, rather than brittle. Remember that this may take quite some time, maybe up to 12 hours, maybe even longer than that.

A bit of trial and error will sort out any teething problems, and the easiest thing to do with your dried tomatoes once they're done is to freeze them. Failing that, consult your nearest venerable Italian great-grandmother for a fabulous dunking-in-olive-oil recipe.

Juice Fill a large pot with coarsely chopped tomatoes, a bit of salt and just enough water to stop them sticking to the base once you turn on the heat. Set your pot on the hob and start it off on a low heat, stirring often. Turn the heat up by small increments once the contents start to disintegrate. Boil gently for about 20 minutes, occasionally mushing with a potato masher. As soon as your tomatoes have all turned to an excellent gloop, switch off the heat and let cool. Then pass your gloop through a blender, then through a sieve with a mesh size small enough to stop the pips passing through, using the back of a spoon to press it down. Stir thoroughly, bottle and freeze. This is streets ahead of the commercial stuff and makes a splendid Bloody Mary.

Bottling Thanks to a suggestion originally made by Oz, the Turkish food scientist that we met some time ago, I always bottle tomatoes in tomato juice, for a richer result, rather than plain water. Slice your tomatoes to about a finger thick and pack as tightly as possible into 0.75 litre spring-top kilner jars (better known these days under the "Le Parfait" brand name). Fill up the remaining space with juice, plus any herbs etc. you may desire, and give the jars a decent shake and a poke to get rid of air bubbles.

When preserving vegetables in this way, *always* cook them in a pressure cooker, as the higher temperatures attainable inside it with its lid clamped on, being greater than 100°C, will kill off any tenacious bacteria that may just survive cooking at room pressure, where the boiling point may be reached at slightly under 100°C (especially if you live halfway up a mountain).

A large pressure cooker will do four 0.75 litre jars together. Once you've filled them, clip the glass tops, with their *new* rubber gaskets, shut. The main advantage of these spring-clip types is that they're self-sealing. During cooking, excess air is allowed to escape but following it, as everything cools, the jars seal themselves by creating a vacuum, so their contents remain sterile until you break the seal. (To do this, pull out the tab on the gasket until it's stretched enough so that the air can get inside. You'll probably need to use a pair of pliers, unless your grip is truly vice-like.)

Before you put them in the cooker, wrap each jar in cloth to stop them rattling about as they cook. If you've got big feet, the bottom half of an old sock does the job perfectly. Fill the space between the jars with water, to the same level as their contents.

Clamp on the lid and heat up slowly, to give time for everything to warm through. Allow 30 to 40 minutes for this, and once your pressure cooker is hissing merrily, switch over the valve from open to the low pressure setting – this usually means five pounds per square inch. Turn up the heat a fraction, and once the requisite pressure is reached, cook for a full ten minutes. After this, turn off the heat, and leave a further ten minutes before venting off the steam, then leave to cool completely.

Tomatoes thus bottled will easily keep for a twelve-month or longer. So you can easily pop open a jar or two at any time of year for the making of a top-grade *sugo*, or whatever other recipe or sauce requires your own best quality, multifarious, sun-ripened, ungassed and unmodified wolf peaches.

Wheat *Triticum aestivum vulgare*

Despite all gastronomic evidence to the contrary, we still have hanging on in our language the expression "the greatest thing since sliced bread". I last overheard this phrase being used several months ago, whilst sitting in The Artillery Arms, that famous traditional hostelry found in Bunhill Row, EC1. Two cunning businessmen were updating strategy over a modest drink: "but what about Malcolm?" said one, to which his colleague replied, "don't you worry about Malcolm, Malcolm really likes you, he thinks you're the greatest thing since sliced bread."

Which reminded me of a long-cherished strategy of my own, to write a science fiction novel set in the not-too-distant future, on a planet very much like the one to which we're all currently bent on laying waste. The whole purpose being to drop in somewhere the line "the greatest thing since *the abolition* of sliced bread".

Why be so churlish on this point, you may well ask? After all, the average UK sliced loaf at least has the virtue of cheapness, which considered on its own is no bad thing whatever, because there are very many people with very little money to spend who rely on it every day, wherewith to stuff themselves.

But the churl in me steps forward when I attempt to limn any other of such bread's virtues, because there aren't any. What we're dealing with is an insipid and denatured lump of putty, a pallid echo of a loaf that doesn't even have a proper crust, just a brownish soft rind that might have been sprayed on, and an eerily smooth and even-textured crumb, like something used for repairing holes in walls. As for its stodge or stuffing function, i.e., repairing holes in empty stomachs, I should think that if we could attain the same sense of repletion by stuffing our insides with "bathroom tissue", we may as well would.

There's also the long list of E-numbers and other extras that the makers of our modern bread put into the mix, including some real dingy ingredients like soya, chalk, etc. So that their end-product turns out riddled with additives, a rival to the more cost-effective type of Taiwanese pot-noodle, which at least has the benefit of a plethora of spicy flavours rather than being *utterly bland*.

As a keen bread consumer – long since tired of the dire industrialised stuff that's passed off as the staff of twenty-first-century British life – back in 2002, I decided to grow my own wheat, and make my own bread, and damn the big bad bread bakers. At first,

I thought I'd just grow the odd clump here and there to fill in occasional gaps on the plot. But whilst pondering the idea, came across the following passage in Charles Darwin's *On the Origin of Species*, concerning natural mechanisms which check population growth amongst plants and animals:

> … a large stock of individuals of the same species, relatively to the numbers of its enemies, is absolutely necessary for its preservation. Thus we can easily raise plenty of corn and rape-seed, &c., in our fields, because the seeds are in great excess compared with the number of birds which feed on them; nor can the birds, though having a superabundance of food at this one season, increase in number proportionally to the supply of seed, as their numbers are checked during winter: but any one who has tried, knows how troublesome it is to get seed from a few wheat or other such plants in a garden; I have in this case lost every single seed.

With these words from the wisest of the wise, the message concerning wheat was clear – don't grow a little bit because the birds will have it.

So, I needed to act large. Vast. With no such spare acreage on my own plot I went back, cap in hand, to Fiona MacKie on Plot 6. Fiona, as I hope you may recall, had lent me her plot a year or so previously for the spud experiment described in the Comfrey Dumpty chapter, whilst she spent the summer in India, torching stuff on the banks of the Holy Ganges.

Déjà vu time. "Can I borrow your plot later this year for a wheat experiment?" I asked, somewhat brazenly. "You're very welcome," came Fiona's immediate response, "I'm going off to Egypt, anyway. Usual rules about the parterre. OK?". Once more she waved a hand in its general direction and I could see that progress had certainly been made, since the mound of nettle-grown rubble now wore a weighted sheet of blue polythene, which had been put down for some time and was breaking up in the sun.

Thus it was that I set myself up as a "prairie farmer", and once again found myself clearing Fiona's plot of rough grass and other weeds, to the extent on this occasion of a square, five metres by five. For an escapade in wheat.

Next, I bought six small packets of wheat seed which weighed in total 600 grammes. Rather than "broadcast" this in the ancient way I sowed it fairly thin, in rows about 30 centimetres or a foot apart, 40 grammes per five metre row. The whole point of this being to allow for hoeing-off weeds in between. Since this was a "winter wheat" I sowed it in September, so it would sprout up, sit over the cold months then get away next spring.

It could hardly have worked better. For one thing, it turned out to be slug-proof. This was partly due to timing, as winter wheat gets established during the autumn season, when slug activity slumps, and also due to the fact that being a grass species it has a naturally high carbon-to-nitrogen ratio, so comes very low down on the average gastropod's hit list. And it faced little weed competition, again for timing reasons: having crept up in slow increments for the first months of its life, it rushed away in the spring, as expected, before much else had even woken up. Weeding between the rows thus became a cinch – barely needful at all.

One last point about the biology of green plants I need to mention is that botanists, who seem ever fond of neat binary classifications (dicot/monocot, and the like), often divide crop plants into determinate and indeterminate forms. Determinate plants are those in which new meristem growth ceases with flowering, so that a single phase of seed production comprises their final act. Indeterminate ones carry on producing fresh stems and buds alongside their flowers. Weather permitting, they'll continue making new seed many times over.

Wheat is most determinedly determinate. Its lifecycle is straightforward, plain to see, as it germinates, grows grassy leaves, shoots up high flowering stems, sets abundant seed and then emphatically dies.

Perhaps that's what we find so wonderful about wheat. There's something profoundly pleasurable about checking on its progress as it grows and sets its upright, fruitful heads, to fade from green to a beautiful gold, rippling – as it really does – in the breeze. Who amongst us genuinely hates to see a field of ripe grain? Or even a patch? More than one plotholder at Fitzroy has since told me they were tickled pink by the sight of my tiny, 25 square metre "prairie". Since this feedback was at no time requested, but freely volunteered, I don't think they were just being polite.

However, I'm convinced that simple determinacy explains only a fraction of wheat's allure, and I wonder if our enthusiasm for it isn't another of those features of experience surviving from the past through being hard-wired into the human mind, like a love of prospects and refuges, or cosy hovels, as we've already seen, or of fire, come to think of it. All such things are impressed into the common psyche, assuming such a thing exists, by the long, long usage of our ancestors, stretching back "for time out of mind".

Starting in the Near East, 12,000 and more years ago, the local habit of gathering seed from wild wheat types like Einkorn and Emmer gradually evolved – through practices such as destruction of competing plants and selection of the best grain – into full-on horticulture. Wheat growing was therefore the foundation stone of Eurasian farming, without which it's unlikely the rest of the agricultural edifice, such as animal husbandry, woodland clearance and permanent settlement, would ever have been built.

Archaeologists have often speculated on the reasons why the human species ever gave up the freewheeling life of the hunter/gatherer for the hard graft of the farmer. Well, we do value abundance, no less than our ancestors did, and once they'd realised that their own ingenuity and effort could produce a regular surplus, they clearly thought the game worth the candle.

So it was with my own wheat project, as least as far as growing was concerned – no trouble at all – likewise the harvest, an hour's work with a sickle, and another hour to tie the cut stems into sheaves, or *stooks*. It was only then that the problems began, as processing the grain proved far harder than growing or harvesting it.

I knew enough to realise that in separating wheat from straw I'd need to "thresh" my stooks and that this would require a "flail". Not the sort of item stocked by B&Q. Never fear, I'd discovered a reference telling me how to make one, in an old anthology of rural tales. A flail, I read, being a simple affair, a tough stick of ash attached to another of holly, hard as flint, with a rotating hinge between the two called a capel, made out of a ram's horn boiled and bent into a circle with a loop, burnt through with a hot iron to fit an attaching thong made out of a cured eelskin and linked with another short loop, this time of rawhide pinned with a blackthorn peg. Fine. No problem…

…although. Sometimes, on the odd occasion, we do need to cut a corner or two, and lacking ram's horns, rawhide, eels and the like I instead joined up my ash and holly sticks with parts of my old worn-out leather belt. As strong a hinge as I could make at short notice.

Armed with this device, I set one of my wheat stooks down on a piece of clean tarpaulin laid on top of the parterre. Having tossed out a few nettles and half-bricks, it was the levellest place around. I then proceeded to give the head of the stook a good thrashing – "no work for a fool", as my old anthology had said.

I swung the ash handle high and brought the flailing holly end down upon the stook with main force. Whack! And again – whack! And again – wha… what? I looked up, just in time to view the arc of declivity of a perfect parabola, drawn through the air by my spinning holly stick as it broke free from the perished belt, to land with a small crash into a rhubarb bed five plots away. Total hinge failure on third whack, and luckily for me there was no-one else about, because I might've accidentally brained them by flying holly. Quite apart from embarrassing myself.

Eventually, and it *was* eventually, I bashed the grain out using the retrieved holly end as a primitive hammer, with a big log of wood as a kind of anvil. It took for ever. "No work for a fool." By the time I was finished I really *was* finished, and all I could do was lie down in the grass and mutter quietly to myself, as the sun set.

The total weight, or *yield*, of that wheat from my five by five metres, came out at 13.235 kilogrammes in all, an amazing increase over a mere 600 grammes of seed, so it seems to me.

Next up, to get it ground into flour. But before moving on to this I need to stand back for a minute for a potted plot history. National as opposed to local, this time around.

Why do we have allotments at all? I don't want to dig too deep here, but, if you ask people about what they think on the topic, far and away the commonest reply, if you can elicit any answer whatsoever, is that allotments exist because of Adolf Hitler, i.e., the country under siege, with U-Boats sinking most of our food imports, meaning doughty urban gardeners putting on tin hats to "Dig for Victory" on bomb sites, ducking down amongst the turnips whenever doodlebugs droned overhead.

Well of course I'm not saying this didn't happen, but it all began a bit earlier, in a time back beyond the reach of current folk-memory (which generally stretches back just two or three generations), and in a country that's only patrolled nowadays by lonely historians. The key word uncovered by their researches being "enclosure", which meant exactly that: fencing out from the land the same common public who'd previously had tillage and pasturage access to it. Somewhere to grow basic foods and/or to fatten their cow or pig. These rights were hijacked, permanently, with little or no compensation.

Almost invariably, enclosure was carried out for the purpose of enriching the local bigwigs, at the expense of everyone else, with a battery of specious arguments being advanced to cover the fact that their real motive was greed. The dispossessed commoners weren't always left quite bereft, since many of them stayed put and became labourers for that same gentleman-farmer who'd taken away their access to the land. But the downside was that they were paid only a pittance, and with the loss of their common rights they had also lost whatever margin of economic independence in the way of grain, vegetables, dairy products or bacon, which these rights had once given them.

All over England, the spread of enclosure gathered pace throughout the eighteenth century and reached its highest pitch of intensity during the first half of the nineteenth.

At the same time, industrial advance was combining with economic and technical changes to agriculture itself. The impacts of this were various, and often piecemeal, but over time they triggered huge changes to the old patterns of rural life. One important such change being the increase in arable in many districts, and less rearing of animals. This meant erratic, seasonal wages, through the course of an average year, for very many a poor labourer who'd previously had regular work in looking after the farmer's cattle, which in contrast to only growing grain, had provided an all-year-round job.

Such persons often had to throw themselves on the doubtful mercy of "parish poor relief" for large parts of the year, i.e. were seasonally unemployed. And in a downward cycle that benefited nobody at all, those unemployed labourers who could find nothing profitable to do had to rely on the taxes paid by the local gentry to keep them from starvation, whilst those same gentry were obliged to reduce whatever wages they still needed to pay out even further, to cover their tax bills. Etc., etc.

Following the end of the Napoleonic Wars in 1815, wheat, eggs and other cheap imports, from France and elsewhere, were quickly resumed, contributing to a long-term national slump in prices, which further stretched the finances of the gentleman-farmer. His profits on some of those same goods were cut to the bone without, apparently, the cheaper imports doing anything to relieve the increasing dereliction of many of his casual employees.

The final straw that broke such employees' backs was the introduction of a new type of mechanical flail known as the threshing machine. This could do the work of a very large number of men, who despite their skills were only equipped with muscle power and their outmoded ash-and-holly sticks. No contest. Once the threshing machine had arrived their poverty duly increased, as the need for their labour vanished. This eventually bit down so hard on them that they rebelled.

By 1831, acts of arson such as barn-burning, and the destruction of threshing machines, had become commonplace. The land was in uproar and riot, particularly in those mainly arable counties of the south and east, where the redundancy that followed mechanisation had most sharply been felt. Here, the arch-rebel, one Captain Swing, stalked the country, firing off his notorious letters, to the gentry in general, and to threshing-machine owners in particular.

Here's a sample, by no means the most bloodthirsty, of what was threatened to those obstinate landowners who failed to help the local poor:

> Sir
> This to inform you what you have to undergo jentelmen if providing you Dont pull down your messhenes and rise the poor mens wages the maried men give tow and six pence a day the singel tow shilings or we will burn down your barns and you in them this is the last notis
> from Swing

Needless to say, this sort of thing was ill-received by the powerful class of people to whom it was addressed. Captain Swing's very elusiveness was, presumably, the cause of much of the fear and loathing aimed in his direction. Wherever that direction might be, no-one knew. The fact that he didn't actually exist was no impediment to those magistrates and other jentelmen who at the time hunted him, or at least his semblance, up hill and down dale. But most of them must have realised they were chasing a shadow and that it was, ultimately, one cast by their own complacency.

As reported by one Wiltshire labourer, suspected of riot: "We don't want to do any mischief, but we want that poor children when they go to bed should have a belly full of tatoes instead of crying with half a belly full."

Not too much to ask, really. And as a great chorus of pleas as pitiful as this one rose through the land, allotments were invented to answer them, with provision of allotment land speeding up hugely in the riotous Captain's wake. No doubt the landowners who gave up a few miserable acres of their most marginal land for the purpose had mixed reasons for doing so. Moved by threat, by compassion, by both. But whatever their reasoning, Swing's grim promise of mayhem and revenge had woken everybody up to the serious advance of rural destitution, and a new consensus amongst the wealthy regarding provision of land for the poor was one of the riots' principal effects.

Thus, it became widely accepted that providing allotments would extend hope to the poor, by re-establishing a measure of economic independence which their irregular earnings were insufficient to supply. And that this would, in turn, not only restore their pride, finances and morals (not necessarily in that order), but also could achieve such laudable ends at little outlay of cash, which in any case would be more than offset through the lowering of taxes paid for poor relief, once the system was up and running.

Many of these early rural allotments were girt about with peculiar regulations. Weekly religious observance was often a requirement – no church, no plot. In spite of such qualifications, in many areas the allotment system certainly took off. By their own efforts, labourers who qualified could bring about a real improvement in their standard of living, and could even think once more of acquiring the cow, or pig – maybe even both at once – that their lost rights of common had once provided.

What did this new breed of rural allotment holders prefer to grow on their plots? Potatoes had by now become the most usual crop, but this was as much out of necessity as of choice, since the "tatoe" was often regarded (as in the Wiltshire labourer's quote, above) as a low-grade famine food.

The crop-of-choice for many plotholders was their *real* favourite, which was wheat. And through much of what remained of the nineteenth century, wheat always ran a close second to spuds as the commonest allotment crop.

Strange to say, wheat yields from such plots were often higher than those achieved by the professional farmer, because plotholders proved so assiduous in scraping dung off the roads, which could be plentiful, especially after a big drove of cattle had passed through the neighbourhood.

A crucial reason for this love of wheat held by the common man was, I should think, the fact that in most areas of the country it was still quite easy to get your personal grain supply ground into flour. You'd simply pay a visit to the nearest miller, that legendarily bumptious and solitary local broker/dealer, who for an extortionate share of your product would grind it up for you.

The miller certainly often had a selfish and cheese-paring reputation, and it's intriguing to wonder whether, and to what extent, his smaller clients found themselves fleeced. Most of them, at best, would have been semi-literate and semi-numerate. If the Swing letter quoted above is anything to go by, it's clear that not even the mysterious Captain himself amounted to much as a scholar.

If you've ever read such old memoirs as Flora Thompson's *Lark Rise to Candleford*, or George Ewart Evans's *Ask the Fellows Who Cut the Hay*, one of the most striking things about the world they depict is that even when things were going their way, life for most nineteenth- and early twentieth-century rural villagers was a matter of many friends, and hardly any money. For the miller, of course, the situation was usually the reverse. Hence, in the old folk song, the bleak self-sufficiency of *The Jolly Miller of Dee*, which jogs along in some such version as this:

> There lived a jolly miller once
> Beside the river Dee.
> He worked and sang from dawn till dark,
> No bird more blithe than he.
> And this the burden of his song
> Forever used to be:
> "I care for nobody, no not I,
> And nobody cares for me.

> I live for my mill, which is for me
> As both of child and wife.
> I would not give this living up,
> For any other life.
> And whilst no lawyer nor doctor none
> Yet had two pence from me.
> I care for nobody, no not I,
> And nobody cares for me."

Whoever first scrawled this brilliantly dark doggerel seems to have regarded personal isolation as a familiar (not to say dominant) figure, in the pattern of daily existence. Appen they mun be one o' they newly fangled existentialists.

However, what ever might have been the true level of philosophical gregariousness, or of honesty, of millers past and gone, I soon found out that history had caught me napping. Having grown my own grain, I discovered that it's no longer an option to get it ground into flour, somewhere just around the corner.

The remaining old wind and water mills which used to do the job are often preserved today as expensive des. res. monuments, but I'll wager there's not a dozen in the entire country can still do their original job of grinding corn. Guess there's just not the demand for it these days.

I made a few long-distance enquiries of modern millers, by telephone. But when I mentioned I'd only got 13.235 kilos of grain to grind, the unbearable lightness of its weight met with the deepest incredulity imaginable:

"You're *beyond* joking – we can lose more than that off the chute in *ten seconds…*"

"This is one of those spoof calls sir, isn't it? Your voice sounds just like that Chris Tarrant's…"

"No, you plank! I'm not an actual miller, I run a Venetian-blind cleaning business. '*Miller' is my surname*, not my *occupation*!"

For a brief while I toyed with the idea of acquiring some suitable lumps of rock and turning stone carver, to make my own handmill or *quern*, having seen examples of various ancient types, both "saddle" and "rotary", in archaeological books. In fact, I had once had a go on a rotary quern (for all of *ten seconds*), which was set up as part of an interactive exhibit on ancient farming in the Barbican House Museum at Lewes, Sussex. However, as soon as I thought "quern" I thought "flail", and reminded of that particular recent disaster, decided not to bother.

Nothing else for it. I was stuck, and to get out from under a creeping desperation, emptied my piggy-bank of its bottom dollar, to buy a brand new kitchen-scale electric mill from America. Unlike here, there still is in the US a recognisable tradition of home-grown wheat. Also in Australia, so I discovered, since the model I was eventually sent was the one wired for down-under domestic voltages which, unlike American ones, are the same as those used in the UK. The makers also threw in a top-of-the-range breadmaking machine with 25% off.

In spite of this generous discount, I daren't even whisper how much these two items set me back. And can hardly yet bear to mention the skulduggery of that gang of criminals extortionists, masquerading as H.M. Customs & Excise, who brazenly solicited me for a bribe – to the tune of a further £48.50 – before I could collect my goods. A payment which they described, using the debased, guttural language of terminal cynicism, as "import duty". *Deranged* economics – my finances have scarcely recovered even today.

I'll trouble you with few details of my bread-making efforts, because in spite of my two excellent machines, my home-sown, grown and ground grain failed time again to rise to the occasion. Every loaf turned out like a brick: certainly as heavy, almost as dense and scarcely more palatable. Our forebears must have been a tough crowd indeed to survive on such ponderable matter, as I did for almost a year, until all my grain was used up, along with most of my teeth.

I tracked down the reason for my brick-like bread, eventually, in Elizabeth David's *English Bread and Yeast Cookery*. Nothing wrong at all with my two fine Australo-American machines, nor, I'm glad to say, with my basic wheat growing method.

Basically, the heavy cause was climate, because the doubtful British summer isn't up to producing in the grain the high levels of nitrogenous *gluten*, which is what gives the flour its elastic powers, to rise in the dough and stay that way during baking, and so produce a light loaf. Which is what modern tastes, including I'm sorry to say my own, prefer. Despite the odd fine day, or odder still, fine fortnight, the UK just isn't hot enough, or dry enough, for long enough, to produce sufficiently glutinous grain. Knowing which, in a moment of mad heresy, almost makes a body long for global warming.

Hohoho. Not really…

I began this section with some searingly critical remarks about the British sliced loaf, and what with all the joys and tribulations of my single attempt at raising wheat, still can't make up my mind whether I should eat those opening words or not. An 800-gramme loaf of thick-sliced white stodge, at the time of writing this, cost me 49 pence. I was quite happy to spend this nugatory amount in bread money, just to remind myself of the true nature of the stuff. 49 pence. Take it or leave it.

By the way, if you do grow your own wheat, and find you can't get it ground without risking bankruptcy, or else discover that the bread you get out of it doesn't quite fit the bill, bear in mind there's always frumenty. Back in the Middle Ages this was the original pauper's gruel, though it has been jazzed up of late, as in the following recipe:

A modern frumenty
Ingredients (Serves 4)
8 oz whole grain wheat
$\frac{1}{2}$ pint water
$1\frac{1}{2}$ pints milk
1 oz currants
1 oz sultanas

1 oz ground almonds
2 large beaten egg yolks
2 oz light brown sugar
¼ pint rum

Method

Soak the currants and the sultanas in the rum for at least two hours before cooking.

Put the water, wheat and half the milk in a saucepan and bring this to the boil, reduce the heat and simmer for 25 minutes. Then cover it, and let it stand for 15 minutes.

Add the ground almonds, the rest of the milk and the rum-soaked fruit (and the rum) to the wheat mixture. Bring to the boil again. As soon as this happens, lower the heat and add the egg yolks, stir in the sugar, then remove from the heat without letting it boil again. Leave to stand for a few minutes, then serve.

If it tastes horrible, add some more sugar or even better, slide some more rum under it. But be careful not to overdo this last bit or else, like the Mayor of Casterbridge in Hardy's novel, you may find yourself flogging your loved ones to a passing seaman.

Karl Marx *Carolus marxius*

Highgate Cemetery, N6, is a necropolis of two halves, divided straight down the centre, north to south, by the public road known as Swains Lane. Formerly Swines Lane.

In tomb terms, the western half is the more elaborate. It even boasts its own set of catacombs. Unfortunately, it's been closed to casual public scrutiny for quite some time and is accessible only by guided tour. This being a precautionary injunction, as the western side, even today, is known to be haunted by a school of Transylvanian vampire zombies, itching to recruit new members to its ranks by bushwhacking the lone visitor, on an opportunistic basis. In other words, not the kind of place you'd expect to find the mortal remains of the Father of Modern Socialism. Nor will you. Because Karl Marx, who was born in 1818 and found peace in 1883, is buried, alongside a hundred thousand or so fellow Victorians of lesser eminence, in the other – eastern – half.

His headstone, surmounted by a huge bronze bust of the man himself, is still quite a tourist attraction, once reputed to be the most frequently vandalised monument in all London. Though nowadays it's less often attacked, and is also much less a goal of genuine pilgrimage than it used to be, when the communism that Marx's political writings inspired was still a going concern.

Marx's side of the boneyard is somewhat more user-friendly than the limited access western half, and is open to the public without the same need for safety in numbers. However, if you ever go there, you'll still need to run the gauntlet raised by the efficiently ferocious breed of female dragon that guards the entrance. As you enter through the eastern portal of heavy, creaking iron, try if you can to keep your cool, as one or more of these vivid, livid creatures lunges towards you from out of their lair, which is just inside the gates to the left, the shed-like tomb of polished pink Aberdeenshire granite, marked Strathcona and Mount Royal. Be warned, the intensity of their fury is undiminished by the fact that most are long past pensionable age. They won't stand for any nonsense.

To swell the dragons' hoard, their principal hunger appears to be for nothing more ghastly than cash, although they also take a vigorously interrogative interest in any visitor whose baggage might conceal a camera, meaning a photography permit. So they can charge extra.

The best defensive tactic is to reveal not the least tremor of fear. And if you can stoop to it, a show of grovelling obeisance – of the sort normally reserved by humbler folk for chance encounters with Royalty – can sometimes quench their fiery breath.

It may well be that the purpose of these dragon-guards isn't to collect entrance fees at all, but to dissuade the faint of heart from entering. However, if you can get past them, the cemetery is well worth a look, and not simply because Karl Marx happens to be permanently resident. The Victorian Age was well-supplied with expert stonemasons, and many thousands of examples of their best work are to be found here. All sizes and shapes, since the iconography of death in those days was nothing if not eclectic.

Wandering the network of paths between the headstones we find, amongst other rocky symbols of mortality: many draped and undraped urns; likewise broken and unbroken columns, these often garlanded with stone foliage; anchors, and chains similarly bust; obelisks; and then angels – rueful, triumphant or reclining – also *putti*; scrolls and open books; the occasional pyramid, lamb, wolf or bird; here, a pilgrim ascends, and there, a curious female figure re-enacts Bernini's *The Ecstasy of Saint Teresa*. Crosses were also very popular, as you'd expect, and the cemetery holds a fine range: plain, celtic, maltese, of lorraine, fitchy, rustic, recumbent or combining two or more such styles and again, often garlanded, wreathed or both; draped with folds of cloth or with angels; or with children; or even depicting the agony of Jesus Christ himself.

All packed in tight, with scarcely a hand's-breadth between, and many of huge height, although I hesitate to say phallic, which seems somewhat blasphemous. Also somewhat glib. But whatever our response might be, gazing at this petrified forest of monumental masonry, those who made it are no longer here to explain what they meant by it.

One thing that's quite clear, is that it's a forest within a forest. Like all the other major London cemeteries of the time, Highgate was founded as a speculative venture, and was expected to pay for itself without subsidy, through its sale of last resting places. The problem the speculators eventually faced was that as most of these places were filled, so the funds began to dry up, and as the nineteenth century turned into the twentieth, and several generations passed away, there was no longer enough money to pay for a full complement of gardeners.

The eventual result being a forest of ash trees (*Fraxinus excelsior*), which sprang up unchecked amongst the largely paid for and forgotten tombs. The astounding vigour of these trees is a tribute, both to the sticky fertility of the London clay, and no less so to the vast numbers of the dead, their accounts settled for eternity, who lie beneath. The reason being that the huge quantities of calcium, phosphorus, etc., supplied by the decaying bones of these departed – crammed together like sardines – boost the rate of tree growth amazingly, way above the levels you'd expect in an ordinary wood.

A further such boost was inadvertently supplied some time back in the 1970s, when funds were at last found to clear the trees and open out the space. Whoever organised this felling clearly had no idea that the ash is one of our more successful coppice species. Chop it down but leave its roots intact, and far from killing you'll only encourage it. Within a few years it'll have driven up half a dozen new trunks where only one had been before. Keep chopping and you risk immortalising it: there are coppiced ash trees in some Essex and Suffolk woods that have lived for over a thousand years.

The results of the 1970s felling are still visible in much of the cemetery today. A dense growth of over-mature ash poles, elegant grey trunks beyond number, writhing up towards the light from amongst the ornate stonework, and in an increasing number of cases, cracking apart the tombs and heaving over the taller monuments at hazardous angles. Add to this a copious growth of ivy, spreading over all, and it's a garden of earthly delights for modern lovers of the Gothic. Not that I'm such a dedicated fan myself, but there's still something wonderfully Phantastickale and Eyrye about the place, in its entanglement of wood and stone.

On my last serious visit to Highgate Cemetery, a bright and breezy February day in 2001, I wasn't there to goggle, gothically or otherwise, but to actually do some work. Why this should be came about like this: as mentioned, having started on the plot not even able to recognise basic vegetable types, after two or three years I had found out what they looked like and the basics of how to grow them. From there, I'd developed a wider interest in nature and in environmental issues, and graduated to my Environmental Science degree at UNL. A further five years and I'd graduated again, properly this time, and amongst other things had come away from the unbosky purlieus of Holloway Road, N7, with an interest in conservation management.

To me, as a practical sort of chump, this meant doing some recognisably practical conservation-type work. So on leaving UNL, I'd immediately signed up with the local conservation volunteers, and by the time I got to Highgate, had already enjoyed several hair-raising months scooting about with my co-volunteers in a minibus, to local nature reserves and similar places, wherever vegetation had got out of hand. On arrival, we'd all jump out to hack down trees and brambles and anything else that stood in our way, or clear sludge out of ponds, and so on. In the process, I became interested in "woodland crafts", which basically meant: what could be made out of the materials our labours produced?

Not that I could think of an immediate use for pond sludge. But some of the trees we cut down might, I thought, prove handy for something or other. So, by the time I arrived at Highgate Cemetery on that particular February occasion, I'd hatched a cunning plan. Our task for the day was to thin out as much of the thicket of tomb-toppling ash poles as we could manage. And rather than simply pile them into heaps (our usual practice), I'd bribed the other volunteers – with promises of an entire lunchtime's worth of beer and pizza – to lift as many logs as we could fit onto the roof rack of the minibus, and then, by making a short detour on our way back to base, to drop them off just over the other side of the hill, at Fitzroy Park.

Before you can cart your tree, you first of course need to fell it. So alongside my fellow volunteers, each of us equipped with a blunt bowsaw and a time-expired yellow plastic safety hat, I set to work. Beer and pizza notwithstanding, this was a keen bunch of people, and the workrate was as fast and furious as ever, so that soon the whole cemetery (eastern side) rang with our cries of "Tim-buurrrr!"

Our scanty training told us that a trunk with a 9-inch diameter was about the thickest you could cut with a bowsaw (blunt or otherwise). But we'd always push this limit. I remember, in particular, a trio of 15-inch thick monster poles which we felled right alongside Marx's tomb, taking care – with the aid of a rope, hauled on just as they fell – not to bounce them off his bronze bonce. Which we managed to do quite safely, though it was touch-and-go a couple of times.

Well, it was a great day, a conservation classic. We got through a great deal of neo-gothic trees, and in due course I found myself back at the plot, the proud possessor of a heap of seven-foot long ash coppice poles.

Once I'd learnt how to split them along their length (the ancient art of "cleaving"), I was away. There followed various raised beds, compost bins, some cumbersome and not very comfortable furniture, hay rakes, the useless flail as previously described, even a coracle, amongst other rustic items. Also more cleft sticks for stakes and other plant supports than you could… ahem… shake a stick at.

I also tried my hand at making charcoal, a short-term success, until I was halted in this particularly smokey track by our representative of local government then in charge of the plots. Who told me frankly that if I carried on with it I'd be prosecuted under the provisions of the Clean Air Act, and cashiered off the site.

In spite of this setback, in pursuing my rustic crafts, more fun was never had by a clothed person. Which is a convenient point to get back on track, after an inordinately long diversion, and tell you about my sixth and final crop.

The growing of mushrooms on allotments has become a much-decayed practice of late. This is a pity – and I'm speaking here from personal knowledge, from the carefree days of my youth, spent plucking the elusive chanterelle (*Cantharellus cibarius*) from the wooded foothills of the Cairngorms – since freshness amongst edible fungi, whether wild or home grown it matters not, is no whit less of a delight than it is with things like sweetcorn and asparagus, as we've already seen. Leave your mushrooms for a few days only and much of their delicious fungal pungency disappears. Which is why most people think they're naturally *bland*. They're not. But by the time they reach you, along the normal commercial routes, what they are is naturally *old*.

Casting a beady eye again into my Waverley's *Complete Guide to Home Gardening*, which dates from the 1940s, I discovered some simple words of encouragement: "Anyone who can obtain fresh stable manure can grow mushrooms."

There follow some blindingly simple instructions, along the lines of: heap up some manure, wait a few weeks, add *spawn* (i.e. "mycelium" – see later), wait a few more weeks, then gather the crop. Easy-peasy. The mushroom seems to have been a familiar allotment or garden crop, back then.

Waverley is talking about the field mushroom (*Agaricus campestris*), far and away the most commonly consumed fungus in the UK and the one most often available in the shops. Indeed, if one out of every ten thousand mushrooms eaten here were something different, I'd be surprised. Its natural habitat is undisturbed pasture of the richer sort, and since this species is so amenable to being cultivated by the amateur grower it seems surprising that it so seldom any longer is. Having said that, I've never yet grown *A. campestris* myself and don't know anyone who has tried. Strange that it should so thoroughly have vanished from the nation's plots.

This may be connected with the deep suspicion held by the majority of people in this country towards any edible fungi, that isn't *guaranteed* to be safe. Given our general state of ignorance on the subject, this invariably means we're confined to those dull old things bought from the shops. Unlike, say, the Hungarians or the Italians, we've no great tradition here of collecting mushrooms from the wild. Obviously, this attitude is changing, but lacking such a tradition puts us at the very foot of a steep learning curve, when it comes to recognition. There are exceptions, like the chanterelle, but the fact remains that many a mushroom species (and there are several thousand in the UK) looks very much like many another, whether edible or not. Quite a few are poisonous, and one or two genuinely deadly, so a reckless attitude can land you in trouble. The best advice is to avoid eating any species for which you cannot make a 100% positive ID.

Aside from difficulties of identification, there is I think something more to our usual distrust of wild mushrooms. Which is that they're *weird*. As food, whether wild or cultivated, fungi are after all in a class of their own. And in biology, they're in a "Kingdom" all their own – a strange realm – one that to my mind, though it may sound perverse, is obviously neither animal nor vegetable, but *both*.

What do I mean by this? Unlike green plants, and very much like animals, mushrooms don't do photosynthesis – they can't carry out the miracle of converting carbon to carbohydrate using sunlight, any more than we can. So, like us, they need to make use of the stored carbon that is either fixed by plants or taken on board by other creatures via eating plants. There are three basic ways the fungi achieve this, the first being parasitism, about which I've nothing more to add since we've already encountered it in such murderous forms as the potato/tomato blight, *Phytopthera infestans*.

Other mushrooms are saprophytes, meaning they grow on dead matter, both plants and animals, though a great number of species favour wood as their substrate, which they "eat" by spreading their roots, or hyphae, through it. These release degrading enzymes, which break down the cellulose and other complex molecules of which the wood is comprised, thus releasing their stored carbon and other nutrients for absorption by the fungus. Fungi such as these are hugely important in nutrient cycling, by forming the first line of attack on newly dead wood, etc., thus earning them the biological title of "primary decomposers".

The third tactic employed is symbiosis, in which the fungus positively co-operates with a living plant host by growing amongst and around its roots. Symbiotic fungi can carry out various functions for the plant, chief of which is their ability to take up nitrogen from the soil, which they then exchange with the plant for the carbohydrates they can't make, thus contributing to mutual success. Essentially the fungus is acting like the nitrogen-fixing bacteria hosted by leguminous plants, which we touched on in the case of broad beans.

The full complexities of symbiosis are still a matter of debate amongst the experts, although it's now known that up to 90% of plant species benefit from fungal "partners", and that in quite a number of instances, the plants simply can't do without them – in the absence of their mushroom auxiliaries, they'd fail to grow at all.

As fungal hyphae spread, they often combine to form a dense mat of mycelium, which continues to absorb and to store sufficient food supplies to enable the fungus to reproduce and to disperse, which it does by poking its spore-laden fruiting bodies out into the open air. These, of course, being the "mushrooms" themselves, the part of them which we ourselves – having made our 100% positive IDs – actually eat.

When it comes to edibility, as mentioned above, shop-bought mushrooms are a very safe bet, though usually old and flavourless. And eating wild mushrooms is clearly a chancy business for anyone inexpert at telling good from ill. But there is obviously a third mushroom-securing method which has the advantage of combining safety with freshness, i.e. grow your own. Home grown mushrooms, having somehow disappeared from sight since the Waverley days of the 1940s, are currently undergoing quite a revival, not just the field sort but more exotic types. This is thanks, amongst others, to the HDRA, through their *Chase Organics* catalogue, which offers a number of new fungal delights, including shiitake (*Lentinus edodes*), also *Hericium erinaceus*, which is sometimes called the hedgehog or lion's mane, and the versatile oyster mushroom (*Pleurotus ostreatus*). "Versatile" here meaning that unlike many species which are specific to certain types of (dead) tree, the oyster mycelium can make use of almost any cellulose-based substrate, so long as this is no longer in the land of the living, from whatever type of wood, to straw, even old bits of cardboard.

It was this last point that attracted my attention. Offcuts of ash pole fall well within the scope of such versatility, and I had these in plenty, left over from my various adventures in woodland crafts. The original plan had been to turn all such odds and ends into charcoal, but since the Council's comprehensive smoking ban had thwarted my efforts in this direction, well, you can probably guess the rest…

I stacked up my ash leftovers in the shade next to the shed, into a neat pile. As it built up, I packed the interstices of the logs with top-grade Rosewood black gold. And also with bits of oyster spawn, purchased from Chase Organics. The spawn itself arrived by post, direct from the supplier, lying in several layers of plastic wrap, somewhat like a slab of rubbery white cheese. By way of "planting", all that was required was to pare off lumps and stick them in amongst the other stuff.

Chief amongst these logs were the three sawn-up 15-inch monster poles, carefully cut down from next to Marx's tomb, which had proved too fat, tough and twisted for cleaving into anything more useful. So all went for mushroom food.

It worked beautifully. Within a year I had all the oyster mushrooms I could possibly eat, their shell-shaped greyish caps poking out in large clusters from amongst the butt ends of the pile of offcuts. No ID problems there. The flavour is certainly fresh and pleasant, definitely of mushrooms, and slightly nutty. Excellent in an omelette, although I have to admit, they are on the chewy side. Next time around, I'm determined to give the ordinary field mushrooms a go.

Dust to dust. To ashes. To fungus. To omelette. And that, ladies and gentlemen of the jury, is how I ate Karl Marx.

As well as – you may be assured – quite a few other, less eminent Victorians.

Does this sound like a boast, the sick bragging of a necrophiliac? I say not. Whatever we eat, we rely on the recycling of nutrients to supply it. Nature has devised a thousand ways to keep turning over nitrates, phosphates and the like. If it hadn't, supplies would have run out long since, and life on our planet would have starved to death hundreds of millions of years before the human race was even a twinkle in the Creator's eye.

Nutrient cycling was here long before and will continue for long after we've all gone under the sod. We are all outgrowths of it, no more nor less than any other living thing. Whether we choose to recognise it or not, this involvement comprises our one genuine claim to immortality, which is a fact that we can't alter, whatever style of monument to ourselves we might care to put up.

Such being my Six of the Best allotment crops. Since I began this long chapter by celebrating all things fresh and diverse available from off the plot, these six examples given above will have to stand as exemplars for the rest. Variations on the theme are practically limitless, I would say, in spite of the constraints of climate and other vicissitudes with which, as gardeners, we're constantly required to deal.

When I consider what my fate has turned out to be – that of an obsessed plotholder – it occurs to me that maybe I did pick up something from that terrible *Music and Movement* after all, other than fluff from the assembly hall floor. An intimation of my future, barely recognised at the time or understood, but it was there nonetheless, as I lay down amongst the other fresh faces of my infants' school, waiting for that distant voice to tell me when I could grow up.

It amazed me to learn, recently, that much the same acorn-to-oak exercise is still inflicted on the nation's children today, in schools up and down the land. This I find hard to believe – all that *hiss*, *crackle* and *pop* – perish the thought! One can only hope that the kids are better equipped to enjoy it, these days, more than we ever did.

A Word Edgewise

Anyway, that's about the lot, so far as this account goes, of my dozen-odd years spent so far, as an gardener at Plot 3, Fitzroy Park Allotments, Highgate, London N6, England. And whilst I've read a few books over the years, quite a few, in fact, it's only in scribbling these final lines that I can start to convince myself I've been up to the job of actually writing one. A task which has occupied more of my time over the past year-and-a-bit than I've really had to spare. So it's all been a quite a rush, and I hope this doesn't show too badly in the text.

Readers with an especially strong literary bent, may have noted a dim echo, in the first two paragraphs of this story, of the opening lines of *The Adventures of Augie March*, Saul Bellow's magnificent Chicago epic, which is one of the greatest novels of the last century and, in my view, of all time. Not that my own jottings can hold a burnt match to Bellow's wonderful work, though there is – so I would argue anyway – a slight coincidence of theme.

Augie March is a young man in search of "a worthwhile fate", and the adventures that follow, in the meandering course of this search, have much to do with his refusal to conform to the role that others have in mind for him, as again and again he refuses to step inside the alien mould, and walks out on the expectations of those who'd put him in it.

By accident, so it seems, I've discovered my own worthwhile fate right here on the plots. Besides the top-grade fruit and veg., good enough in themselves as they are, there's this other thing to consider. Because if I stop for a moment to dwell on the not infrequent past occasions that I've screwed up my chances in life: in work, in love, and so on, I find, from out of this hilariously miserable, general wrack – lashed together to rise above it – that I'm in lucky possession of a raft of experience of a different and far happier sort. This rough craft is the direct product of my allotment experience, comprised in more-or-less equal parts of the pleasure of being out among nature, of learning and good friendship, and of the many and varied rewards of a not too arduous type of gardening work. Which has kept me buoyant, at least, over the years.

In some areas of our lives – maybe too many – second, third, fourth chances don't always appear when we hope they would. But gardening itself ever defies this dismal fact. A new season always comes around, holding out its fruitful promise. If I were in a more sentimental frame of mind I might be tempted next to say something along the lines of nature being forever giving, forever generous, etc. But in reality nature is nothing of the sort, of course, and you'd be rightly wary of such a stab (feeble poke, more like) in the direction of anthropomorphism, should I attempt to make it.

What nature has, really, in full measure, are the twinned and complementary qualities of *resilience* and *rhythm*. Half a billion years or so of the evolution of complex life forms guarantees the former. Whilst the latter is derived, in our familiar temperate latitudes, as elsewhere in the world, from the annual repetition of climatic patterns, to which whatever exists has always had to adapt.

So that whenever we put our gardening hats on, and not forgetting our stout pair of boots, we're assured of a regular go to put right whatever it was that didn't work out as planned the last time around. Our knowing this isn't necessarily a joy in itself, but so long as we've the strength, and are able, and can plan our activities to fit in with it, it's surely not a bad beginning.

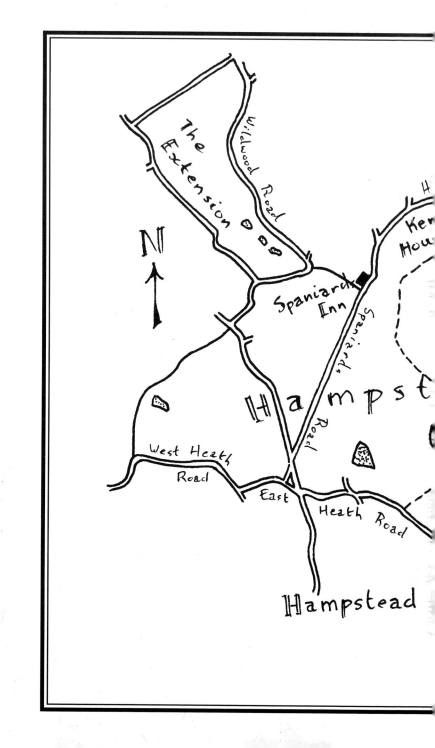